Thera in the Bronze Age

D1479108

American University Studies

Series IX
History

Vol. 187

PETER LANG
New York • Washington, D.C./Baltimore • Boston
Bern • Frankfurt am Main • Berlin • Vienna • Paris

Phyllis Young Forsyth

Thera in the Bronze Age

PETER LANG
New York • Washington, D.C./Baltimore • Boston
Bern • Frankfurt am Main • Berlin • Vienna • Paris

Library of Congress Cataloging-in-Publication Data

Forsyth, Phyllis Young.
Thera in the Bronze Age / Phyllis Young Forsyth.
p. cm. — (American university studies. Series IX, History; 187)
Includes bibliographical references and index.
1. Thera Island (Greece)—Antiquities. 2. Bronze Age—Greece—Thera
Island. 3. Akrotiri (Greece)—Antiquities. 4. Volcanoes—Greece—
Thera Island. I. Title. II. Series: American university studies.
Series IX, History; vol. 187.
DF221.T38F67   939'.15—dc21   97-13093
ISBN 0-8204-3788-3 (hardcover)
ISBN 0-8204-4889-3 (paperback)
ISSN 0740-0462

Die Deutsche Bibliothek-CIP-Einheitsaufnahme

Forsyth, Phyllis Young:
Thera in the bronze age / Phyllis Young Forsyth. –New York;
Washington, D.C./Baltimore; Boston; Bern; Frankfurt am Main;
Berlin; Vienna; Paris: Lang.
(American university studies: Ser. 9, History; 187)
ISBN 0-8204-3788-3 (hardcover)
ISBN 0-8204-4889-3 (paperback)

The paper in this book meets the guidelines for permanence and durability
of the Committee on Production Guidelines for Book Longevity
of the Council of Library Resources.

© 1997, 1999 Peter Lang Publishing, Inc., New York

All rights reserved.
Reprint or reproduction, even partially, in all forms such as microfilm,
xerography, microfiche, microcard, and offset strictly prohibited.

Printed in the United States of America

For Jim

"Always and Ever"

ACKNOWLEDGEMENTS

I am greatly indebted to many people and organizations for their assistance in writing this book. The University of Waterloo supported my fieldwork with a sabbatical leave in 1991–1992; its Small Grants Subcommittee of the Social Sciences and Humanities Research Council of Canada also helped with two grants-in-aid. Major funding was provided by the Social Sciences and Humanities Research Council of Canada, without whose four-year grant the project could not have been undertaken. Work in Europe was greatly facilitated by the Badisches Landesmuseum in Karlsruhe, the Allard Pierson Museum in Amsterdam, the Rijksmuseum in Leiden, the French School of Athens and the Canadian Archaeological Institute at Athens. I am especially grateful to the Badisches Landesmuseum, the Hellenic Republic's Ministry of Culture (TAP Service), the Archaeological Society at Athens, the Thera Foundation (Idryma Theras-Petros M. Nomikos) and Professor Christos Doumas for their permission to reproduce artwork from Thera. I would also like to thank Lena Levidis of the Thera Foundation for being unfailingly helpful.

I owe much to Floyd McCoy for help and encouragement on matters geological, to Sheila Ager and Susan Downie for their work in the fields and quarries of Thera, and to Susan Downie once again for her editorial assistance. But above all, I am most grateful to my husband, James J. Forsyth, who not only shared in the demanding fieldwork but also formatted the text and drew all the figures; without his patience, support and help this book would not have been written.

Finally, there are many researchers whose work has made my own possible. Foremost among them are the late Spyridon Marinatos and Christos Doumas, the current excavator of Akrotiri. Without their vision and hard work there would be no tale to tell. I would also like to acknowledge the outstanding achievements of Nanno Marinatos, whose works about Thera are both prolific and provocative, always forcing the prehistorian to look at data in new ways. Finally, I would like to thank John Younger and all the contributors to Aegeanet for their scholarly debates and willingness to share ideas and information; they are a true "community of scholars." Any defects in this book, however, remain mine alone.

TABLE OF CONTENTS

LIST OF FIGURES

LIST OF PLATES

PREFACE

Lying approximately 100 kilometers north of Crete, the volcanic island of Thera ranks among the most awe-inspiring places of the world. Wildly beautiful but ever threatening, it bears witness to one of the greatest natural disasters in human history. Only in the last thirty years, however, have scholars begun to unlock the secrets of its past, mainly through the continuing excavation of the Bronze Age site called Akrotiri.

There is a tremendous amount of general interest both in this excavation and in the island itself. Since the late 1970s I have been invited to speak to many academic and non-academic audiences about Thera and Akrotiri. The lively question period that inevitably ensues always includes a request for the titles of relevant and readable books in English. Aside from Christos Doumas' *Thera: Pompeii of the Ancient Aegean* (1983), however, very little of a non-specialist nature is presently available, and even Doumas' book is now hard to obtain and out of date in light of the progress made at Akrotiri since 1983. As a result, in 1990 I finally gave in to the request of many people that I myself write a book for both students of the Aegean Bronze Age and the general public.

The result is a book that attempts to synthesize and interpret the work that has been done in many fields and reported in specialized journals or in conference proceedings. For those wishing to know more I have included comprehensive notes and a bibliography concentrating for the most part on works in English. My aim throughout this compact volume has been to reach as wide an audience as possible. I leave it to readers to judge how successful I have been.

CHAPTER ONE

GENESIS: BIRTH OF AN ISLAND

Euphemus, rejoicing in the prophecy of Jason,
threw the clod of earth into the sea,
and from it arose an island, Kalliste.
(Apollonius IV. 1756–1758)

In Greek myth, the island of Thera had a readily comprehensible, although unusual, birth. According to Apollonius of Rhodes, Euphemus, one of the Argo-
nauts, had been given a clod of earth by the god Triton; soon after, Euphemus
cast this clod into the sea and at once arose the island called Kalliste, later to
be known as Thera (IV. 1551–1764). In reality, however, the birth of Thera
was much more complicated and much less instantaneous.

The Santorini complex of islands (Thera, Therasia, Aspronisi, Palaea
Kameni and Nea Kameni) is the product of millions of years of geological
evolution in the Aegean Sea [see Figure 1]. Approximately thirty million years
ago the Aegean Sea did not even exist: in its place stood a mountainous landmass, commonly called Aegeis, which stretched from the Ionian Sea through
Crete to Asia Minor. Around thirteen million years ago, however, a complex
system of geological faults led to the break up of this landmass and to the
formation of the modern Aegean Sea. Thus, the islands of the Aegean are in
reality the peaks of submarine mountains which formerly stood high and dry
on Aegeis.

The geological stresses that destroyed Aegeis were also responsible for
the formation of a chain of volcanic islands lying to the north of Crete and
extending from the Saronic Gulf to western Asia Minor. The major eruptive
centers along this chain are the islands of Melos, Thera, Kos, Yali and
Nisyros. Volcanic activity in general commenced around three to four million
years ago, but, in the particular case of the Santorini complex, it is believed
that eruptions began only 1.6 to 1 million years ago.[1] Prior to this, the island
consisted solely of a small non-volcanic outcrop composed of limestones, marbles and schists. Fragments of this so-called basement formation can be found
today in the southeastern part of the island of Thera, and include Mount
Profitis Ilias (at 565 meters the highest point on the island), Mesa Vouno and
the adjacent Sellada, Gavrillos ridge, the areas around Pyrgos and Gonia, and
Cape Athinios. A reconstruction of this basement would suggest an island of
roughly 9 x 6 kilometers.[2] Offshore and to the northeast lay the tiny island of
Monolithos, a 29 meter limestone outcrop that would become part of Thera
only in the Late Bronze Age [see Figure 2].

Figure 1: Modern Thera

The first site of Theran volcanism was the Akrotiri peninsula in the southwestern part of the modern island;[3] here, periodic eruptions from multiple submarine vents deposited such vast amounts of lavas and pyroclastics that a new island came into existence [see Figure 3]. Today, the remnants of these Akrotiri volcanoes can be seen at Balos, Kokkinopetra, Mavro and Mavrorachidi. Shortly thereafter, around one million years ago, the so-called Thera volcanoes began to build a complex of their own in the area of the present-day caldera [see Figure 4]. Three massive eruptions, occurring over a long period of time, created the largest volcanic complex yet seen at Santorini and started

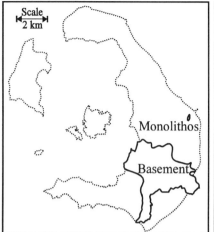

Figure 2: Original Islands

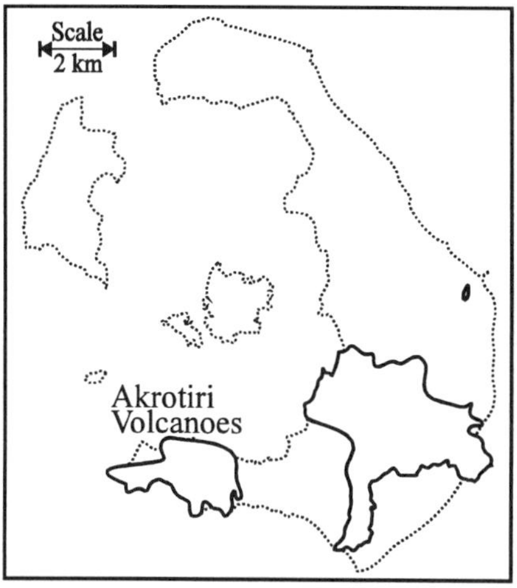

Figure 3: Akrotiri Volcanoes

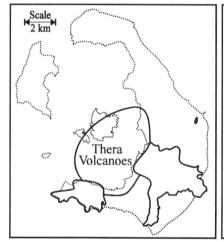

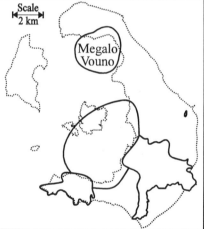

Figure 4: Thera Volcanoes

Figure 5: Megalo Vouno

the process of unifying the island. Towards the end of this eruptive cycle, however, another volcanic complex began to rise in the north, creating the Megalo Vouno lava shield [see Figure 5 above]. In time, all three volcanic complexes (Akrotiri, Thera and Megalo Vouno) grew together, and, along with the still exposed basement rocks, formed a single island [see Figure 6]. The geological stage was now set for a massive eruption that would drastically alter the topography of the new landmass.

Approximately 100,000 years ago, a violently explosive eruption, known

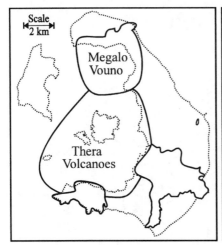
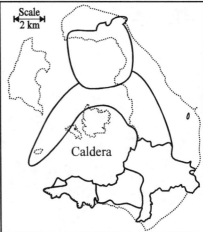

Figure 6: Unified Complex   Figure 7: Lower Pumice 2 Caldera

today as Lower Pumice 1, deposited an average of 30 meters of debris over the
central and southwestern parts of the island. This, however, was only the
forerunner of an even more explosive eruption that took place perhaps a
thousand years later: Lower Pumice 2, which left behind a deposit approximately 60 meters thick. In fact, so much debris was ejected that the magma
chamber emptied and collapsed inwards, forming a caldera in the southern part
of the island [see Figure 7 above]. This Lower Pumice 2 caldera remained a
prominent feature of the island's topography into the Late Bronze Age, and
still exists as the southern basin of the modern caldera.[4]

Despite the fact that milder volcanic activity continued in the north,
where the Megalo Vouno lava shield was slowly being enlarged, the formation
of the Lower Pumice 2 caldera is thought to signal the end of one eruptive
cycle at Santorini, and the beginning of another.[5] Indeed, the overall development of the island complex is marked by a pattern of alternating constructive
and destructive volcanism: major explosive eruptions, such as Lower Pumice 1
and 2, are usually followed by the construction of new lava shields or cones.[6]
Thus, approximately 80,000 years ago, increasing volcanic activity began to
reshape the northern, western and central parts of the island.

In the north, near the still active Megalo Vouno center, the cone now
called Mikros Profitis Ilias produced enough debris to raise itself to a height of
ca. 315 meters. To the west, meanwhile, new volcanic vents opened near the
modern Cape Trypiti in southern Therasia; generating mainly lava, these
Therasia volcanoes significantly enlarged the island in the northwest [see

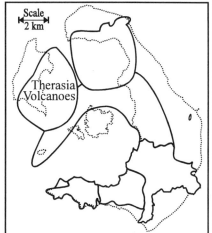
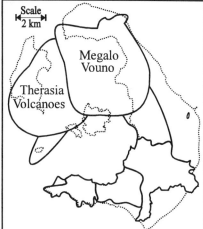

Figure 8: Therasia Complex   Figure 9: Northern Lava Shields

Figure 8 above]. In the central part of the island, however, the Thera vol-canoes generated the next major explosive event: the so-called Middle Pumice eruption, ca. 79,000 years ago. This violent eruption deposited up to 67 meters of volcanic debris over a large part of the island and may have created the small Skaros caldera to the northwest of the modern town of Fira.[7] These Thera volcanoes continued to be active on an irregular basis for some time to come.

Both during and after the Middle Pumice eruption, gentler effusive ac-tivity continued to alter the topography of the northern part of the island by creating overlapping lava shields [see Figure 9 above].[8] The Megalo Vouno complex became increasingly active, and the Skaros volcano now seems to have come into existence. Stretching from Mikros Profitis Ilias to the modern town of Fira, the Skaros volcano produced copious amounts of a very fluid lava over a long period of time. Meanwhile, to the northwest, a similar type of effusive activity was also taking place, now originating from a vent located somewhere in the region of the modern channel which divides Therasia from Thera.[9] At times referred to as the Oia volcano, this eruptive center produced lavas that eventually mixed with those of Megalo Vouno.

This gradual reshaping and enlarging of northern Santorini continued for thousands of years. The island, however, was not free of more explosive and destructive activity during this lengthy period: for example, roughly 54,000 years ago, the so-called Vourvoulos eruption deposited up to 5 meters of debris. Even more explosive was the almost contemporary event called the

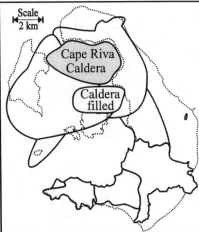

Figure 10: Northern Caldera   Figure 11: Cape Riva Caldera

Upper Scoriae 1 eruption, which left behind a deposit of ca. 20 meters. The small Skaros caldera, associated by some with the Middle Pumice eruption, might just as easily have been created as a result of this activity. In either case, there is little doubt that, by this time, a second caldera (the first being that created by the Lower Pumice 2 eruption) did exist, with its center lying in the northern part of the modern caldera [see Figure 10 above].[10] This small caldera was eventually filled by the extensive lavas produced by the Skaros volcano.

Then, around 37,000 years ago, while the Skaros and Therasia lava shields were still being constructed, the Upper Scoriae 2 eruption took place. A more massive explosion than its namesake predecessor, the Upper Scoriae 2 event deposited about 70 meters of volcanic debris. The ca. 19,000 years that followed this upheaval saw volcanic activity on Santorini restricted to constructive lava flows in the areas around the Megalo Vouno, Skaros and Therasia complexes.

Around 18,000 years ago, however, another massively explosive event occurred: the Cape Riva eruption, which takes its name from the modern Cape Riva on Therasia where the vent seems to have been situated.[11] Some 44 meters of debris rained down upon the island; indeed, the volume of debris expelled seems to have weakened the vent's magma chamber, leading to collapse and the formation of a new caldera of uncertain size in the northern part of the island [see Figure 11 above].[12] Although the Skaros volcano continued to produce lava flows until approximately 13,000 years ago, the Cape Riva eruption was the last major explosive event prior to the Late Bronze Age (LBA) eruption.[13]

Given our growing understanding of the eruptive history of the Santorini complex, it is now feasible to attempt to reconstruct the topography of the island in the period immediately preceding the Late Bronze Age event. Most importantly, the once popular theory that the pre-eruption LBA island was round in shape and dominated by one or more tall central strato-volcanoes is no longer tenable. The rejection of this theory is due, in large part, to the work of G. Heiken and F. McCoy, who, in 1984, postulated the existence of a pre-LBA caldera in the southern half of Santorini on three grounds. First, the volume of volcanic debris from the LBA eruption had been estimated at roughly 13 cubic kilometers,[14] whereas the volume of the caldera thought to have been created by that eruption was ca. 60 cubic kilometers. Given the fact that calderas are the products of magma chamber collapses, the total volume of the erupted material ought to equal the volume of the resultant caldera; the large discrepancy in the case of Santorini (i.e., 13 vs. 60 cubic kilometers) could be explained, according to Heiken and McCoy, only if one or more calderas had already existed before the LBA eruption.[15] Second, it had long been known that the modern caldera was in fact composed of two basins of unequal depths: to the north of the present-day Kamenis the caldera had a depth of ca. 380 meters, while to the south of the Kamenis its depth was ca. 280 meters. Such a discrepancy could be explained if the two basins were seen as the products of two separate collapse events. Finally, the analysis of air-fall debris (tephra) found plastered onto the caldera-facing cliffs of southern Santorini in several localities indicated that these cliffs had already been in existence before the LBA eruption: "distribution of these deposits implies that there was a circular, 6-km-diameter depression located here [i.e., in the south] before the Minoan eruption...The presence of phreatomagmatic tuffs [i.e., fine rocks created when water meets hot lava] implies that this depression was flooded then, as it is now."[16] This depression corresponds to the shallower southern basin of the modern caldera, and Heiken and McCoy concluded that this basin could have been the caldera formed at the end of the Lower Pumice eruptions. Thus, in their view, only the deeper northern basin could be directly attributed to the Late Bronze Age eruption.[17]

As for the topography of northern Santorini prior to the LBA event, Heiken and McCoy argued that three overlapping lava shields (i.e., those of Therasia, Megalo Vouno and Skaros) had combined to form an extensive landmass [see Figure 12].[18] However, whereas Heiken and McCoy had envisioned a broad, low plain in the north, others more recently have argued for a flooded

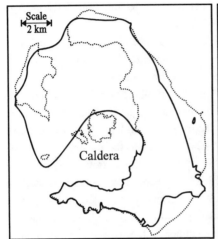

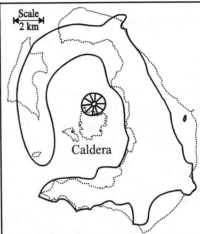

Figure 12: LBA Thera,
after Heiken and McCoy:1984:8460

Figure 13: LBA Thera,
after Friedrich et al:1988:567

depression in the north as well as in the south. In 1988, W.L. Friedrich et al.
presented evidence for a pre-LBA depression, shallow and flooded, in the
north, with an island of undetermined size (a "proto-Kameni") occupying the
center [see Figure 13 above]. It was beginning to look as though a significant
portion of the modern caldera had been in existence before the LBA eruption.[19]

During the Third International Congress on Thera (September 1989) the
question of the island's topography just prior to the LBA eruption received a
great deal of discussion. While Heiken, McCoy and M. Sheridan argued that
the topography of Thera before the LBA eruption was "dominated by a
flooded caldera that formed a bay in the south-central part and low hills in the
northern part of the island," they significantly added that "there also may have
been a small caldera or calderas" on one of the three overlapping lava shields
of the north.[20] In their opinion, however, the northern basin of the modern
caldera was still to be viewed essentially as the product of the Late Bronze Age
eruption.

Nonetheless, other researchers had come to believe that a large caldera
had been generated in the north by the Cape Riva eruption. T.H. Druitt and V.
Francaviglia, for example, had discovered pumice from the LBA eruption
plastered against the modern caldera wall at Cape Apanofira (below Fira), and
had concluded that "the cliff surface at this locality is part of the denuded wall
of an ancient caldera formed during the 18 ka Cape Riva eruption. This occur-

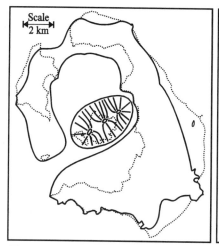

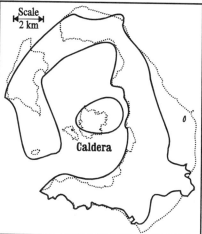

Figure 14: LBA Thera,
after Druitt and Francaviglia:1990:367

Figure 15: LBA Thera,
after Eriksen et al:1990:148

rence [of the LBA pumice] confirms that the Megalo Vouno, Skaros, and Therasia shield complexes had already partly collapsed well before the onset of the Minoan eruption."[21] Thus, they favored a reconstruction of Santorini that featured a large northern caldera and a central island [see Figure 14 above].

This revised topography of the pre-LBA eruption landmass was also supported by U. Eriksen et al. on the basis of a study of stromatolites, gastropods and marine travertines from Santorini.[22] Indeed, their own reconstruction of the island featured a caldera even larger than that proposed by Druitt and Francaviglia [see Figure 15 above]. Thus it was now being argued that *both* basins of the modern caldera must, in part, pre-date the LBA eruption. According to this hypothesis, the LBA eruption began in a vent on the central island and in time caused the creation of a still more extensive caldera.

In the course of discussions during the Third International Congress, McCoy also directed researchers' attention to the so-called Suez Quarry in northern Therasia, where inward-dipping Minoan tephra deposits afford evidence of a "deep valley between present-day Therasia and Oia, in a position about where the Cape Riva caldera would have been;" this led McCoy to postulate a northern embayment in that area.[23] His observation, taken in conjunction with Druitt's discovery of LBA pumice plastered on the caldera cliffs below Fira and Friedrich's analysis of the shallow-marine stromatolites, provides substantial evidence for the existence of a partially flooded caldera in the northern half of Bronze Age Santorini. The major questions remaining are:

(1) how large (and how deep) this northern caldera would have been, and (2) whether it was physically joined in any way to the older southern caldera. Connected with the latter question is the postulated existence of a central, proto-Kameni island, generally believed to have existed because the LBA eruption had clearly begun on a landmass.

Answers to these questions were suggested by D.M. Pyle's revised estimate for the volume of the LBA eruption at between 27 and 30 cubic kilometers.[24] This estimate requires a larger landmass in the area of the

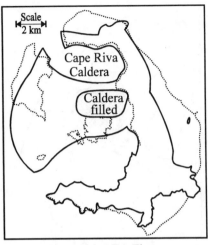

Figure 16: LBA Thera: Alternative Model

present-day caldera than the central islands proposed by Friedrich, Druitt and Eriksen, and so another model of the topography of pre-eruption Thera is now possible: if we admit the likelihood that the present gap between northern Therasia and Thera had been created, at least in part, during the Cape Riva eruption (rather than being totally the product of the LBA event as commonly believed),[25] we can envision an island with a caldera in the south (the Lower Pumice 2 caldera), a smaller caldera in the north (the shallow, partially infilled Cape Riva caldera), and a large landmass separating the two that included a depression where the former Skaros caldera had been [see Figure 16 above]. This landmass, composed of young and rather inhospitable lava shields, would have presented a striking contrast to the older, more fertile land in the southern Akrotiri peninsula, which would have offered the first inhabitants of the island reasonably good arable soil as well as an adequate water supply.[26] Indeed, the large number of Bronze Age sites concentrated on the Akrotiri peninsula confirms the attraction this region must have had for early settlers.

To the east of the Akrotiri peninsula, Gavrillos ridge, Mount Profitis Ilias, Mesa Vouno and the Sellada would have been (as they still are) dominant topographic features, defining the pre-LBA coastline of the southeastern part of the island; the thin soils of these rocky outcrops, however, would have made them less attractive to human settlement than the Akrotiri region. Moving northwards, the landscape would change into younger, rugged, and more barren terrain, the product of the lava shields punctuated by Mount

Mikros Profitis Ilias, and, still further north, by the Megalo Vouno complex with its two prominent cinder cones.[27] Similarly stark would have been the postulated central landmass connecting modern Thera with Therasia, which at that time extended further south, reaching its end around present-day Aspronisi; between this western landmass and the Akrotiri peninsula lay a shallow channel approximately 2200 meters wide.

Except for such prominent features as Mount Profitis Ilias, Mesa Vouno, Megalo Vouno and Mikros Profitis Ilias, the actual surface landscape of the pre-LBA eruption island "has changed dramatically with the addition of substantial thicknesses of pumice to the valley floors and in particular around the outer coastline, which has been extended in places by more than one kilometre" as a result of the Bronze Age eruption.[28] This enlargement of the coastal areas is most graphically illustrated by the incorporation of the once independent islet of Monolithos into the Santorini complex at the end of the LBA event. Thus, detailed reconstruction of the Bronze Age landscape prior to the eruption is rendered difficult by the loss of valleys and low hills to the LBA pumice blanket which created today's relatively flat and featureless ground surface.

Reconstruction of the climate, flora and fauna of the pre-eruption island is also difficult. There is indeed a general consensus that the climate has remained relatively stable (i.e., generally mild, with a great deal of wind and high levels of sunshine), although Oliver Rackham has argued that, before the arrival of human settlers, Santorini was not quite as arid as it is today. He adds, however, that the island would not have stood high enough to generate much rain; in fact, he estimates that Thera would have had to stand at least 200 meters higher in order to support abundant vegetation.[29] What little vegetation was present on the island before the LBA eruption seems to have been confined to patchy woodlands of oak and lentisk, along with some olive trees and tamarisk. As for native fauna, Rackham argues that the Cape Riva eruption would have eradicated all local mammals.[30] The resultant lack of browsing animals would have been beneficial to the development of whatever woodlands then existed.

As far as present knowledge allows, such was the state of Santorini before the arrival of human beings. While certainly not a fertile paradise, the island did offer, especially in the Akrotiri peninsula, enough arable soil to sustain limited cultivation, and the sea was ever close at hand, with its abundance of fish and its potential for trade and/or piracy. And so, at some point in the Late Neolithic Age, the first human settlers arrived to take advantage of these modest conditions.

The Neolithic Period

While there is ample evidence that the Greek peninsula was inhabited during the Palaeolithic Age (over 100,000 years ago), there is no evidence to suggest any permanent occupation of the Cycladic islands [see Figure 17] until the Middle to Late Neolithic Age (approximately the fifth millennium B.C.). This, however, does not mean that the Cyclades were of no importance to the early inhabitants of the mainland. Indeed, in at least one respect, the island of Melos (ca. 90 kilometers NW of Thera) was extremely important—namely, as the Aegean's basic source of the versatile volcanic glass known as obsidian. Used in the manufacture of sharp weapons and tools (especially blades), obsidian was easily accessible on Melos and was being imported to the mainland by the end of the Palaeolithic (ca. 8000 B.C.).[31] It follows that, even in this early stage of Greek prehistory, seafaring must have been advanced enough to carry cargo from the islands to the mainland. Most likely using the islands themselves as stepping-stones, small vessels would have moved among the Cyclades in search of fish and other natural resources; as J.F. Cherry has stated, "the finding of obsidian on Melos was merely a chance by-product of a much more widespread pattern of movement and exploration among the islands."[32] It is even possible that these early explorers made landfall on Thera in order to exploit its abundance of pumice; pumice, however, is less durable than obsidian, and no remains of Theran pumice have yet been found on the mainland in Stone Age contexts.

Excavations at the Franchthi Cave in the Argolid of the northeastern Peloponnese attest to the continued importation of Melian obsidian from the end of the Palaeolithic through the Mesolithic Age (ca. 8000–7000 B.C.).[33] Yet, despite this long period of contact, the Cycladic islands, including Melos itself, were not yet attracting permanent settlers. Simply put, there was no need for Palaeolithic or Mesolithic peoples to move to such relatively barren and remote locations: no population pressure was forcing migration, nor did the islands themselves offer much beyond their removable natural resources (e.g., obsidian, pumice, marble, fish); in fact, their paucity of flora and fauna would not have sustained a basic hunter-gatherer lifestyle. It was only with the Neolithic Age and the rise of agriculture that the Cyclades would come to play a larger and more central role in the development of Aegean civilization.

After the Neolithic Age began (sometime between 7000 and 6000 B.C.), the dominant economic centers in Greece became the regions of Thessaly and Macedonia, where conditions were very favorable for agriculture. As had been the case in the past, the Cyclades, mainly because of their fragile ecology

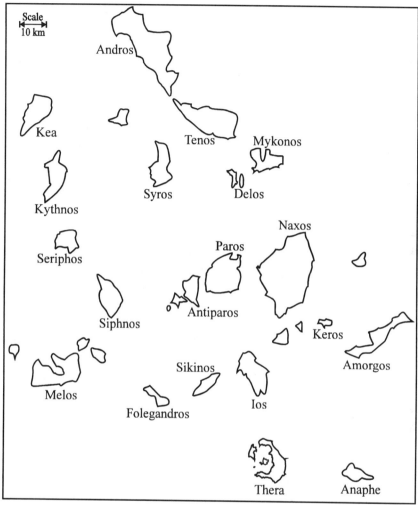

Figure 17: The Cyclades

(e.g., poor soils and a lack of rainfall) and their geographical isolation, remained on the periphery of Aegean civilization. Fortunately, as time passed, technological advances in the design of ships made it easier and safer to reach the islands, and by the fifth millennium B.C. small Cycladic settlements began to appear, although these must have been isolated enclaves in otherwise vacant landscapes. By the end of the fifth millennium, two factors combined to generate increasing settlement of the Cyclades: (1) a growing population on the mainland encouraged migration to what had been less attractive, marginal environments, and (2) a growing interest in metals encouraged the exploitation of Cycladic resources.

Once established, however, many of these small settlements would not have survived long without the emergence of regional exchange networks to ensure that such local problems as crop failure, drought or a lack of mates would not doom their existence. Indeed, given the precarious nature of life on these islands, trade was indispensable for permanent settlement,[34] and, as a result, what may be termed an exchange mentality soon developed in the Cyclades. Pointing to studies of the islands of Polynesia, Cherry has stressed that "exchange is a specialised adaptation which allows populations to exploit regions which, from a basic subsistence perspective, have only marginal value," and has even speculated that trade may have been a primary motive in the settlement of at least some of the Cyclades.[35] While it is not yet possible to determine the extent of emerging trade networks in the Neolithic Aegean, there is evidence of Melian obsidian reaching contemporary Asia Minor, and of emery, most likely from Naxos, reaching Egypt in the fourth millennium B.C.[36]

The key site which has opened a window on this early phase of Cycladic settlement is Saliagos, now a rather unimposing islet, but then a promontory on the land bridge connecting the large island of Paros with neighboring Antiparos.[37] Dated to the Late Neolithic period, Saliagos seems to have been settled by immigrants from mainland Greece or Asia Minor who practised mixed farming (growing barley and emmer, as well as raising goats, sheep, pigs and oxen) and fishing (excavation brought to light more than 30 kinds of shellfish, in addition to tunny and other fish). The settlers were also involved in exchange: they imported emery from Naxos and obsidian from Melos, leading Christos Doumas to suggest that Saliagos may have served as a distribution center for Melian obsidian.[38] The inhabitants' dwellings were small, stone-built structures, and were apparently protected by a fortification wall. It has been proposed that this small settlement lasted as long as 400 to 500 years before its extinction, due possibly to an ecological disaster such as repeated crop failure.[39]

Recent excavations at Grotta on the north shore of Naxos have uncovered a Late Neolithic settlement that has much in common with Saliagos. Two uncontaminated Late Neolithic strata have been identified, with numerous obsidian tools and with pottery remains very similar to those of Saliagos. Even the location of the settlement resembles that at Saliagos: a coastal village on a promontory, part of which is the present-day islet of Palatia. However, on the basis of some pottery judged by the excavator to be a bit later in date than that of Saliagos, it has been postulated that the settlement at Grotta did not go out of use at the same time as Saliagos, but continued into a later phase of the Late Neolithic.[40]

The last phase of the Late Neolithic (often called Final Neolithic) saw the establishment of a small settlement at Kephala on the island of Kea, not far from mainland Attica, the most likely source of its inhabitants. Usually dated to around the mid-fourth millennium B.C., Kephala was a small village of ca. 40–80 people located on a barren promontory by the sea.[41] The inhabitants, like those at Saliagos and perhaps at Grotta,[42] lived in small, stone-built houses, buried their dead in stone cists, and engaged in mixed farming as well as fishing. Their participation in a nascent Aegean trade network is probable in light of finds of not only Melian obsidian, but also copper and lead, and in light of the site's proximity to the mainland.

Saliagos, Grotta and Kephala, while perhaps the best studied, were not the only Cycladic settlements of the Late Neolithic Age. Growing archaeological evidence points to other similar settlements: on Kea additional sites have been located at Ayia Irini and Sykamias; the island of Mykonos seems to have had at least one and possibly two Neolithic sites, while Antiparos, in addition to Saliagos, had a Neolithic settlement at Vouni; Naxos also may have had another settlement at Sangri.[43] As for Melos, the source of the obsidian that helped fuel Aegean trade, a Neolithic settlement has been found at Agrilia. What, then, can be said of a Neolithic presence on nearby Thera?

T.H. Van Andel and C.N. Runnels, in their reconstruction of the principal Neolithic sites and trade routes of the Aegean, did not include the island of Thera, despite its proximity to Melos, and, in 1981, Cherry had postulated that Thera had not been occupied until the third millennium B.C.[44] However, recent work by P. Sotirakopoulou has convincingly demonstrated an earlier, Late Neolithic presence on the island.[45] In examining the pottery sherds from Akrotiri, Sotirakopoulou first focused on a fragment of dark-burnished ware with white-painted rectilinear designs which had counterparts at Saliagos. She concluded that this sherd, which resembled Aegean Late Neolithic pottery in its shape, technique and decoration, provided evidence of human activity at the site prior to the start of the Aegean Bronze Age.[46] At the Third International Congress in 1989, Sotirakopoulou argued for a continuous occupation of the Akrotiri site from around the mid-5th millennium B.C. based on her study of 16 sherds with white rectilinear designs on a dark surface. The find sites of these Late Neolithic sherds were also of significance: 12 of the 16 were found either in or near Xesté 3, at the southwesternmost part of the current excavation area; moreover, an additional 10 sherds which looked Neolithic were discovered in two rooms of that building.[47]

On the basis of this ceramic evidence, Sotirakopoulou concluded that "the southwesternmost area of the site was the place of the first installation in Late Neolithic times and continued to be the nucleus of the settlement throughout the Early Cycladic period, in the course of which it gradually extended east and north-eastward."[48] The current excavator of Akrotiri, Christos Doumas, agreed that at least a small village had existed on the site in the Late Neolithic Age.[49]

The next question to consider, then, is why the site at Akrotiri was chosen for settlement at this time. Certainly its geography must have been an important factor: although obscured today by the deposits of the Late Bronze Age eruption, the site lay on the ridge of a small hill (ca. 20–25 meters above sea level) close to the sea,[50] in the southernmost part of the island. Its gentle slope towards the southern coast would make the site accessible from the sea; indeed, there seems to have been a good harbor to the west, between the present-day hills of Mesovouna and Mavrorachidi.[51] Even today, with the proposed site of the ancient harbor erased by volcanic fill, the southern side of the Akrotiri peninsula provides a safe anchorage for ships, and is well sheltered from strong northerly winds by the prominence to the north which now bears the modern village of Akrotiri. Thus, as Doumas has pointed out, Akrotiri was much more advantageously located for maritime pursuits than any other prehistoric site so far found on the island.[52] Moreover, the Akrotiri peninsula, being the earliest volcanic part of the island to be formed, provided older and richer soil for agriculture than the younger regions to the north. In sum, the site of Akrotiri was most suitable for the three economic activities that would come to characterize the Late Neolithic Age: farming, fishing and exchange.

That nautical activities indeed played an important role in the selection of Akrotiri as a Neolithic village site is also suggested by the fact (mentioned above) that most of the Late Neolithic sherds so far found have come from the southwesternmost part of the site, that is, the part closest to the sea. While mixed farming must have existed in nearby fields, the site was especially useful to seafarers. In fact, from the point of view of geography, the island of Thera was very well situated in terms of a nascent Aegean trade network: its proximity to Melos enabled its inhabitants to participate in the exchange of obsidian.[53] Moreover, given that obsidian from Melos reached as far south as Crete at this time, there is no reason to exclude Thera, the Cycladic island closest to Crete, from a Neolithic exchange network. Indeed, postulating the existence of a series of landings (some 20 to 50 kilometers apart) criss-crossing the Aegean, Thera would have been well placed for participation in such a network, and the site of Akrotiri in particular was well suited to serve as a trading station.[54]

It is possible, however, that the village at Akrotiri became more than just a passive node in an Aegean Neolithic trade network (e.g., receiving Melian obsidian and facilitating its movement to the next node), since the island of Thera possessed a valuable commodity of its own: pumice. The usefulness of pumice in antiquity is well known: as P. Faure pointed out at the First International Congress, pumice was commonly employed as an all-purpose abrasive (especially vital in the polishing of stone), as a cleanser of skin and teeth, as a depilatory agent, as a tool for the preparation of hides, and even as pigment.[55] Excavation has in fact brought to light pieces of pumice in Neolithic levels on Crete, especially at Knossos, where both the West and Central court areas contained pumice in the context of cosmetic and industrial materials.[56] Post-Neolithic levels showed a continued use of pumice both at Knossos and at several other Bronze Age sites on Crete, including Mallia and Zakros. In addition, Colin Renfrew reported at the same Congress that pumice had been found in Neolithic levels at Saliagos.[57] There were, however, three sources of pumice in the Neolithic Aegean: Thera, Nisyros and Melos. To what degree Theran pumice in particular was mined and exported to other places is difficult to determine, but there is no reason at the moment to rule out the exploitation of their pumice resources by the Neolithic settlers of Thera.

Given the current state of exploration on Thera, as well as the massive destruction caused by the LBA eruption, it is impossible to know whether the site at Akrotiri was the only significant settlement of the Neolithic Age. J.W. Sperling has noted that two black burnished bowls found in the Fira Quarry could belong to either the Final Neolithic or the Early Bronze Age,[58] but otherwise the island looks as if it were generally uninhabited outside of the Akrotiri peninsula. Such a picture would be in keeping with the situation on other Cycladic islands, where, as has been noted, very few settlements existed. In fact, Cherry has estimated that, at the end of the Neolithic Age, less than 10% of the Cycladic islands were settled at all, despite advances in seafaring, and Renfrew has estimated the entire population of the Cyclades in the Neolithic at only 3000.[59]

Yet, in spite of the small scale of settlement in the Cyclades in this period, a foundation was successfully laid for the more prosperous age to come: the Early Bronze Age. Archaeologists see cultural continuity in the transition from the Neolithic to the Early Bronze Age in the Cyclades, rather than an influx of new and different peoples. In short, the Early Bronze Age population of the Cyclades consisted of "the descendants of the Neolithic population and their culture is simply the development of the culture of their ancestors."[60] Such cultural continuity is indeed reflected at Akrotiri, where a small Neolithic hamlet developed into a larger Early Bronze Age settlement.

CHAPTER TWO

THERA AND THE EMERGENCE OF THE CYCLADES

Dating the Early Bronze Age (EBA) in the Cyclades is controversial: its beginning has been placed as early as 4000 B.C. and as late as 2500 B.C., its end as early as 2200 B.C. and as late as 1800 B.C.[1] However, as scientific dating techniques have become more refined and reliable, and also as additional Cycladic EBA sites have been identified and excavated, there is emerging a general consensus that the Cycladic EBA as a whole lasted approximately 1200 years, from ca. 3200 to 2000 B.C. During this lengthy period, the Cycladic islands experienced significant growth: not only did the number of settlements rise to ca. 140 from the dozen or so known in the Neolithic but also the population of the islands increased from a postulated maximum of 3000 in the Neolithic to around 7000.[2] This population, moreover, was distributed over many islands that had shown no evidence of human occupation in the Neolithic. Clearly, something was occurring which drew more settlers to more islands where they began to enjoy an increasingly rich material culture, as evidenced especially by the grave goods found in EBA cemeteries.

The lure of the Cyclades in the early EBA could not simply have been additional arable land, for superior farmland was still available on the Greek mainland at the end of the fourth millennium. Nor could it have been the cultivation of the vine and olive, whose products seem to have played a relatively small role in the Cycladic EBA economy.[3] Rather, the key factors propelling the Cyclades into prominence must have been their raw materials (e.g., metals and marble) and a geographical location which made them perfect centers for maritime trade, now facilitated by improvements in ship-building technology, as manifested in the long vessels depicted on Early Cycladic artefacts. These Cycladic longships opened up the Aegean Sea to the islanders as never before. Now it was possible for both traders and pirates to range further afield, and trade and piracy were to take their place alongside agriculture and animal husbandry as major economic activities in the history of the Cyclades for the rest of antiquity and even beyond.

Trade and piracy, however, depend for their existence on the presence of highly valued goods deemed necessary or desirable by a consuming population. In the Neolithic, obsidian was just such a commodity and it continued to be traded during the Early Bronze Age. Likewise, such materials as marble, emery and pumice continued to be exploited and exchanged. There came into predominance, however, a commodity that far outweighed these in value: metal. While the Cyclades could not offer a great deal in terms of prime agricultural land, they did possess the metal deposits required for the tools, weapons and luxury items of the Bronze Age: copper from Kythnos and Seriphos; lead from Kea, Seriphos, Siphnos, Melos, Kimolos, Antiparos, Mykonos, Anaphe and perhaps Thera;[4] and silver from Siphnos, Kimolos and Syros. Taken in conjunction with the copper, lead and silver deposits at Laurion in southern Attica, these Cycladic resources encouraged the development of a trade network in which ships could safely "island hop" throughout the Aegean, taking on and discharging valued ores or metal artefacts at each stop. Thus, while some Cycladic trade stations do indeed date back to the Neolithic, it is no surprise that most emporia in the islands were established during the Early Bronze Age.[5]

This metallurgical revolution of the EBA was crucial to the development of Cycladic civilization. Not only were improved tools and weapons produced but also a new way of life: for example, the extraction of metals and trade in metals required general laborers and sailors who may have moved to various islands in search of a better economic livelihood, resulting in population dispersal to and growth in the Cyclades; craft specialization arose, conferring economic gain and prestige on those with the requisite skills; luxury items were produced, giving rise to a new type of wealth; and entrepreneurial activities led to the creation of more complex communities. The seafarers of this new Aegean world would soon make contact with extra-Aegean peoples, thus becoming exposed to new cultures and ideas that would in turn enrich their own.

The Early Cycladic (EC) Period

This expanding world of Cycladic civilization in the Early Bronze Age may seem far removed from its humble Neolithic beginnings but the transition from Neolithic to Early Bronze Age, as seen in the so-called Early Cycladic I (EC I) period, was so smooth that EC I has in fact been characterized as an extension of the Neolithic in all but pottery styles.[6] The major change involved the replacement of sparse Neolithic hamlets by a denser pattern of settlements that even appeared on previously unoccupied islands. While this process obviously required the movement of people from one place to another, the old theory that the EBA in the Aegean was precipitated by the arrival of immigrants from the East (especially from Asia Minor) has been generally discredited. Instead, it is now recognized that the Aegean EBA witnessed a redistribution of population from within its own confines and, hence, maintained cultural continuity.[7]

The EC I period is mainly known from settlement sites evidenced by cemeteries and occasional chance finds. In general, settlements of this phase were established near the sea (as would be expected in a society engaged in maritime activities) and were unfortified, suggesting that their control of the sea provided the inhabitants with ample security. Each settlement was probably an independent unit, with some housing fewer than 30 people.[8] The houses themselves (probably composed of one or two rooms) were apparently made of perishable materials and thus have left few traces in the archaeological record.

It is the cemeteries located close by each settlement that have provided most of our knowledge of this formative period. Generally set on low hills, these burial places are characterized by cist graves in which the corpse was placed in a tightly contracted position, with knees drawn up to the chin. At first used for single burials, some cist graves eventually contained multiple inhumations, with this practice becoming more common in the succeeding phase known as Early Cycladic II (EC II). Significantly, this type of burial can be traced back to the Final Neolithic: similar cist graves have come to light at Kephala, once again attesting to a process of local Cycladic evolution.

Although these cemeteries were small, with only ca. 15 graves each, the goods buried with the dead provide an important source of data on such matters as personal/family wealth, the belief in life after death and the existence of a cult of the dead. It seems clear that the family of the deceased, if their wealth allowed, felt obligated to provide him/her with artefacts that were needed in the next world, most commonly pottery. As a result, virtually all of our knowledge about EC I pottery comes from burials: these "offerings" consist of coarse fabrics in various shapes, with burnished surfaces and incised rectilinear patterns often filled with a white paste-like substance. Stone vessels also appear in some of the graves, usually in the form of bowls or beakers. However, by far the most famous stone artefacts of this period are the marble schematic figurines which only suggest the human form *sans* head, arms and legs. Metal objects, on the other hand, are not yet part of the burial assemblage.

The ensuing Early Cycladic II period marks the acme of EBA Cycladic civilization and features larger settlements with an increased number of inhabitants who seem to have enjoyed a higher standard of living than their EC I ancestors. The settlements themselves show no radical change: they are for the most part still coastal and unfortified; houses remain small, with only one or two rooms, but are now increasingly built of stones and mortar. Cemeteries continue to be located on sloping ground near the settlements and cist graves remain the basic form of burial, with multiple interments becoming more common as the population increased.

There are, however, some significant changes in EC II that help to explain the growth and prosperity of the period. Probably the most important of these was a new capability in metallurgy, graphically evidenced by ore-working activity at Siphnos (lead and silver) and Kythnos (copper), the latter being the earliest known copper smelting site in Greece.[9] The demand for the products of this revolutionary material led to increased trade not only within the Aegean itself but also with Asia Minor and perhaps even with the Near East, both of which were likely sources of the tin needed to create high quality bronze.[10] This increase in trade led to an internationalism never before experienced in the eastern Mediterranean, and the Cycladic islanders, with their long tradition of seafaring, must have participated in an expanding trade network that now connected the Cyclades, the Greek mainland, Crete, Asia Minor and the Near East.

A clear indication of the existence of such a trade network is the occurrence of EC II artefacts in quantity beyond the immediate confines of the Cycladic Aegean. Recognizably EC II exports (e.g., pottery, stone vessels, marble figurines) have been found on the Greek mainland, especially in Attica; in the northeastern Aegean, especially at Poliochni on Lemnos, at Thermi on Lesbos and at Troy; in southwestern Asia Minor; and in Crete.[11] In fact, the site of Ayia Photia in northeastern Crete has yielded an extensive cemetery with strong EC II links, leading some to suspect the presence here of an actual Cycladic enclave, whose purpose was most likely mercantile.[12] It seems clear that whatever trade contacts may have existed among eastern Mediterranean cultures in EC I are insignificant when compared to the expansive interconnections of EC II.

The higher standard of living which EC II brought to the Cyclades is manifested in pottery, stone vessels, marble figurines and metal objects. While coarse burnished ware is still found, finer fabrics were developed: e.g., "Patterned Ware" used dark paint to decorate its smooth, light-colored surface with rectilinear designs and "Glazed Ware" had its fine light-colored fabric covered with a dark glaze. New shapes also appear, such as the jug, the small two-part cylindrical container called the pyxis, and the rather enigmatic "sauceboat" and "frying pan."[13] That these vessels show marked similarities with the pottery of mainland Greece is evidence of the close contacts between the two regions in EC II.

Stone vessels also appear in new shapes, including spouted bowls, the cylindrical pyxis and the stemmed cup—artefacts which reflect both an improved technical ability and a higher quality of life. The best known stone artefacts of this period, however, are not vessels but the folded-arm figurines virtually synonymous with EC II. Generally made of high quality marble from the island of Paros, the folded-arm figurines are much more naturalistic than the schematic figurines of EC I and are characterized by 5 or 6 "varieties" with differing head and body shapes/proportions. Normally female and ranging from a few centimeters to life-size, these marbles are usually highly polished, perhaps using pumice, and were originally painted. While most commonly found buried in cist graves, some folded-arm figurines have come from settlement sites, and so the form may have had a non-funereal function as well; as in the case of the EC I schematic figurines, there is still much debate over the precise function of these sculptures.[14] Somewhat more comprehensible are the marble figurines of male musicians, such as harpists or flute-players, which are still among the finest pieces of small-scale marble sculpture ever produced.

Finally, given the prominence of metals in this period, the existence of high quality metal artefacts is not surprising. Bronze weapons in particular seem to appear for the first time in the Cyclades in EC II and most commonly take the form of daggers and spearheads. The new importance of such weapons, however, suggests conflict, and the existence of an expanding trade network must have encouraged the profession of piracy. Trade emporia as well as ships at sea were inviting targets for these marauders, perhaps turning EC II into an age plagued with piracy, as reflected in Thucydides' assertion (I.8) that the Cycladic islanders were once formidable pirates. Piracy thus may have been a factor in the disturbances that were to mark Early Cycladic III.

Early Cycladic III, the final phase of the EBA in the Cyclades, is not yet well understood, but it appears to consist of a period of turbulence followed by one of recovery. For this reason, EC III is sometimes subdivided into EC IIIA and EC IIIB, with the former incorporating a disturbance of uncertain dimensions that befell the islands after the prosperity of EC II.[15] The signs of this disturbance may be seen in the settlements, pottery, stone and metal artefacts and external connections of EC IIIA.

According to R.L.N. Barber, approximately 75% of settlement sites in the Cyclades seem to fall out of use between EC II and EC IIIA.[16] At the same time, a new type of settlement appears: the hill-top fort, surrounded by walls that protect tiny houses crowded within. While some of these fortified villages are near the sea, others are built in more remote, defensible locations. All indications are that the inhabitants of these settlements lived in fear of attack. One of the best studied EC IIIA hill-top forts is that of Kastri on Syros, where two defensive walls (an outer and an inner) protected an area of ca. 3700 square meters. The houses within were small in size and in number (fewer than 50 in all) and were crowded together, with some even backing onto the inner defensive wall with its projecting semicircular towers. Such defensive measures, however, were to no avail: the settlement at Kastri ended its life with a violent destruction at the close of EC IIIA.

To solve the problem of what had created such a hostile environment attention became focused on both the pottery and metal remains of EC IIIA. With regard to the former, two classes of EC IIIA pottery were identified: the so-called "Dark-faced" and "Kastri" groups. It is often claimed that the Dark-faced Ware belongs to the local Cycladic tradition, whereas the Kastri Ware shows non-Cycladic affinities, i.e., not only does the Kastri group display a new type of slipped and burnished fabric but it also introduces a number of new shapes. In general, those who have studied this group tend to see an Anatolian influence or origin.[17] In 1988, however, Christos Doumas drew attention to similar pottery found not on mainland Asia Minor but on the North Aegean islands, especially Lemnos and Lesbos, and proposed that the makers of the Kastri Ware, which is characteristic of the hill-top forts, were "refugee-pirates" from these northern islands. In his view, the North Aegean islanders had established contact with the Cyclades by EC II and, when their homelands suffered serious disruptions ca. 2100 B.C., they moved south *via* Euboia and Attica to the Cycladic islands, "where they hastily settled on some remote coastal hill-tops which they fortified in their own way."[18]

This theory has gained favor as a result of recent metallurgical analyses of artefacts associated with the hill-top forts. That new metal types with Anatolian features had been introduced to the Cyclades in EC IIIA was long recognized, and lead isotope analyses carried out on metal artefacts from Kastri revealed a large proportion of the tin-bronze abundant at Troy and at Thermi on nearby Lesbos, thus lending support to the hypothesis that the inhabitants of the fort at Kastri were Anatolian refugees who had fled destructions in Lesbos, Lemnos and/or the Troad.[19] These newcomers allegedly disrupted life in the Cyclades to such an extent that some Cycladic islanders were forced to emigrate to Crete or to mainland Greece. Eventually, however, the hill-top forts were destroyed and the Cycladic islands recovered from this upheaval in EC IIIB.

While still popular in some quarters, this theory has recently been challenged by J.L. Davis, who points out several weaknesses: e.g., the site at Kastri has not yet been fully published, making it impossible to determine with precision the degree of Anatolian influence; moreover, the excavations at Ayia Irini on Kea have demonstrated that "the Anatolian features in the ceramics are displayed in only a small minority (about 10%) of the pottery in use." Davis adds that "it is now generally agreed that the Anatolian ceramic types that characterize the Kastri Group are of southwestern Anatolian, rather than Troadic, derivation." He concludes that Anatolian types of pottery and bronzes of apparent Anatolian origin need not indicate more than increased trade between the Cyclades and the eastern Aegean.[20] Increased trade between these two regions, however, does not account for the destructions of the hill-top forts at the end of EC IIIA. If foreign invaders are indeed to be ruled out, there exist two other possible culprits: piracy and internal conflict.

The expansive trade routes of EC II must have seen the passage of ships carrying highly valuable and prestigious objects. That piracy would have flourished at such a time is predictable, and pirates would attack not only ships at sea but also vulnerable coastal trading stations. This raises the possibility that the hill-top forts of EC IIIA were places of refuge built to protect islanders from the increasing attacks of marauders, and the destruction of these forts would then be the work of these same marauders. If, moreover, the pirates were themselves Cycladic, traces of them might be hard to pick out in the archaeological record, resulting in the unclear picture we now have of EC IIIA.

It is also possible that internal discord brought about the destruction of the hill-top forts. Kastri itself has recently been described by S.W. Manning as one of "a few special sites [that] seem to have had the capacity for long-distance trade," and as a result was one of the "main beneficiaries of the exchange of prestige items."[21] These special sites would have been home to a wealthy and powerful elite, and outside their walls would have lived the poorer members of the community. Conflict between the "haves" and the "have-nots" might have plagued many a Cycladic island in the EBA and at times even led to rebellion and the destruction of the strongholds of the rich.

Whatever the precise cause of the troubles that befell the Cyclades in EC IIIA, the period that ensued was one of recovery: EC IIIB sees the emergence of larger settlements to replace the scattered villages of the past. On many, if not most, of the islands one major settlement gradually becomes dominant (e.g., Akrotiri on Thera, Ayia Irini on Kea, and Phylakopi on Melos) and smaller settlements begin to disappear. As a result, while the total number of settlement sites decreases, those that exist take on the appearance of more sophisticated centers. That most of these larger settlements were coastal and unfortified would indicate that the problems of EC IIIA had been resolved.

There are changes in other respects also: the diagnostic pottery of EC IIIB, for example, is a new "Geometric Ware" which displays an increased use of painted decoration, with a strong tendency towards dark-colored geometric designs on a light-colored ground; in addition, several new pottery shapes appear. Change can even be seen in the appearance of new burial practices alongside the traditional cist grave, namely, the use of the rock-cut chamber tomb and the burial urn.

Despite being a period of recovery, EC IIIB never reached the cultural heights of EC II. "Classic" Bronze Age Cycladic civilization remains synonymous with EC II, when its basic features were fully formed and the islands enjoyed considerable prosperity. By the end of the Early Bronze Age, however, the Cycladic islanders' freedom of the seas would have been challenged by the growing maritime power of Minoan Crete to the south.

Thera in the Early Bronze Age

The island of Thera generally shared in the pattern of development seen in the Cyclades as a whole during the Early Bronze Age. At Akrotiri there seems to have been a smooth transition from Neolithic to Early Bronze Age and continuous occupation of the site into the Middle Bronze Age (MBA). The evidence is mainly ceramic: potsherds from every phase of the EC period have been found during the excavations.[22] The EC I sherds come from pyxides, funnel-necked jars and the pear-shaped vessels considered transitional between EC I and EC II. From the more prosperous and more populous EC II, Akrotiri has appropriately yielded a greater number of sherds from a greater variety of shapes, including funnel-necked jars, jugs with dark-painted decoration on a light ground, bowls with flat rims, black-coated drinking cups, sauceboats and wide-mouthed jugs.[23] EC II is also marked at Akrotiri by a folded-arm figurine uncovered in Room 5 of Complex Beta in 1971, as well as by three small figurines recovered from Xesté 3 in 1992. From debris east of Complex Delta came EC II marble vases, but of even greater significance was the discovery of nine marble male figurines that Christos Doumas believes may have been found by the inhabitants of Akrotiri when they were rebuilding the city after the early seismic destruction of the Late Bronze Age (see Chapter 6); apparently recognizing the importance of their find, the inhabitants placed these figurines on a small stone mount in the open air.[24]

Transitional between EC II and EC III is the material recovered from a rock-cut vault discovered in the process of installing pillar pit #6.[25] The material from this structure is sealed, i.e., uncontaminated by later activity, as is the pottery discovered in the enigmatic "Fire Deposit," which contained sherds from both EC IIIA and B.[26] The EC III ceramics at Akrotiri include jars, storage vessels, wide-mouthed mixing bowls, rimmed bowls, pans and pyxides. The EC IIIA Kastri group is represented by spherical pyxides, tankards, bell cups, open bowls, jugs and pedestalled cups. From EC IIIB come cups, jugs, conical pyxides and various types of jars.

Thus the ceramic evidence indicates clearly that Akrotiri was occupied without a break throughout the Early Bronze Age. However, as was the case in the Neolithic, most of the EC sherds are concentrated in the southwestern part of the excavated site, which must have been the nucleus of the EBA village.[27] As Akrotiri ceramicist Panayiota Sotirakopoulou has noted, "the Early Cycladic sherds coming from the West House, the most completely excavated building of the site up to this moment, are two and a half times fewer than those of the incompletely excavated Building G" to the south.[28]

With regard to architectural remains of the EBA at Akrotiri, an investigation of pillar pit #17 northeast of Complex Delta uncovered evidence of EC occupation in the form of a rock-hewn, grave-like chamber; several such chambers are now known and EC artefacts have been found in association with them. In addition, in 1987, examination of a stratigraphic sounding made outside the West House yielded evidence of older architectural remains, not only from the Middle Cycladic (MC) period but also from the Early Cycladic: a wall was located in association with EC sherds. Once again the continuity of occupation at Akrotiri was confirmed.

To the west of the Akrotiri excavation stands the hill called Mount Archangelos, dominating a plain which would have served as a natural passage from Cape Akrotiri (at the end of the peninsula) to the settlement at Akrotiri itself. On Archangelos, Doumas reported seeing sherds of the Kastri type,[29] perhaps attesting to the existence of a small EC settlement in this strategic position. Another possible EC site in the Akrotiri area is the cemetery of "pre-Greek graves" (called *sepulcra antiquissima*) mentioned by F. Hiller von Gaertringen as lying (apparently) east of the modern village of Akrotiri.[30] Given the proximity of the site at Akrotiri, an EC cemetery in this region is not out of the question, and recent explorations in the nearby Mavromatis Quarry even suggest a possible EC settlement in that area.

The Akrotiri peninsula, however, was not the only settled region of Thera in the Early Bronze Age: at least four sites outside of the peninsula are presently known. Unfortunately, it is not always possible to determine exactly which phase/phases of the EBA each of these sites belonged to, but, in general, EC II and EC III are the best represented, thus suggesting that on Thera, as on the other Cycladic islands, a sparse settlement pattern in EC I was followed by remarkable growth in EC II and by consolidation in EC III.

What seems to have been an Early Cycladic cemetery was uncovered in the 1930s by the mining of pumice in the Fira Quarry, just south of the modern town of that name. Slab-covered cist graves were found in which skeletal remains were contracted in the usual EC fashion. Moreover, the contents of these graves resembled those of EC cist graves found elsewhere in the Cyclades: figurines and other artefacts of marble, and both stone and ceramic ware. These burial assemblages were apparently dispersed after their discovery, with some coming to rest in the Fira Museum and others finding their way to northern Europe.

Two schematic marble figurines are now on display in the Fira Museum. While no documentation is presently available,[31] these look very much as if they belong to EC I. That the cemetery from which they came continued to be used in EC II is indicated by a folded-arm figurine also in the Fira Museum. Moreover, a steatite pyxis from this cemetery is considered to be of Early Minoan II (EM II) form,[32] thus pointing to contact between Crete and Thera in EC II, the period, as we have seen, of an expanding Aegean trade network. That trade did in fact take place between Thera and Crete is also attested by an Early Minoan II incised clay pyxis now in the possession of the École Française d'Athènes.[33] I.A. Sakellarakis sees the provenance of this import as the plain of Messara in southern Crete and notes that, in Early Cycladic II/Early Minoan II, a number of Minoan artefacts appear in the Cyclades for the first time.[34] Since Thera was the Cycladic island most accessible to Crete, evidence of EC II/EM II trade would indeed be expected there.

Although their precise find sites are uncertain, other EC II figurines have been found on Thera: for example, a folded-arm figurine, now in the Copenhagen National Museum, was obtained by Ludwig Ross in 1837 in the village of Megalochori.[35] Given that the extensive exposures of the pre-eruption LBA surface now seen in the Megalochori Quarry, to the west of the village, have yielded large quantities of sherds and pieces of obsidian, the existence of an EC settlement and attendant cemetery in that area seems probable. In addition, Renfrew notes another folded-arm figurine from Thera and places its find site on the caldera rim in the vicinity of Fira;[36] thus this artefact probably came from a quarry in which an EC cemetery had been unearthed.

The most famous Cycladic figurines found on Thera, however, are not folded-arm figures but rather the two seated harpists now residing in the Badisches Landesmuseum in Karlsruhe, Germany.[37] Found apparently in the Fira Quarry in 1838, these musicians were part of a funerary assemblage which also included four marble vessels (two bowls and two footed cups) typical of EC II. While their stylistic differences suggest the hands of two sculptors, the figures are possibly the products of a single workshop and must be considered among the finest Cycladic sculptures yet found [see Plate I]. Their presence in an EC II grave must imply significant wealth/status on the part of whoever owned them; clearly, at least some inhabitants of Thera shared in the widespread prosperity of Early Cycladic II.

On the basis of these early discoveries alone, it could be postulated that at least two settlements existed in central Thera during the Early Bronze Age: one in the vicinity of Fira, the other perhaps to the west of Megalochori. At present, the only architectural remains that could conceivably be linked to either of these settlements is a wall segment discovered in the Fira Quarry.

The existence of a third EC settlement in this region of the island has been suggested by the discovery of about a dozen tombs in the Karageorgis Quarry, on the caldera rim west of Messaria, between Fira and Athinios. Uncovered by bulldozers, these tombs presented a classic case of rescue archaeology and in the end only one was in fact excavated, yielding pottery from Early Cycladic IIIB to Middle Cyclacic (MC), including the diagnostic EC IIIB Geometric Ware.[38]

Also from the EC IIIB/MC period are the substantial architectural remains recently uncovered at Ftellos, in the Papageorgiou-Chiotopoulos Quarry, ca. 1 kilometer south of Fira. Here were found "the remains of at least two dug-out buildings ... one of [which] has been completely excavated and yielded ceramic wares dating from EC IIIB ... to MC, but in disturbed deposits."[39] EC IIIA Kastri Ware has also been reported at this site,[40] so that occupation throughout EC III seems assured. The excavated structure itself is unusual in having been subterranean, dug out from top to bottom and likely covered with a roof of clay-coated branches; apparently no longer in use at the time of the LBA eruption, this structure remains enigmatic.

In light of these two recent discoveries, it now seems probable that at least four settlements were located in this part of the island in the Early Bronze Age. Unlike the Akrotiri peninsula, this region had little to offer in terms of arable soil; what, then, was its attraction? Given our new understanding of the topography of the pre-eruption LBA island, an intriguing possibility presents itself: all these settlements were apparently located not far from cliffs created long ago during the various caldera collapse events. As suggested by W.L. Friedrich and C. Doumas, these cliffs may well have provided access to rich mineral deposits that remained subterranean and inaccessible elsewhere on the island. For example, lead could be found at Athinios, iron oxide and talc at Cape Plaka, and malachite and azurite at Cape Therma.[41] The exploitation of such resources could have provided the inhabitants of nearby settlements with a unique source of wealth.[42]

In summation, during the Early Bronze Age Thera grew from its modest Neolithic roots into an important node in the emerging Aegean trade network. The EC II period saw it experience the same prosperity as other Cycladic islands, while, in EC III, it seems to have been spared the disruptions endured elsewhere. By the close of EC IIIB, one major town, Akrotiri, had arisen in accordance with the general pattern of that age; its participation in trade is confirmed by petrographic analysis of its vessels, both local and imported, which "represent a sophisticated and wide-ranging ceramic assemblage ... [revealing] contact with other contemporary cultures, both in the immediate Cycladic region, and probably farther afield."[43] While farming certainly continued to play a vital economic role in Theran society, it was trade that enabled the site at Akrotiri to grow into a major center and to continue to thrive in the Middle Cycladic period.

The Cyclades in the Middle Bronze Age

The Aegean Middle Bronze Age (MBA) witnessed complex change in the relationship among the Cyclades, Crete and mainland Greece. Over the course of approximately 400 years (ca. 2000–1600 B.C.), the Cyclades, especially the islands in the south, fell increasingly under the growing influence of Minoan Crete, where the first palaces now came into existence. A long process of Minoanization was to commence, but the Cycladic islanders never completely surrendered their own cultural identity, perhaps because the prosperity and vibrancy of the Early Cycladic Age had provided them with a strong sense of self that not even powerful neighbors could erase.

The continued existence of a truly Cycladic culture in the Middle Cycladic period (MC) of the Middle Bronze Age has not always been recognized: G. Papathanassopoulos, for example, once wrote that developments in the Cyclades in the Middle and Late Cycladic periods were "nothing more than ramifications and influences of the Minoan and Mycenaean civilisations in the Cyclades," adding that, at the end of the Early Bronze Age, "the new naval power in the Aegean, Crete, swept away the autochthonous civilisation of the Cycladic islanders and thence forth only a few survivals of its high artistic level are discernible in the cultural course of the islands, where Minoan, and later Mycenaean art dominated all aspects of their existence until the close of the Bronze Age."[44] The belief that Cycladic culture in some sense disappeared after the EBA was fostered by two observations: (1) the development on Crete of an influential Minoan culture and (2) an apparent reduction both in overall population and in numbers of settlement sites in the Cyclades themselves.

While the growing power of Crete is undeniable, the argument that fewer people and fewer settlements in the Cyclades indicate a period of decline in the Middle Cycladic era is open to question: as has been shown above, the general prosperity and most likely the overall population of the Cyclades peaked in EC II, while EC IIIA brought disturbances that seriously disrupted life in at least some of the islands; EC IIIB then saw the dawn of a period of recovery which continued into the Middle Cycladic era. Thus, rather than being characterized as a period of decline, the Middle Cycladic is more accurately described as an era of continued recovery and consolidation: MC sites are not only more numerous than those of EC IIIB, they are also larger and more sophisticated.[45]

While the disruptions of EC IIIA would thus help to explain why, when taken in the aggregate, there seem to have been fewer settlements in the Cyclades in the MBA than in the EBA, another factor was a growing pattern of nucleation: most of the islands in the MC feature a single dominant settlement. Yet even this trend is really the continuation of a process that can be traced back to EC IIIB, when, for example, the site of Phylakopi on Melos emerged as a substantial center. This site is probably the best known of all MC settlements and, in fact, the destruction of the "first city" (Phylakopi I), apparently by earthquake, at the end of EC IIIB is taken to mark the break between EC and MC in traditional Cycladic chronology. The MC settlement that arose on the site (Phylakopi II) was carefully laid out, with well built houses of 2 to 4 rooms protected both by the promontory on which the settlement lay and by a fortification wall which defended the exposed side of the town. Likewise, the site of Ayia Irini on Kea, which seems to have housed almost the entire population of the island in the MC period, saw the construction of fortification walls: an early MC wall with a bastion at the entrance to the city and a late MC wall with square or rectangular towers.[46] Since some major MC sites do not appear to have been fortified, local factors must have played a role in determining the defensive posture of settlements. However, it should be noted that the congregation of an island's population in a single large center may in itself have been carried out as a protective measure, since one main site is more easily defended than many scattered, smaller villages.

In general, Middle Cycladic settlements follow the Early Cycladic tradition of being located on or near the sea, indicating continuity in the inhabitants' interest in maritime activities. While such locations obviously offered opportunities for engaging in transport and trade, they were also vulnerable to sea-borne attack, requiring at least some towns to build fortifications as a protective measure against piracy and/or military attack by aggressive neighbors (perhaps including Crete).[47]

The advantages of access to the sea, however, far outweighed the disadvantages, and the Cycladic islanders continued their mercantile role within the Aegean: as Oliver Dickinson has stated, "there is much evidence for exchange patterns involving the Cyclades, Aegina and the central parts of the mainland throughout the MBA," adding that "certain settlements...appear to be key points, 'emporium' sites that may have acted as conduits for commodities from wide areas."[48] The major indicator of such trade is, of course, pottery, whether it be Cycladic pottery found elsewhere or foreign pottery found on the Cyclades themselves. Indeed, the MC period is best known today by its pottery, both local and imported, and the study of these artefacts reveals the economic realities of the Cycladic Middle Bronze Age, namely, strong links between the islands and the Greek mainland, especially in the early MC, followed by growing Minoan influence in the islands during the late MC.

Christos Doumas once suggested that, in the realm of art, the Middle Cycladic was noteworthy only for its pottery,[49] and it is true that MC potters produced outstanding vessels of many types: a Dark Burnished Ware characterized by a lustrous coat in colors shading from black through brown to red; the Cycladic White Ware with its fine fabric decorated in matt black paint; and the late MC Black-and-red (or Bichrome) Ware, which featured a combination of elements from both Dark Burnished and Cycladic White, with a predilection for burnished red elements and the depiction of birds. Cycladic vessels of these and other MC types exported to the Greek mainland in the early Middle Helladic (MH) had a pronounced impact upon the development of local MH pottery: Cycladic White imports, for example, have been identified at MH Lerna in the Peloponnese and seem to have exerted a strong stylistic influence upon the local MH Matt-painted Ware.[50] In turn, MH pottery exerted its own influence upon Cycladic ceramic art, especially in the shapes of vessels.[51] Indeed, Middle Helladic pottery is so common at MC sites that J.B. Rutter has postulated "consistent and extensive contacts in the early MBA between the Cyclades and an area from the northeastern Peloponnese to Boiotia."[52] These early MC ties to the Greek mainland continued into the late MC, when increasing contact with Minoan Crete becomes evident in the ceramic record.

Evidence of exchange between Crete and the Cyclades in the Middle Bronze Age not surprisingly takes the form of: (1) Cycladic pottery found on Crete and (2) imported Minoan pottery found on the islands. With regard to the former, the catalogue provided by S. Stucynski convincingly demonstrates the relative rarity of early MC vessels in early Middle Minoan (MM) contexts: for the MM IB period we find only sherds of a Cycladic White jug with curvilinear decoration from Knossos; for the ensuing MM II period there are no

Cycladic imports listed.[53] It seems apparent that, in the early MC, Cycladic vessels, along with the goods they contained, were much more likely to be sent north to the mainland than south to Crete.

As for Minoan pottery found in the Cyclades, some examples of Middle Minoan I–II vessels have been discovered at Phylakopi II, Ayia Irini and, more recently, Akrotiri, but certainly not enough to dispel the general impression of relatively modest contacts between Crete and the Cyclades in the early MBA. This situation, however, changes significantly in the MM III/late MC era, when contact between the two regions becomes intensive.

As Stucynski's catalogue shows, MC vessels in MM III contexts have been discovered at Pyrgos, Kommos and Knossos; at the last-named site sherds of at least 12 MC "bird jugs" were found in the MM III Temple Repositories excavated by Arthur Evans.[54] In addition, a significant number of Cycladic imports in MM III contexts were identified in recent re-examinations of sherds stored in the Stratigraphical Museum at Knossos.[55] In all, over 40 imported Cycladic vessels have been identified at Knossos in MM III deposits, many of them assignable to either Melos or Thera, the Cycladic islands closest to Crete. That these vessels served as containers would indicate that Cycladic products were now reaching Crete in significant quantities;[56] that Minoan products were in turn being sent to the Cyclades is attested by MM III vessels found on the islands as well as by local Cycladic ware displaying Minoan influence. Barber sums up the situation well by noting that "there is a much stronger incidence of Cretan imports in the islands and of Cretan influences on Cycladic shapes and decoration. It seems clear that the Cyclades were being increasingly drawn into the orbit of Crete."[57] However, it would be misleading to equate growing Minoan influence at the end of the MBA with the disappearance of a Cycladic identity or culture: local pottery styles continued to exist, cist graves were still in use, and each island retained its own specific individuality. This essential "Cycladic-ness" of the islands would even survive into the Late Cycladic/Late Minoan period, when Minoan influence reached its greatest extent in the islands.

Middle Cycladic Thera

At the end of the Early Bronze Age the settlement at Akrotiri was already well established and on its way to becoming an important economic center. The transition to the Middle Bronze Age did not interrupt this progress and, during the Middle Cycladic period, Akrotiri continued to grow, both internally (in terms of its size) and externally (in terms of trade).

The internal development of the town can be seen in the distribution of
MC material (either architectural or ceramic) over the site. It is clear from
Doumas' 1978 plan of the excavation (which shows the find sites of both EBA
and MBA remains)[58] and from later discoveries that the town expanded
towards the north. Whereas EBA material is most common in the southwest,
MBA finds stretch from south to north, indicating a settlement that included
the areas of the present Xesté 3, Complexes Beta and Delta, the West House,
and the House of the Ladies.[59] Indeed, despite the fact that few systematic
explorations of the Middle Cycladic level underlying the Late Cycladic town
have as yet been carried out, Angelia Papagiannopoulou has suggested that, on
the basis of MC ceramic finds alone, the MC town had approximately the same
size and layout as the Late Cycladic (LC) town destroyed in the eruption.[60]
While such an assertion remains open to question, especially in view of the
fact that the size of the final LC town is still unknown, there is no reason to
doubt the existence of a good-sized MC town at Akrotiri, covering much of the
area presently excavated.

Architectural remains of MC Akrotiri have been detected at several locations and it seems clear that some of the LC structures on the site stand above
MC predecessors. The West House provides a good example of this phenomenon: a stratigraphic sounding made at the northwest corner of the building
brought to light a wall, approximately 2 meters long, belonging to a structure
obviously older than the existing West House and dated by ceramic finds to the
late MC period.[61] Additional soundings along the south wall of the West
House also uncovered older architectural remains in the form of another wall
associated with late MC sherds, while a section opened along the east wall
located yet another MC wall. Moreover, soundings made under the LC floors
of Rooms 3A and 6 of the West House provided additional evidence of earlier
(MC) walls on the site.[62] It thus seems certain that there are three architectural
phases represented in the area of the West House: an EC phase, an MC phase,
and the LC West House itself. Similarly, the foundations of the House of the
Ladies reflect an MC phase, while excavation in Room 16 of Complex Delta
has uncovered earlier MC walls. There are also traces of MC foundations in
the square south of Room 15 as well as to the east of Room 3 in Complex
Delta. It has even been established that at least some of these MC buildings
were adorned with wall-paintings: found in the MC level were fragments of
painted plaster which may have borne a non-pictorial style of decoration, perhaps simple monochrome surfaces or bands of color; some geometric motifs,
such as the spiral, have also been attested.[63]

More curious architectural remains are the many rock-hewn cavities now known throughout the site. The first to be discovered (in 1969) was the "Fire Deposit" mentioned above, with pottery remains dating from EC III to early MC. Since then similar cavities have been located, containing MC vessels along with signs of fire and even remains of charcoal. Papagiannopoulou has suggested that these MC pots were heirlooms that were placed in the hollows and fumigated in a ceremony of some kind. However, west of Xesté 5 and northeast of Complex Delta, several such hollows came to light that seem to have been used by MC potters for the storing and cleaning of clay.[64]

More plentiful than architectural remains, however, are the Middle Cycladic ceramic finds: the MC pottery of Akrotiri at present consists of approximately 15 complete vessels and several thousand sherds. Sometimes uncovered in the course of digging the pillar pits or in trial stratigraphic soundings, most of this material comes from debris levelled to construct the final LC town and is thus unstratified. As a result, it is not yet possible to distinguish the ceramic phases of MC Akrotiri. Nonetheless, the major MC pottery types noted elsewhere are present: Dark Burnished, Cycladic White and Black-and-red (Bichrome).

This Middle Cycladic pottery shows a wider range of shapes than the preceding Early Cycladic ware: at least twenty-nine distinctive shapes have been identified, with some of the more common being jugs of different types. This growth in pottery shapes in the MC must reflect a new demand for vessels with highly specialized functions, and such a demand would correlate well with the increasingly urban nature and prosperity of MC Akrotiri. In fact, some of the highly specialized shapes which evolved in the MC were so successful that they continued to be produced into the Late Cycladic period: examples include the loop-handled bowl (perhaps used as a measure), the bird jug, the conical cup and the nippled ewer (a type of pitcher featuring representations of female breasts). Indeed, an outstanding nippled ewer, decorated with swallows, has been found intact in a cavity in the bedrock under the West House and thus seems securely dated to the Middle Cycladic period.[65] Another West House find of the late MC also deserves mention: a large oval storage jar bearing two separate designs, one of dolphins and flying birds, the other of a bull and two goats in a mountainous landscape; this is, beyond doubt, one of the finest MC vessels yet found at Akrotiri.

Kathleen Bolton once observed that "local ceramic traditions die hard, particularly in the Cyclades," while Gerald Cadogan noted that much of the Late Cycladic I pottery from Akrotiri had an archaic look.[66] As a result, it is sometimes very difficult to determine whether a particular vessel should be assigned to late MC rather than to early LC.[67] This uncertainty is complicated by the absence at Akrotiri of any clear break between late MC and early LC I, when a major earthquake levelled the town. As has long been recognized, the debris layer created by that event contained *both* MC and early LC I pottery.[68] Even after the earthquake, when the town was rebuilt and the influence of Late Minoan Crete reached its peak, local Middle Cycladic styles and shapes of pottery continued to be produced in quantity.

That Akrotiri was a trading center by the end of the Early Bronze Age has been postulated above, and the Middle Cycladic period saw the town maintain its external contacts with both mainland Greece and Crete. The main evidence is, once again, that of pottery, and large numbers of Middle Helladic (MH) and Middle Minoan (MM) vessels have been found in the course of the current excavations. In the case of relations with Middle Helladic Greece, a number of imported MH-style vessels seem to attest to the Cycladic-mainland links already noted above. However, some of these vessels were found in the Late Cycladic I final destruction level, resulting in uncertainty as to whether they are "heirlooms" from the Middle Helladic or Late Helladic vessels which maintain the MH stylistic tradition.

Fortunately, the recent stratigraphic soundings at the West House have produced MH-style mainland pottery in a context likely to be pure MBA, and hence provide more secure evidence of contact between Thera and the mainland in that period. In light of the existing Aegean trade network, however, one must acknowledge that such contact need not always have been direct: the products of each area could have been transported throughout the Aegean by merchants from various places, including other Cycladic islands, who landed at each node to take on and to off-load cargo. What the ceramic evidence does prove, then, is that the Greek mainland was certainly part of this Aegean trade network in the Middle Bronze Age.

Another participant in the network was the island of Crete, and early contact between Thera and Minoan Crete in the MBA is well attested by fragments of Middle Minoan II Kamares Ware found both at the present excavation site and at Potamos, just to the east. At the latter site Robert Zahn had long ago discovered a sherd of imported Kamares Ware, while, at Akrotiri itself, Spyridon Marinatos recorded finding two imported Kamares sherds in a pillar pit in 1972.[69] By 1990, M.H. Wiener could write that, at Akrotiri, "classical Kamares appears regularly in the pits dug to support stanchions or test for bedrock. These sherds appear to be almost entirely Knossian, of the highest palatial quality; and to come mostly from cups and bridge-spouted jars, sent or brought from Knossos to Akrotiri as fine ware."[70] Pottery imported from Crete continued to reach Akrotiri in the late MC/MM III period and is a common find in the transitional phase of late Middle Cycladic/early Late Cycladic I, when new Late Minoan IA style vessels began to arrive on the island. These MBA imported wares influenced local potters on Thera, who tried not only to imitate their style but also to adopt Minoan pottery shapes.

That trade between Crete and Akrotiri was reciprocal in nature is indicated by discoveries of Middle Cycladic Theran ware at Knossos itself.[71] Moreover, sherds made of a clay very similar to that used on Thera have come to light at Kommos in southern Crete in an MM III context, leading Philip Betancourt to argue that there was contact between the Cyclades and southern Crete at the close of the MBA.[72] Thus there is ample ceramic evidence for trade between Crete and Thera in the Middle Bronze Age; the Late Bronze Age would see an even closer relationship evolve.

Middle Cycladic finds/sites outside Akrotiri itself are growing in number as exploration of the island continues. MC pottery has been discovered at Ftellos, at the Karageorgis Quarry and at the Mavromatis Quarry, three sites already showing signs of occupation in the Early Bronze Age. The first named site, dated to the transition from EC to MC, has yielded a well preserved Cycladic White pot and some fragments of Dark Burnished Ware. In the Karageorgis Quarry, graves dated from EC IIIB to late MC also contained Dark Burnished and Cycladic White vessels, some intact. Finally, MC finds at the Mavromatis Quarry near Akrotiri, including traces of walls and tombs, are said to extend over five hectares.[73] If this estimate proves to be accurate, the Mavromatis site must represent either a separate town or, more likely, the continuation of Akrotiri itself.

Crete and the End of the Middle Bronze Age in the Cyclades

From all the evidence available, the Middle Bronze Age saw the development of major towns in the Cyclades. That these towns were generally located near the sea, with access to good harbors, argues for the continued prominence of maritime activity in the islands; that at least two such towns had fortification walls points to the existence of some danger, probably sea-borne. One can conclude that both peaceful exchange and hostile sea-raids played large roles in the lives of the MBA Cycladic islanders. As there is no evidence to suggest any political unity among the islands, Cycladic mariners were most likely involved in raiding each other's domain, as seems to be reflected in Thucydides' famous statement (I.5) that "in ancient times the Greeks and the barbarians who inhabited the coast and the islands, when communication by sea was more commonplace, became tempted to turn to piracy under the leadership of their most powerful men...They would descend upon a town with no walls to protect it,...and would plunder it." J.A. MacGillivray has even asserted that Middle Cycladic Phylakopi, Ayia Irini and possibly Akrotiri were essentially pirate towns.[74] This thesis, however, is difficult to prove, in that the material evidence of contact/exchange (e.g., pottery from one place found at another) is silent as to whether it arrived by peaceful trade or by hostile seizure.

In addition to Cycladic contact with the mainland and with Crete, trade certainly existed among the islands themselves in the MBA: Middle Cycladic Melian pottery, for example, has been found on Siphnos, Naxos, Tenos, Delos, at Ayia Irini on Kea and at Akrotiri; Theran pottery in turn has been identified at Phylakopi.[75] Direct contact with more distant ports of call, however, may have become less frequent as Minoan Crete increasingly established itself as the middle-man between the eastern Mediterranean and the Aegean world.[76] There can be little doubt that Crete now enjoyed direct contact with Syria, Palestine, Mesopotamia, Asia Minor, Cyprus and Egypt. In stark contrast, evidence for direct contact between the Near East and the Cyclades is almost non-existent.[77] The conclusion is obvious: Crete had now become *the* major Aegean node in an eastern Mediterranean trade network and would control the secondary diffusion of eastern products within the Aegean. This raises the very difficult (and controversial) question of the political relationship between Minoan Crete and the Cycladic islands at the close of the Middle Bronze Age: was this the period during which, according to tradition, King Minos of Crete cleared the Aegean Sea of pirates and established Minoan hegemony, i.e., the start of the so-called Minoan thalassocracy? Certainly, as the Late Bronze Age gets under way, the Minoan presence on the Cycladic islands, including Thera, is more pronounced than ever before.

CHAPTER THREE

THERA AND CRETE IN THE LATE BRONZE AGE

According to tradition, Minos was the first to establish a navy. He became master of the Hellenic Sea, ruling over the Cycladic islands, and founding colonies on most of them. He drove out the Carians, and made his own sons rulers; thus he did what he could to eradicate piracy in those waters. (Thucydides I.4)

Perhaps the most vexing and divisive problem pertaining to the Late Bronze Age in the Aegean is the extent of Minoan control over the Cycladic islands. Scholars are increasingly being drawn into one of two camps: the "Cycladic nationalists" (who minimize the power of Crete over the islands) and the "Minoan imperialists" (who maximize it).[1] The latter camp is bolstered by ancient Greek historians who wrote of a Minoan "thalassocracy" or rule of the sea: not only Thucydides but also Herodotus and Diodorus Siculus proclaim Minos of Crete the ruler of the Aegean. Thucydides depicts Minos and his navy as driving out the Carian inhabitants of the islands, while Herodotus, attributing maritime supremacy to Minos of Knossos (III.122), states that the islanders did not pay him tribute but rather manned his ships when needed (I.171). Presenting a more complicated scenario, Diodorus Siculus (V.84) records that, before the time of the Trojan War, Minos of Crete sent many colonists to the Cyclades, which (he claims) were as yet uninhabited; then, after the fall of Troy, the Carians gained control of the sea and seized the Cyclades. Only after this did the increasingly powerful Greeks drive out the Carians and take over most of the islands. In sum, while these ancient authors do not present a consistent picture, they do seem to be reflecting a very old tradition in which the Minoans exercised great power in the Aegean.

That Minoan Crete had significant influence over at least some of the Cycladic islands in the Late Bronze Age is undeniable: at the sites of Phylakopi on Melos, Ayia Irini on Kea and Akrotiri on Thera, architecture, metalwork, wall-painting and pottery all show a great degree of "Minoanization" in Late Cycladic I (LC I). For example, while local pottery styles continued in LC I, and were not radically different from those seen in the late Middle Bronze Age, they now existed alongside a growing number of Late Minoan IA (LM IA) ceramic imports from Crete and local imitations thereof. Moreover, the inhabitants of these three islands even adopted the Minoan Linear A script and the Minoan system of weights and measures. To many, all this is strong evidence that the Cyclades, or at least some of them, were "colonies" of Crete and that a Minoan Empire (probably ruled from Knossos) extended from the

Aegean to the Dodecanese and the coasts of Asia Minor. It has consequently been argued that Akrotiri and other prominent island sites were major parts of an empire created mainly by Crete's need for secure access to raw materials, especially copper and tin, and also to exotic luxury items desired by its ruling elite.[2]

However, even those who envision large numbers of Minoans actually settled in the Cycladic islands note that "the safeguarding of trade routes and establishment of colonies need not necessarily involve political control from the homeland;" in addition, they clearly recognize the survival of Cycladic culture at the very time when the power of Minoan Crete was at its greatest height.[3] It is in fact this survival of Cycladic culture in the LBA which fuels the Cycladic nationalists. For example, Christos Doumas has argued that "Late Cycladic culture is a natural continuation of Middle Cycladic. Foreign influences, either Minoan or Helladic, left their mark, but the character of indigenous culture was never substantially altered."[4] In other words, the Cyclades were never subsumed into a "Greater Minoa."

Much of the often heated controversy about a Minoan thalassocracy hinges on the politically-charged word "colony." Yet, as Keith Branigan has pointed out, there can be different kinds of colonies: e.g., the settlement colony, in which foreigners establish and populate a town on previously vacant land; the governed colony, in which a foreign administration is imposed by force upon a previously existing settlement; and the community colony, in which a significant proportion of a settlement's population is composed of foreign immigrants.[5] Given that Phylakopi, Ayia Irini and Akrotiri all housed Cycladic populations long before their Minoanization in the Late Bronze Age, they cannot have been settlement colonies of Crete. In fact, the only widely acknowledged Minoan settlement colonies are those at Kastri on Kythera and at Trianda on Rhodes, both founded to facilitate trade.[6] Accordingly, only governed or community colonies would seem to be applicable to the three major "Minoanized" Cycladic settlements named above.

While governed colonies cannot at present be ruled out, the community colony model, with its significant proportion of foreign immigrants (in this case, Minoans) living within an established settlement, seems best to fit the archaeological evidence at Akrotiri and elsewhere in the Cyclades. For example, a Minoan presence would explain how Minoan architectural features in buildings, Minoan iconography on wall-paintings, Minoan (or Minoanizing) pottery and even the presence of Linear A could co-exist with strong local Cycladic elements.[7] Minoan immigrants to the Cyclades might then play an economic rather than a political role, perhaps as merchants engaged in trade (either freelance or as agents of the Minoan elite) or as skilled craftsmen producing high quality products suitable for export. They would, over time, most likely intermarry with the local population, creating a mixed elite that based its wealth on trade. Consequently, the Minoan thalassocracy need not have been anything more than an economic relationship between Crete and the Cyclades in which the latter would benefit not only from Crete's own resources, high quality products and sophisticated culture, but also from Crete's contacts with areas beyond the Cyclades themselves.

Within the Aegean world, the Cyclades continued to maintain direct contact with the Greek mainland, with at least Kea, Melos and Thera forming what has been called a "Western String" network between Crete and Greece.[8] For the Minoans, trade with the mainland was vital, for in Attica were found the abundant metal resources (copper, lead, silver) required by Crete. That Cycladic islanders may have taken on the role of middlemen in this trade is suggested by the presence of mainland Late Helladic I (LH I) imports on Kea, Melos and Thera. Indeed, at Ayia Irini on Kea imports from the mainland equal those from Crete in LC I and outnumber them by LC II. Moreover, there are a significant number of Late Helladic sherds at Phylakopi and Akrotiri, sites farther from the mainland.[9] This contact with the early Mycenaean world is also reflected in Late Cycladic pottery found on the mainland itself, especially in Attica and the Argolid.[10] There can thus be little doubt that the LC I islanders' world encompassed the Greek mainland as well as Crete, and it is likely that Cycladic ships carrying Cycladic as well as Minoan products played an important role in the economic and cultural development of the mainland.

Cycladic contacts with the eastern Mediterranean, however, must have been somewhat constrained by Crete's emerging role as "gatekeeper" to the Aegean. Crete certainly enjoyed direct contact with Egypt and the Near East, as recent discoveries of Minoan-style paintings at Alalakh in Syria, Kabri in Israel, Miletus in Turkey and Tell el-Dabʻa (Avaris) in Egypt have made clearer than ever before.[11] Some of the Near Eastern products flowing to Crete, including prestigious luxury commodities such as ivory, gold and ostrich eggs, would be secondarily redistributed to the Cyclades. Thus Late Bronze Age Cypriot pottery has been identified on both Melos and Thera, while the excavations at Akrotiri have yielded pottery from LBA Kos as well as a Syro-Palestinian amphora and fragments of Syro-Palestinian gypsum vessels.[12]

Accordingly, whether or not a Minoan thalassocracy in the political sense ever existed (either over the entire Cycladic world or simply over those islands of more strategic importance to Crete), there did come into being what may be termed a Minoan economic orbit, and the Cyclades in the early LBA were enjoying a new prosperity that must have been fostered by the growing wealth and influence of Crete. After the destructions at the late MC/early LC boundary, apparently by earthquake, Phylakopi, Ayia Irini and Akrotiri were rebuilt on larger and more sophisticated scales, and the islanders resumed producing and exporting local goods: Cycladic bird jugs and nippled ewers, for example, are found on Crete in LM I contexts.[13] Phylakopi, Ayia Irini and Akrotiri had now become key nodes in a network of trade stations that allowed seafarers to sail safely in a loop that united Crete, Thera, Melos, Kea and the Greek mainland. Indeed, only such a scenario reasonably accounts for the wide distribution of Minoan, Mycenaean and Cycladic products throughout the Aegean. Trading as part of a Minoan-dominated regional economic network, the Cycladic people were greatly influenced but not completely overwhelmed by the powerful civilization to the south; while adopting and adapting much that was Minoan, they still maintained their inherent Cycladic identity.

Crete and Thera: A Special Relationship

Near the beginning of Late Cycladic I, at a time when early LM IA Minoan pottery was arriving on Thera, a serious earthquake struck the southern Aegean. Not only Thera but even Crete suffered massive damage, with Knossos itself being severely affected. Farther afield, the islands of Kos and Rhodes also show signs of seismic damage at this time.[14] On Thera, the ruined settlement at Akrotiri had to be rebuilt, and the wealth of the new town, as manifested in its more sophisticated architecture, its elaborate wallpaintings, its pottery and the other artefacts now being brought to light by excavation, makes it very clear that the early LC I earthquake did not seriously disrupt the economy of the island. Foreign contact quickly resumed; that most of this contact involved Minoan Crete is attested by the fact that Akrotiri is by far the most Minoanized settlement yet found in the Cyclades.

Geography alone would account for a special relationship between Thera and Crete: as the southernmost of the Cycladic islands, Thera was only a day's sail from Crete, making contact between the two relatively easy. From Thera, Minoan products could be distributed throughout the entire Aegean, carried by Minoan and/or Theran vessels. Thus, by LC I, Thera had become a vital part of the pan-Aegean trade network dominated by Crete, and Akrotiri, with its harbor facing south towards Crete, was the main beneficiary.

Nonetheless, the Minoanization of Akrotiri was not complete. While many features of the town certainly do reflect Minoan influence, local Cycladic features persist. An illustrative case study involves ceramics. It has been estimated that only ca. 7.5% of all the pottery found at Akrotiri are LM IA imports from Crete and that local vases account for ca. 85–90% of the total.[15] In her detailed study of the local painted pottery from the volcanic destruction level, Marisa Marthari has isolated three main types: (1) vessels that imitate Minoan prototypes, though with some degree of independence; (2) vessels that combine Minoan elements with local tradition; and (3) vessels that continue the local Cycladic tradition.[16] Those vessels that blend Minoan and Cycladic traits (type 2) result in something novel, e.g., the white-coated surface decorated with dark brown paint that gives Theran White Coated Ware its name or the polychrome ware with its subjects taken from nature (e.g., swallows, dolphins, goats). Even the most strongly Minoanized pottery (type 1) exhibits a freer spirit, especially in the use of floral motifs such as reeds and lilies. Thus, LC I ceramic painting at Akrotiri retained its local character despite influences emanating from Crete.

A similar situation exists with respect to the shapes of vessels, with some seen as Minoan or Minoanizing and others as purely Cycladic or even purely Theran. For example, the conical cups which are found in large numbers at Akrotiri represent a Minoan form that the Therans adopted for their own use.[17] On the other hand, some types of LC I pottery from Akrotiri seem purely Cycladic, e.g., the nippled ewers, the rectangular "trays" known as kymbai and the famous bird jugs. Their continued presence, not only on Thera but also elsewhere as exports from Thera, attests to the persistence of the local Cycladic tradition.

Likewise, wall-paintings from Akrotiri reveal both Minoan and local elements. When these paintings were first discovered, scholars stressed their Minoan iconography, pointing, for example, to the depiction of men in red skin tones and women in white skin tones, of women in Minoan-style clothing, of the typically Minoan horns of consecration, of monkeys and griffins, etc. It thus seemed to some that the Therans had either learned the art of painting on plaster from the Minoans or had Minoan artists decorate their walls.[18] However, both E.N. Davis and E. Sapouna-Sakellaraki have drawn attention to the local Cycladic features of these wall-paintings, especially to the use of a white background—a feature not found in Minoan frescoes. Davis even asserts that the "Theran style [of wall-painting], based on painting on white, is a consistent and distinct one. None of the painted walls can be attributed to a Minoan artist, nor does any painting appear closely to imitate a Minoan one. This suggests an evolved tradition."[19] Given the observations made by both sides in this debate, what these paintings (as well as the pottery) demonstrate is a synthesis of Minoan and Theran art that created something unique. Even the small amount of jewelry found so far at Akrotiri attests to a similar synthesis: local styles continue but show mounting Minoan influence. Christina Televantou has examined the jewelry depicted on the wall-paintings as well as the actual beads, rings and pins unearthed, and has concluded that traditional, local Cycladic craftsmanship continued, although absorbing Minoan influence, especially with regard to shapes and materials.[20]

The architecture of Akrotiri likewise blends two traditions, one local, the other Minoan. The Minoan features include rooms with pier-and-door partitions (called polythyra), sunken chambers known as adyta or lustral basins, light wells and horns of consecration atop buildings. Even the differing functions of the storeys seem Minoan, with workshops and storerooms below and living quarters above. Yet it should be noted that such a division in function between house levels reflects a pragmatic approach to common problems of daily life and thus need not have arisen as a direct result of Minoan influence. Local features can be seen in the tendency to use projecting cornices to mark the division of storeys and in the use of ashlar blocks to frame wall openings. In addition, the overall plan of Akrotiri appears to be more haphazard than those of comparable towns on Crete, suggesting a long established Cycladic tradition.[21]

Of course, trade with Crete was essential to the continued prosperity of Late Bronze Age Akrotiri, as its adoption of both the Linear A script and the Minoan system of weights and measures attests. Some of the commodities of that trade must have been perishable, such as timber, textiles, unguents, pigments, spices and foodstuffs. Others, however, were durable and have come to light on both Thera and Crete. In addition to the LM IA pottery mentioned above, stone vessels were imported from Crete: Peter Warren has estimated that 22% of the stone vases found on Thera originated in Crete. In return, tripod mortars made on Thera were exported to Crete.[22] Crete, however, especially needed one vital commodity: metal. Indeed, with respect to the bronze that underpinned its wealth, Crete depended upon imported copper and tin, making the security of its trade network of utmost importance.[23]

While it has long been recognized that copper was being exported from Cyprus by the Late Bronze Age, there is growing evidence that this extremely important metal was also available much closer to home, namely, at Laurion in Attica, and that Laurion rather than Cyprus was the major source of copper for the Minoans.[24] In addition, Laurion produced silver-rich lead ores, with the result that the Western String of Kea, Melos and Thera provided Crete with secure access to metal ores.[25] In fact, litharge found at Akrotiri points to a local industry in silver smelting. Since Thera itself apparently had no local source of silver, it would appear that silver-rich ore from Laurion was exported for finishing elsewhere and that the finished products would then be traded throughout the Aegean and even beyond. Given that similar evidence for metallurgy has been found at Ayia Irini on Kea, the islands of the Western String served not only as trans-shipment centers for raw ores but also as manufacturing centers producing high quality metal goods. Because of its geographical proximity, Akrotiri in particular became Crete's major link in the all-important quest for metals.

Thera in Late Cycladic I

On the basis of the archaeological evidence, the town at Akrotiri must have been the dominant settlement on Thera both economically and politically. Its size alone indicates its uniqueness: Akrotiri is thought to have covered some 20 hectares, making it 10 to 20 times larger than either Ayia Irini on Kea or Phylakopi on Melos.[26] Moreover, in comparison to Kea and Melos, both of which also had single dominant centers, Thera "reveals a more complex picture of dense and diffuse rural settlement, organized in villages, hamlets, villas and isolated farms" that echo the general settlement pattern of Crete.[27] The topography of the island, however, limited settlement in the north, which was more rugged and less fertile than the older and smoother terrain in the south. It was especially in the Akrotiri peninsula, then, that Late Bronze Age farmers found good arable land, while fishermen and traders found sheltered harbors.

The hinterland of the town at Akrotiri stretched from Cape Akrotiri eastwards towards the modern village of Emporion. At Cape Akrotiri, not far from the modern lighthouse, Spyridon Marinatos investigated a ravine which yielded both MC and LC sherds.[28] Just over two kilometers to the east, Mount Archangelos stands guard over the plain below: here Christos Doumas reported finding evidence of Late Cycladic occupation and the large number of sherds lying on the top of the hill suggests prolonged use of the site.[29] To the north lies the site of Katsades, where remains of LC I painted storage jars have been found and approximately where, in 1870, a trial trench dug by H. Mamet and H. Gorceix turned up pre-eruption walls and pottery.[30] This area in general was very suitable for farming and was probably occupied by a small rural hamlet or perhaps several scattered farmsteads. In fact, slightly to the east, a recent road cut leading to Vounari Kaparies has revealed excellent Bronze Age soil exposures that include traces of walls and pottery *in situ*.

To the northeast, at the edge of the caldera, is found the site of Balos, also explored in 1870 by Mamet and Gorceix, who found two buildings of the pre-eruption period, one of which had partly collapsed into the caldera in the course of the eruption [see Figure 18].[31] The buildings were free-standing and separated only by a narrow passageway. The larger of the two (the western building) measured ca. 9.7 x 9.4 meters and was built of rubble stone and timber; a coarse plaster, painted yellow, lined its interior walls. It had at least four rooms: the two largest in the north and two smaller ones to the south.[32] The southeastern room contained two narrow closet-like areas, a built-in cupboard and the skeleton of a goat. The smaller (eastern) building also contained animal bones (of both sheep and goats) on a floor of earth covered with straw, and probably served as a stable. To its north extended a small yard, bordered by a parapet-like wall on the east. In clearing these structures, the French team also came upon fragments of obsidian, a copper saw and a large number of pots which are now housed in the French School at Athens. Some were storage jars that had contained barley, peas and lentils. The pottery, similar to that found at Akrotiri, dates the complex convincingly to the LC I period. Doumas has speculated that the site was part of a suburb of Akrotiri (only about 1 kilometer away), while others have interpreted it as an independent farmstead complex.[33] However, since it now appears that a caldera had existed in this region prior to the LBA eruption, it is possible that there was a small port at Balos and that these buildings stood at the top of a path leading down to this inner harbor.

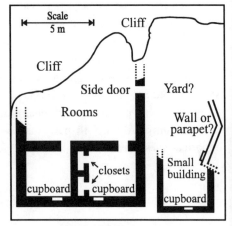

Figure 18: Balos,
after Fouqué:1879:119

To the south of Balos, and serving as the western boundary of the postulated harbor of Akrotiri, stood Mavrorachidi, a small hill whose almost flat summit bears traces of a pre-eruption building as well as potsherds, pieces of marble and metal, and small fragments of painted plaster. Doumas has suggested that a watchtower stood here in the Late Bronze Age, although the presence of marble and painted plaster could also point to a villa.[34] Much more extensive LBA remains, however, were brought to light in the nineteenth century some 600 meters to the east of the Akrotiri site, in a ravine known both as Potamos and Kamara. In 1899 the German excavator Robert Zahn seems to have discovered the ruins of a storage area that once was part of a house. Rough blocks of lava made up the walls and a lava flagstone near the front of the structure was apparently used in the grinding of grain, as were the numerous grinding stones also found here. Other discoveries included part of a gold necklace and LC I large storage jars.[35] Doumas has argued that the building at Potamos was originally part of the Akrotiri settlement because "the ground between the excavation and the Potamos Valley does not follow the natural southward slope,...but rises towards the sea, thus creating a concave plateau inland. The plateau can be explained if one supposes that the ground has subsided over collapsed multi-storey houses."[36] Northeast of the Potamos/Kamara ravine Late Cycladic I remains have been found in the Mavromatis Quarry on the edge of the caldera, about 1 kilometer from the Akrotiri excavation; Doumas believes this area might also have housed a suburb of Akrotiri.[37] Whether the influence of Akrotiri extended even farther to the east is at present unknown, but the identification of at least eight LC I sites (in addition to Akrotiri itself) attests to the densely settled nature of the Akrotiri peninsula.

In contrast, other regions of the island seem to have held only scattered hamlets or farmsteads. For example, Doumas' excavation at Ftellos (near Fira) revealed two rooms dated to LC I, as well as a yard and what looks very much like a stable with its roof supported by a central column—hence the identification of the site as a farmstead [see Figure 19].[38] In addition, in a field apparently lying north of Mount Profitis Ilias, Mamet and Gorceix sunk a trial trench that hit upon the remnants of LC I walls. It would appear that one or more buildings had existed at the site, whose exact location is no longer known.[39] A more substantial settlement has been postulated near modern Oia in the north of the island: the Oia Quarry contains good Late Bronze Age soil exposures and has yielded LC I finds, leading Doumas to suggest that here was "the most important north-facing prehistoric settlement on Thera: located not far from the coast, it was probably the main point of contact between Thera and the neighbouring island of Ios."[40]

On the south coast of what is now Therasia, ruins of a small hamlet came to light in 1866. During mining operations in the Alaphouzos Quarry, approximately 50 meters inland from the modern coast (but quite inland prior to the eruption), Bronze Age remains were first noted by local inhabitants and then investigated scientifically by F. Fouqué in 1867. Fouqué reported a total of six free-standing structures, spread over ca. 125 meters east to west, the most impressive of which was a roughly 12 x 11 meter house with a large yard

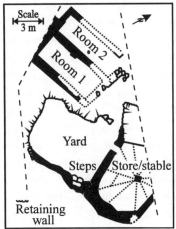

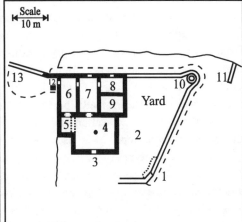

Figure 19: Ftellos,   Figure 20: Alaphouzos Quarry Site,
after Doumas:1973:162   after Fouqué:1879:96

adjacent [see Figure 20 above]. The structure was well built, featuring ashlar quoins complemented by irregular lava blocks and reinforcing timbers of olive wood. The ground floor was apparently divided into six rectangular rooms, the southernmost of which (Room 4) was spacious enough to need its ceiling supported by a central column; on its west side was a smaller room (Room 5), where numerous clay and stone vessels, stone weights and the skeletons of three sheep or goats were found. However, it was the main room itself that supplied the most important skeleton—that of an older man of medium height, the first known victim of the eruption. The remaining rooms to the north (Rooms 6–9) were smaller, and at least two of these had windows on their northern walls. The adjoining yard (2) was defined by a rubble wall and contained in its northeast corner a peculiar round structure (less than 1 meter in diameter) made of rough lava stone and approached by three steps (10). Although preserved to a height of 1 meter, the structure's function was unclear, with some interpreting it as an altar for sacrifice and others as a support base for a lost construction or even as a cistern. Further to the east was found a wall segment from another building (11) and associated potsherds, while to the west of the house stood a square pillar (12) composed of two ashlar blocks and standing roughly 2 meters high, as well as the remains of another structure/wall. The excavation as a whole yielded a good deal of LC I pottery (including large decorated storage jars), stone vessels, obsidian tools, traces of barley and other foodstuffs, and even an olive press. Unfortunately, the location of this site has long been lost.[41]

The isolated remnant of prehistoric Thera now known as Aspronisi was once part of the southern extension of Therasia and in the Late Bronze Age lay near the entrance to the Lower Pumice 2 caldera. On the basis of potsherds found in large numbers at the interface of the Bronze Age surface and the tephra cover it seems possible that a settlement/farmstead of some sort had also existed here.

The evidence for additional Late Cycladic I sites on Thera is rather more tenuous. For example, a single LC I storage jar was supposedly found in a grave on the Sellada of Mesa Vouno, an LC I vase was alleged to have come from the region of Exomiti at the southernmost tip of the island, and at Cape Koloumvos in northeast Thera LC I pottery was allegedly found in tombs.[42] These vessels, however, may have been plundered from other sites which their sellers desired to keep secret. The site of Megalochori is, however, more problematic: Hiller von Gaertringen referred to a cemetery of the "Kykladenkultur" located somewhere south of the town, and while some think these graves might have been Early Cycladic, J.W. Sperling argues for a Late Cycladic date.[43]

Considering how much of the island was either destroyed in the eruption or so thoroughly entombed by tephra that excavation cannot be carried out, even discounting the somewhat questionable sites named in the paragraph above does little to alter our general picture of Thera in the Late Bronze Age: the island was clearly much more densely populated than the other Cyclades. What the inhabitants grew in a climate that may have been a bit less arid than that of today[44] is gradually becoming clearer as the artefactual and botanical evidence is unearthed and analyzed: basic food crops included barley, wheat, legumes, olives, figs, nuts (especially almonds and pistachios) and, of course, grapes. Honey would have been gathered, and spices such as saffron were also part of the Theran diet; the prominence of the saffron crocus in the art of LC I Akrotiri strongly suggests its value as a cash crop, in great demand abroad not only as a spice but also as a perfume, a medicine and a dye for clothing. Another commodity that might have been exported was linen, as botanical studies have demonstrated the cultivation of flax on the island.[45] The recent identification of a silk cocoon at Akrotiri also hints at high quality textile exports and may help explain the sheer garments worn by several female figures in the wall-paintings from Akrotiri. Indeed, the elaborate clothing seen in these wall-paintings, the large number of loom weights discovered during the excavation, as well as the fact that historical Thera was very famous for its distinctive clothing, all suggest a thriving textile industry on the Bronze Age island. However, given that a great amount of water is used in the preparation of flax, Bronze Age Thera needed a secure water supply in order to maintain a textile industry. While some believe there was a scarcity of fresh water at Akrotiri, N. Kourmoulis has determined that "an unconfined aquifer developed at a small depth below the surface...and was used for the water supply by the population of the island" *via* wells. Evidence supporting the existence of this aquifer is found in one of the wall-paintings from the West House in Akrotiri, in which women are clearly shown getting water from a well.[46]

Animal husbandry was also vital to the life of the island, and the most detailed analysis of animal remains from Thera has been carried out by C.S. Gamble, who distributes the fauna at Akrotiri as follows: sheep and/or goats account for 72% of the total, pigs for 19%, and cattle for 9%.[47] Other fauna exploited for food included fish and mollusks. Especially noteworthy in the latter category is the murex, which accounts for roughly half of the mollusks found at Akrotiri and which was used mainly as bait; however, murex shells were also crushed for the production of purple dye and were occasionally used as flooring.[48]

While it is now possible to reconstruct with a reasonable degree of certainty the crops, animals, diet and even some of the exports of the Late Bronze Age Therans, it remains much more difficult to ascertain the social and political structure of the island. There can be no doubt that skilled craftsmen and merchants existed alongside the farmers and fishermen who must have constituted the majority of the population, or that the infrastructure of the town of Akrotiri (e.g., sewers, paved streets, public squares) suggests a high degree of organization indicative of some type of central authority. It even seems logical to assume that Akrotiri was the political as well as the economic center of the island and that a powerful ruling elite was based within the town. Beyond this, however, difficult questions remain to be answered and only a thorough examination of Akrotiri itself will enable us to suggest, even tentatively, some answers.

CHAPTER FOUR

THE LATE BRONZE AGE CITY AT AKROTIRI

An archaeological investigation on the island of Thera was planned
many years ago by the writer as it was fairly certain that at several
places throughout Thera and Therasia considerable ruins were hid-
den. (Spyridon Marinatos: *Thera I*, 3)

The history of the modern excavations on Thera began, somewhat ironically,
with the eruption of 1866. This event drew the attention of several European
researchers, most notably the French geologist F. Fouqué. In 1867 Fouqué
visited Therasia, where he examined the discoveries made the previous year in
the Alaphouzos Quarry. Moving on to Thera, Fouqué found traces of walls
and numerous potsherds in the Favatas ravine, ca. one kilometer to the southeast of the modern village of Akrotiri. He was followed in 1870 by H. Mamet
and H. Gorceix, who explored both the site at Balos and the Favatas ravine,
where they discovered the remains of two structures and even a fragment of
wall-painting depicting lilies. Mamet also investigated the pre-eruption surface
exposed in a field north of Mount Archangelos and found traces of walls as
well as potsherds. Little else was undertaken until the arrival on Thera of F.
Hiller von Gaertringen in 1896. While Hiller was concerned mainly with
excavating the historical Greek city known today as "Ancient Thera" on Mesa
Vouno, he was aware of the earlier discoveries near Akrotiri; in 1899, one of
his colleagues, Robert Zahn, excavated at Potamos, the ravine located ca. 600
meters to the east of the one previously explored by the French.

A long time then passed before a thorough scientific excavation of the site
near Akrotiri was undertaken. In 1967 Spyridon Marinatos dug at the Favatas
ravine in an attempt to confirm his theory that the Bronze Age eruption of
Thera had been responsible for the destruction of Minoan Crete. His discovery
of a "Bronze Age Pompeii" (as it was called in the press) came quickly: in his
first trenches he hit upon major ruins. The years from 1967 to 1974 saw
Marinatos excavate and publish the finds from several areas of the site. Upon
his death in 1974, Marinatos was succeeded as director of the excavation by
Christos Doumas. At present, ca. 12,000 square meters have been cleared in
an area roughly 150 meters north-south and 80 meters east-west. Most of this
area was accessible to excavation because winter torrents had eroded much of
the blanket of tephra deposits over the years. In fact, the erection of a protective metal roof over the excavation had been a priority of Marinatos, who real-
ized the danger that winter rains presented to the newly exposed ruins.

Only a small portion of the Late Cycladic I settlement has yet been cleared and much data remain to be published. Thus our understanding of the site is in almost constant flux, and it should be acknowledged that future excavation may well alter our general picture of Bronze Age Akrotiri and will certainly alter many details.

The Site at Akrotiri

After the earthquake at the start of Late Cycladic I, the Middle Cycladic city of Akrotiri had to be extensively rebuilt, although the general plan of the town was maintained. The major problem faced by the inhabitants was the removal of debris, which was gathered together in various open areas (e.g., streets and squares) and then packed down. This activity resulted in the ground levels of these open areas being raised to such a degree that, in many places, the inhabitants had to use debris to raise the ground levels of their houses to match those outside. Thus new entrances had to be constructed, and some rooms that had previously stood on the ground floor were transformed into half-basements.[1]

The debris itself was mainly precipitated from upper floors destroyed by the earthquake. This destruction, while severe, presented the people of the town with a unique opportunity to restore their dwellings in a more "modern" style. Thus, interiors were renovated and new, more elaborate wall-paintings adorned some of their walls. These were the buildings later overwhelmed by the volcanic eruption in late LC I and now being brought to light by the current excavations [see Figure 21].

While not the only LC I site on the island, Akrotiri was without doubt the major settlement of Thera, housing several thousand inhabitants within an area estimated as ca. 200,000 square meters. The narrow, winding streets that ran through the town were paved with flagstones and contained the underground stone-lined sewer system which served individual houses. Their irregular layout is very much like that of modern villages on the island, whose labyrinthine streets afford protection from often violent winds and help drain the settlement of rainwater; in more dangerous times, they also provided safety by making enemy attacks more difficult.

The buildings at Akrotiri varied greatly in size, plan, architecture and decoration, each reflecting its function and the wealth/status of its occupants, with the fine ashlar structures (the "xestai") being the most impressive. In general, however, most structures were built of rubble stone, clay and wooden reinforcements, no doubt to minimize earthquake damage. Their external

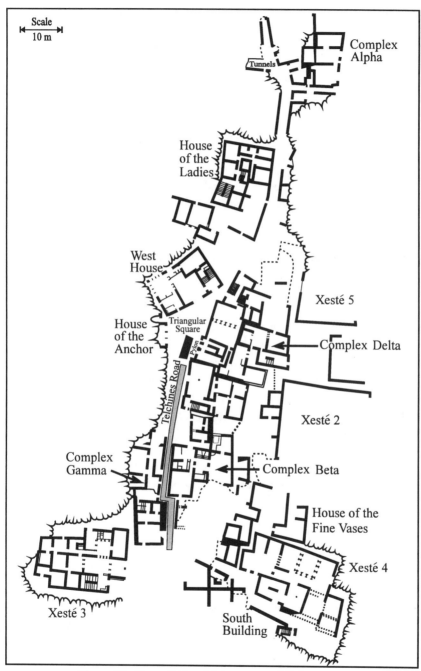

Figure 21: Plan of Akrotiri (courtesy of C. Doumas)

facades, usually two or three storeys tall, were coated with the straw-tempered clay also found on the inner walls of ground floors and basements, with high quality plaster generally restricted to the interior walls of the upper storeys. Doors and windows often had frames of fine ashlar masonry, with the doors themselves being made of wood and the windows occasionally having wooden grills across them. Windows were normally small on the lowest floor, but large picture windows might break the walls of an upper storey. Partly because of window size, it has become common to interpret the basement and ground floor rooms as service areas (e.g., storerooms, workshops, kitchens and even retail shops), while the upper floors are thought to have contained private living quarters as well as ceremonial and reception rooms.[2] The residents may also have used the flat roof as an additional living or sleeping area, especially during the hot summer months; it is likely that a parapet surrounded the roof to ensure a measure of privacy.[3]

Entrances to buildings featured a window beside the door, no doubt to allow light and fresh air into the vestibule when the wooden door itself was shut. Inside the buildings rooms were divided by partition walls of varying quality: some were substantial structures of stone and clay, while others were more simply made of sun-dried mudbrick. Large rooms used pillars, columns or, in a few cases, the pier-and-door partitions known as polythyra to support their wooden ceilings, and floors ranged from plain beaten earth to elaborate flagstone pavements. There were even floors inlaid with pebbles or fragments of sea shells to create a type of mosaic. Stairways, often located near the main entrance, could be made of either wood or stone, and were supported by wooden beams.

Such, then, were the general features of the buildings at Akrotiri. It seems appropriate to begin a more detailed analysis of the excavated structures with Xesté 3: not only is it the first building on the site to be seen by visitors, it is also the area in which the earliest occupation of Akrotiri has been documented.

Xesté 3

At the southwestern edge of the excavation site lies Xesté 3 [see Figure 22], one of the most impressive buildings yet found at Akrotiri. Built of ashlar masonry with walls reinforced by timber, Xesté 3 has a facade approximately 12 meters long. At least two, and perhaps three storeys high in its western half, Xesté 3 had 15 rooms on its ground floor. But what marks this structure as truly outstanding are the features that it shares with Minoan palaces and villas: in addition to wall-paintings, there are polythyra, an "adyton" (a sunken area sometimes called a lustral basin), and Minoan-like benches. It is thus understandable that Xesté 3 would be commonly interpreted as a public building of great importance to the life of the town.

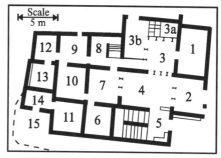

Figure 22: Xesté 3

The plan of the building suggests a division into eastern and western sections, with the former interpreted primarily as a sacred or ceremonial area due to the presence of large rooms, polythyra, elaborate wall-paintings, and, especially, the adyton—the only such ritual area so far identified at Akrotiri. In contrast, the western section seems to have served as a service/storage area: it features smaller rooms with no polythyra and has only abstract wall-paintings in a single room. Any private quarters were most likely located on the upper floor(s) of this area.

The entrance to Xesté 3 was Room 5, at the southeast corner of the facade. Here a doorway led into a vestibule, paved with flagstones and flanked by stone benches, which gave access to a stairway to the upper floor. Both the vestibule and the walls on either side of the staircase bore paintings: the excavators record a life-size male figure in the vestibule, while the paintings by the staircase seem to have depicted a mountainous landscape.[4]

To the right of the staircase was an opening that joined Room 5 to Room 4, which could justly be called the Room of the Polythyra: in the east a polythyron connected it with Room 2, in the north with Room 3, and in the west with Room 7. Thus the entire area encompassed by Rooms 4, 2, 7 and 3 on the ground floor could have served as one large hall with all the polythyra doors open. Such a hall probably had a ceremonial purpose: Nanno Marinatos and Robin Hägg have argued that "rooms with pier-and-door partitions on more than one side can be considered as areas of transit preceding the holy area," in this case, the adyton of Room 3; moreover, they point out that the polythyra could have served as screens, to limit not only access but also light and visibility to the adyton.[5] Indeed, the lamps discovered in Room 4 may attest to the performance of some type of ritual in darkened areas.

In Room 4 the existence of polythyra on three walls severely reduced the wall surface available for painting to the narrow strip above the pier-and-door partitions, thus virtually dictating the painting of a frieze. The resultant composition, a frieze ca. 20 centimeters in width, seems to have depicted an exotic landscape in which swallows were feeding their young and blue-colored monkeys were imitating human beings by playing harps or drawing swords.[6]

Moving north from Room 4 one would pass through the polythyron and enter the area (Room 3) containing the adyton. From similar adyta found on Crete, it is generally agreed that these sunken areas had a ritual function: worshippers would probably have descended into the basin in order to perform rituals and/or make offerings. If the rites conducted in Xesté 3 were secret in nature, the polythyra could be closed and public view of the ceremonies prevented; given the nature of the polythyra, in fact, one could postulate rituals that were open to public view at certain times and at other times were conducted in total secrecy with the closing of the doors.

The paintings on the eastern and northern walls of the ground floor adyton also confirm a religious function for this area. The east wall depicted a small shrine, crowned by "horns of consecration" (the stone bull's horns common at Minoan ceremonial sites). The entrance to the shrine was decorated with spirals on its frame and with lilies on the door itself, which also bore blood that appears to stream from the horns of consecration. On the adjacent north wall were three female figures, roughly three-quarters life-size. The woman closest to the corner where the two walls meet is shown in an awkward pose sometimes interpreted as representing a dancer: while she is clearly moving to the left (towards the other two women), her head is twisted back to look at the shrine on the eastern wall. There are two especially noteworthy features given this woman: first, her head has been shaved, leaving only a few locks, and second, she is draped in a transparent stippled veil that extends from her head to her ankles. Under the veil, she wears a sleeved bodice and a flounced skirt. The woman in the center of the north wall is depicted as sitting on a crocus-bearing knoll, with one hand touching her head and the other reaching towards her left foot, from which blood appears to be dripping. She is dressed in a transparent garment that reveals her upper body, while her lower body is skirted; in her hair appear two distinctive ornaments: a crook-shaped pin and a twig of either olive or myrtle leaves. Approaching her from the left is the third woman, holding a string of beads in her left hand. On her upper body she wears a transparent blouse-like garment that reveals her breasts, while a flounced skirt covers her lower body. Exactly what is being depicted in this narrative remains uncertain, but Doumas believes that an initiation ceremony of some kind is being conducted.[7] That blood drips both from the foot of the central woman and from the horns atop the shrine seems to imply that the shedding of blood played some role in this ceremony. In addition, the landscape suggests that the scene of the ritual may be a hill-top shrine [see Plate II].

The wall-paintings of women in the adyton (technically known as Room 3a) are supplemented by paintings of male figures in Room 3b. At least four life-size males were depicted: three naked youths (one a small boy holding a cup, the second an older boy clutching a piece of cloth, the third a young male carrying a bowl) and a seated adult male who wears a loincloth and holds a large jar. It appears that the three younger males, all of whom have their heads shaved to various degrees, were moving towards the seated man, bringing him offerings. Doumas postulates another scene of initiation, complementing that within the adyton, but involving men; perhaps the youth carrying the piece of cloth will use it to gird his loins in a male coming of age ceremony.[8]

Other ground floor rooms were also accessible from Room 4 and thus might have serviced the adyton area. Room 2, for example, is joined to Room 4 by a polythyron and was also adorned with wall-paintings, namely, a frieze/friezes of rosettes and spirals that stood above the lintels of the polythyron.[9] Room 7, to the west of Room 4, was also joined to that room by a polythyron. While no fragments of wall-paintings have yet come to light, Room 7, with the doors of the polythyron open, would have served as an extension of Room 4, and, moreover, if all the polythyra doors were opened, the complex encompassing Rooms 2, 4, and 7 would have provided a gathering area in front of the adyton some 13 meters long.

There was one other room on the ground floor that seems to have serviced the adyton in some manner: Room 1, north of Room 2 and joined to Room 3 by a doorway. Doumas believes this room to be a relatively late addition to Xesté 3,[10] and it could have been added expressly for the purpose of augmenting the service area of the adyton, perhaps being used as a treasury room.

The upper (first) storey also featured a large area connected by polythyra (Rooms 2, 3 and 4) and seems to have been lavishly adorned, especially the room directly above the adyton on the ground floor: here once stood the wall-painting now known as the "Crocus Gatherers." As was the case on the ground floor, the northern and eastern walls of upper Room 3a bore thematically related scenes: within the general theme of women gathering crocus, the artist depicted two women on the east wall and three on the north. The two women of the east wall are shown in a rocky landscape strewn with clumps of crocus, which they gingerly harvest. The right-hand figure has a shaved head except for one short and one long lock. She wears an earring and two bracelets, and her clothing consists of an elaborate bodice and a colorful flounced skirt. She looks towards the left-hand figure, who has a full head of hair and even more elaborate jewelry and clothing; she is shown harvesting the crocus with her right hand and carrying a basket in her left.

On the north wall, close to the junction with the east wall, is one of three female figures. Though not well preserved, this woman was carrying on her shoulder a basket almost identical to that carried by the woman on the adjacent wall; she is as elaborately dressed and bejewelled as the other women but is distinctive in having a reddish tinge to her full head of hair. She is depicted as moving towards the other figures of this wall and is thus a transitional figure serving to unite the two walls, much like the veiled woman in the room below.

At the western end of the north wall is a woman emptying her basket of crocus flowers into a large container; she is finely dressed in a bodice and flounced skirt and has a full head of dark hair. She seems to depict the final stage in the crocus gathering process: after picking and packing the flowers in small baskets, the women deposit their harvest into a large container. Had there been no other figures in this painting, one might easily conclude that picking crocus was a common activity for the women of Akrotiri and that the artist is simply showing us a scene from the daily life of Bronze Age Therans. However, the remainder of the painting on the north wall warns us that such a secular interpretation is unlikely.

Between the two women already described are three figures, the central one being a mature female who is sitting upon a tripartite structure/platform as though enthroned, and thus is elevated above the women gathering crocus. The rich imagery pertaining to this woman tells us clearly that she is not a figure from daily life: not only is she physically set apart from the other women but she is also adorned with much more elaborate clothing and jewelry; indeed, she wears two necklaces (one depicting ducks, the other dragonflies) and her dress is decorated with crocus flowers. In addition, lines that look like crocus stigmas appear on her cheek. Even more significantly, on her full head of long hair slithers what appears to be a snake. The two creatures that flank her also serve to set this figure apart from ordinary life: she gazes leftwards towards a blue-colored monkey presenting her with an offering, while on her other side there stands a colorfully-winged griffin in a heraldic pose. This female figure is beyond doubt the focal point of the activities depicted on both walls and can be reasonably identified as a goddess [see Plate III].

This composition raises a great number of questions, one of which is the nature of its relationship to the wall-paintings in the adyton directly below. Physically, the two compositions are distinct in that a solid floor separated them; someone in the adyton would have to proceed to the upper floor in order to view its paintings. Yet, from both a thematic and structural point of view, a connection seems probable. For example, both northern walls depict three female figures; on each of these walls the two women at either end approach the central figure. In the composition of the upper floor, the central goddess with her snake is enthroned almost directly above the woman with the injured foot on the floor below; perhaps that woman has been wounded in the foot by a snake, which has subsequently "ascended" to be one again with the goddess. The two compositions, in tandem, would accordingly depict the initiation of a mortal woman into the cult of the Great Goddess, the agent of unification being the sacred snake (for which there is much evidence from both Minoan Crete and Egypt). The real-life ritual for Theran women might thus place the would-be initiate in the adyton for the drawing of blood; she would then leave the adyton, ascend to the upper floor and be translated into the realm of the goddess.

A second question pertains to the prominence of the crocus flower, clumps of which appear in the landscapes of both the upper floor and the adyton. As mentioned earlier, saffron may have been an important cash crop for Bronze Age Thera. Its many uses would create a high demand throughout the Aegean: it was desirable as a spice, as a dye for clothing, as an ingredient in perfume, and, even more importantly, as a multi-purpose drug. In this last respect, it is instructive to note that, in historic antiquity, saffron was seen as a cure-all not only for such diverse maladies as insomnia, inflammation of the eyes, cough, and general wounds but also for specifically female ills, such as sterility and menstrual and uterine problems.[11] At least some of these uses must have been known to the inhabitants of the prehistoric Aegean, who would have regarded the crocus plant as a vital gift from the gods. Its presence in what appears to be an initiation ritual for young women suggests that the coming of age signified by the onset of menstruation is the event being celebrated.

Wall-paintings on the upper floor of Xesté 3 were not confined to Room 3a. In the adjacent Room 3b fragments discovered indicate a composition depicting at least three life-size women on the south wall; their unusual hairstyle (all seem to have their long hair bound up in snoods) differentiates them from the women depicted elsewhere in Xesté 3 and may indicate advanced age.[12] All three appear to be holding flowers (lilies and roses), while lilies and crocuses decorate their clothing. The west wall of this room seems to have borne a painting of a marshy landscape with reeds and aquatic birds, sometimes interpreted as a fowling scene.[13]

At least one other room in Xesté 3 had wall-paintings: Room 9 on the ground floor yielded fragments that are believed to have fallen from above, perhaps even from the postulated second floor. The composition, which covered at least two walls of its original room, seems purely decorative in nature: in the words of Doumas, "Double undulating relief bands passing through painted rings form a network of lozenges, each enclosing four rosettes...The plasticity of the moulding, the precision of the design and the alternation of colours in the rosettes make this...one of the loveliest master-pieces in the art of Akrotiri."[14]

Complex Gamma

Located to the northeast of Xesté 3, Complex Gamma [see Figure 23] has been only partially excavated. Although the complex in general appears to have been badly ruined in the tectonic earthquake that heralded the eruption (see Chapter 6), the excavated rooms of the eastern section are thought to form one building since there is uninterrupted access from one room to another. At least two, and possibly three storeys in height, Complex Gamma faces the western side of Telchines Road, the major north-south street that runs along the crest of the hill on which the town sits.

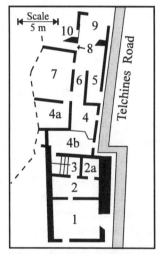

Figure 23: Complex Gamma

In the south, Rooms 1-3 form a distinct unit with unusually thick exterior walls that had been reinforced with wooden beams. These walls, in conjunction with the staircase in Room 3, provide evidence of an upper storey in at least this part of the complex. Fragments of wall-paintings found in the area of Room 1, including a segment featuring a combination of plants and spirals, most likely came from this upper storey.[15] Spyridon Marinatos had interpreted ground floor Rooms 1-3 as a workshop complex based on the stone tools (including hammers and anvils), hearth and benches they were found to contain; he was inclined to attribute the existence of this workshop to the restorers active in the area after the earthquake rather than to the original building.[16] Later excavation, however, would show that work areas of various types were not unusual within the houses of Akrotiri.

North of this industrial unit lay a cluster of rooms that included the main entrance to Complex Gamma, Room 5. As befits an entrance hall, the southern section of Room 5 had a floor covered with fine stone slabs; in addition, the wall separating Rooms 5 and 6 was plastered on both surfaces. That well-appointed rooms existed here is suggested by fragments of wall-paintings featuring rosettes as the dominant motif.[17] Such wall-paintings, in conjunction with fragments of imported Minoan pottery found in this northern area, attest to the existence of an extensive domestic quarter, including a kitchen (Room 9) that yielded animal bones, snails, sea shells and flakes of obsidian. Hence, Complex Gamma was most likely a residence that had a work area incorporated into it; in the interval between the tectonic earthquake and the eruption, this work area was utilized by those involved in the restoration of the city.

Complex Beta

Across the Telchines Road from Complex Gamma lies the group of rooms constituting Complex Beta [see Figure 24], to the north of which extends the agglomeration of rooms known as Complex Delta. How many individual residences are to be found in the Beta–Delta block is a matter of contention: J.W. Shaw, for example, has seen three distinct units: Delta 1–9; Delta 10–16; and Beta 1–8; C. Palyvou, however, convincingly argues that Beta 5, 5a, and 8 were intrusively inserted between Complexes Beta and Delta and post-date the original construction of both blocks.[18] Thus it may be more accurate to distinguish an earlier core of rooms (Beta 1–4 and 6–7) and a later addition composed of Rooms 5, 5a, and 8, which formed an independent unit. This later addition effectively obscured an earlier architectural break between Complexes Beta and Delta. The precise interrelationships of the rooms in Complex Beta, however, may never be clear, as the later devastation of this area by the torrent that carved the modern ravine has prevented a complete plan from being determined. In fact, this devastation has made it impossible at present to locate the main entrance to the building, although the eastern or southern facades are the most likely candidates.

Like its neighbor to the west, Complex Beta appears to have been a well-appointed residence of at least two storeys. At its southern end, Rooms 3 and 4 have been washed away by the modern torrent and have consequently yielded very little data. To the north, however, stand the large and relatively well preserved Rooms 2 and 1. These rooms, discovered early in the excavation, are now well explored and have yielded impressive finds.

On the level of the upper storey, Room 2 is a roughly square room paved

with flagstones and featuring a wood-
en column in the center. When excavated, the circular stone base of the
long-vanished column was found *in
situ*, surrounded by a large number of
ceramic and stone vessels, leading
some to speculate that the column had
formed the focal point of some type of
ritual.[19] Determining whether or not
this room had a cultic function depends to a large extent on how one
interprets Room 1, accessible from
Room 2 by a passageway in the northeast corner.

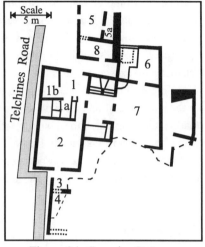

Figure 24: Complex Beta

The upper floor of Room 1 was a
much more complex space than its
neighbor to the south. Its floor also paved with flagstones, Room 1 was
subdivided by interior walls into three areas: Rooms 1, 1a and 1b. The most
important of these seems to have been Room 1, now famous as the "Room of
the Boxing Boys and Antelopes" after the paintings that adorned it. On the
western, northern and eastern walls were depicted six antelopes: two appear
together on each of the west and east walls, while the two on the north wall are
separated by a large window.[20] The animals, roughly life-size, resemble the
impala and are drawn in a sparse manner, outlined in black with only a slight
amount of detail on their heads.

The southern wall of Room 1 was broken by two doorways and a closet
or niche, and thus provided only a short spur for painting on its western edge.
Here were depicted two boxing boys, estimated to be between 6 and 8 years
old. Each child wears a boxing glove on his right hand and, although difficult
to see because of the poor state of preservation of these paintings, each
originally wore a loin-cloth.[21] Their heads have been partially shaved, leaving
only several flowing locks of hair on each. The boy on the left is distinguished
from his companion by earrings, a necklace and bracelets [see Plate IV].

There has been much speculation about the unity and significance of these
wall-paintings. While the thematic connection between the two compositions
remains elusive, their artistic continuity seems emphasized by a common lower
boundary of horizontal bands and by a common upper boundary of blue ivy
running in a frieze around all four sides of the room; in addition, the two compositions seem united by an upper red "wave" that flows around the tops of

the figures. Given the shaved heads of the Boxing Boys, it has been argued that they are engaged in an initiation ceremony, but how the antelopes relate to this is at present enigmatic. As was the case with Xesté 3, however, the architecture and contents of this and the surrounding rooms suggest that Room 1 did have a ceremonial function.

Room 1 itself has three architectural features worthy of note: (1) the large window in the northern wall, which looks out upon a square; (2) the closet/niche in the southern wall, which bore yellow stucco and contained a large number of vessels; and (3) a double door entrance on its eastern wall. In addition, Room 1a, located to the southwest of Room 1, contained unfired brick partitions that subdivided it into three smaller areas. These three areas look like repositories for pottery and indeed contained tables of offerings and other ritual vessels, leading Spyridon Marinatos to claim that Room 1a was a sacred apartment.[22] Room 1b, located to the west of Room 1, was another small area formed by a partition wall of unfired brick; the precise function of this room remains unclear, although Marinatos guessed it might have provided access to the basement below, either by means of stairs or a step-ladder.[23]

The basement area below both Rooms 1 and 2 may thus be relevant to an understanding of the function of this entire section of Complex Beta. The basement under Room 1 was clearly used as a storeroom: flanking a narrow central aisle were two stone benches into which fourteen clay storage jars had been set. Lying on these benches were smaller vessels for removing produce from the jars, as well as stone pestles that would have been used for grinding grain. To the south lay the basement under Room 2, described by Marinatos as a kitchen storeroom.[24] This room was full of pottery that included conical cups, cooking pots, and even an imported Minoan ewer.

On the basis of this evidence, Nanno Marinatos has postulated that upper Room 1 was a shrine which was serviced by repositories in Room 1a and by a "preparation room" in Room 1b, while upper Room 2 could have been used as a ceremonial dining room, especially given the existence of a kitchen storeroom beneath it. Moreover, she argues that the large window in the north wall of upper Room 1 could have served as a means of communication between those within the room and the public gathered in the square outside.[25] She accordingly sees a ritual activity symbolized in the wall-paintings of Room 1, whose common theme is "the idea of contest or competition which differs from serious conflict and only involves a test of strength."[26] Marinatos' inclination to interpret rooms with wall-paintings as shrines, however, raises an important question: were all Theran wall-paintings infused with religious/ritual symbolism or could wall-paintings ever be purely decorative additions to rooms?

It must be recognized that, based on all that we presently know of the Bronze Age in the Aegean in general, religion must have been an integral part of the lives of the inhabitants of Akrotiri. To separate the "sacred" from the "secular" may well have appeared incomprehensible to them, in the sense that everything they experienced could have had a religious dimension. Thus wall-painting would be viewed as an ideological medium by which to express deeply held beliefs. But does the intrinsic religiosity of their lives rule out the existence of purely decorative art? Moreover, does it transform *every* room with wall-paintings into a shrine? In a few cases the iconography of the paint-ings themselves and their architectural contexts make our task easier: thus, for example, not only the subject matter of the wall-paintings but also the presence of an adyton and polythyra made it logical to accept a ceremonial or ritual function for some of the rooms in Xesté 3. Yet, even that imposing building bore a wall-painting in Room 9 which seems purely decorative.[27] What is needed, then, is an evaluation of each wall-painting in terms of both its ico-nography and its architectural context. In this light, there does indeed seem to be a good case for characterizing upper Room 1 as an area that was used for ceremonial or ritual purposes, whether or not it was a "shrine" in the modern sense of the word.

The rooms to the east of 1 and 2 have been much damaged by the torrent. Fortunately, however, Room 6 to the north was found in better condition and yielded fragments of the wall-painting known simply as the "Monkeys." The room itself was a modest ground floor room which contained a large number of vases, including some that had been imported from Minoan Crete. As the first fragments of the "Monkeys" came to light, it seemed clear that they had fallen from an upper room which had been paved with flagstones.[28] The find sites of the various fragments pointed to a composition that had covered at least the northern and western walls of the upper room. Its upper zone had borne a frieze of blue and white spirals bordered by parallel horizontal bands of red, blue and white, while the lower zone featured a series of wavy bands in blue, yellow and red, perhaps meant to symbolize a riverine setting. The middle zone bore the main composition: a group of at least eight blue-colored monkeys shown climbing in a rocky landscape. Also depicted were larger than life-size swallows, as well as reeds, myrtles and crocuses. In addition, there were fragments bearing the heads of two other animals, at first interpreted as dogs but later seen as two calves. As restoration continued, it appeared that the fragments depicting the calves, the swallows and the vegetation were painted on a different scale than that of the monkeys, and so the relationship between the two scenes is unclear; Doumas even speculated that the fragments associated with the calves had belonged to an earlier wall-painting of the upper room.[29] However, a reconstruction of the painting by Nanno Marinatos shows a single composition, spread over at least three walls of the room, with the climbing monkeys on the western and northern walls [see Plate V], and the calves, swallows and vegetation on the eastern wall.[30] Given that a blue monkey is depicted as serving the goddess of Xesté 3 and that ritual vessels were also found in this area, it would appear likely that upper Room 6 had a ceremonial function. However, reconstructing the all-important architecture of this area has so far proved impossible.

An important revelation offered by Room 6 was evidence for wall-paintings that pre-dated the ones on the walls of the buildings at the time of the final destruction. Spyridon Marinatos had already noted faint traces of older painted plaster on the north wall of Room 1, at the bottom of the antelope composition; in Room 6 he discovered fragments of such older paintings in the substratum of the Monkeys composition, although positioned in reverse (i.e., with their painted surfaces facing the wall).[31] The historical significance of this discovery was clear: buildings at Akrotiri had already borne painted plaster on some wall surfaces prior to the earthquake of early LC I; after that event, the walls were covered with new paintings that in places made extensive use of the older plaster that had been damaged. To date, however, these fragments of older paintings have revealed only simple painted bands of a purely decorative nature.

There remains the apparently later block of rooms labelled Beta 5, 5a, and 8. Palyvou has remarked upon the care taken in inserting these rooms: "the group of rooms Beta 5, Beta 5a, and Beta 8 has been squeezed in between Sectors Beta and Delta in such a way as to ensure that no existing window of the surrounding buildings is blocked."[32] These three narrow rooms appear to be architecturally independent of the rest of Complex Beta but could have been joined to it on an upper level. As for the rooms themselves, Spyridon Marinatos suggested that Room 5 may have contained a staircase and that Room 8, to the south, was just an "ordinary" room.[33]

Complex Delta

Located to the north of Complex Beta, Complex Delta [see Figure 25] does not appear to be a single dwelling but rather an agglomeration of at least four architectural units that perhaps grew up around an original core building.[34] Although apparently independent structures at the ground floor level,

these units may have been linked on their upper storeys, thus
making it extremely difficult to
distinguish individual private
dwellings. Moreover, the development of this sprawling
complex has been obscured by
the extensive rebuilding that
took place in this area after the
earlier seismic destruction:
parts of the structure seem to
have been deliberately buried
to create new space for open
squares/courtyards.[35]

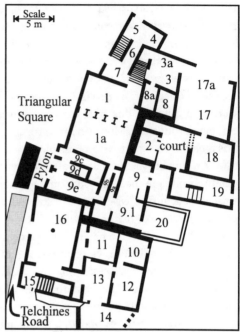

Figure 25: Complex Delta

The extant ruins at ground
level presently consist of at
least twenty rooms. The first of
these was reached early in the
excavation: in 1967 Marinatos
hit upon the northernmost wall
(Rooms 4 and 5), the lower
part of which was built of ashlar masonry; the existence of this ashlar facade
soon led to the structure being labelled Xesté 1.[36] This northernmost wall
formed the southern border of a courtyard/square with an irregularly paved
surface. From this courtyard one could access Xesté 1 through the doorway
into Room 5, which, in conjunction with the adjoining Room 4, is usually described as a vestibule or anteroom; this long, narrow area was paved with flagstones and, as is common at Akrotiri, provided access to a staircase leading to
the upper storey. The staircase was roughly one meter wide and was composed
of eight stone steps, still *in situ*. Ceramic sherds fallen from the upper storey
were found in Room 4 along with intact vessels, one of which bore four Linear
A signs.

The upper storey area reached by the staircase in Room 5 became known
as Room 7 and yielded a circular grinding stone and a semi-circular hearth.
To the right of the hearth and by the outer wall appeared vertical clay pipes ca.
20 centimeters in diameter, thought to be part of a lavatory whose pipes were
connected to the drainage system in the street below.[37] Between Room 7 and
Room 3 to the northeast ran another stone staircase, apparently composed of
three flights of very steep and narrow stairs that ended at the door of Room 3.

The latter room was paved with flagstones and had a niche in its northeast corner; a large number of vessels appeared both on the floor and within the niche. More importantly, however, a hoard of three bronze pitchers and two bronze baking trays was discovered under the paved floor.[38]

Other interesting finds came to light in the upper storey area south of Room 3: here two rooms (8 and 8a) yielded not only ceramic artefacts, including three rectangular clay boxes, but also a group of lead weights, a whetstone, a bronze dagger and a lead object in the shape of a cross. Discovered in the disturbed layers near Room 8 was a tripod table of offerings made of stucco and depicting, in the polychrome style, dolphins in a marine landscape. Room 8 was also distinguished by white plaster with incised patterns on its west wall and by "a kind of primitive mosaic floor made of small sea pebbles mixed with a form of cement."[39]

The major discovery in this northern unit of Complex Delta, however, was Room 1, south of Room 7 on the upper storey, where a polythyron crossed the middle of the room from west to east; when the doors of the polythyron were opened, a spacious room was created. Ironically, it was first thought that this grand room was simply a storage area because it contained six large jars. On inspection, however, it became clear that the inhabitants had deliberately placed these vessels in the openings below the door-frames for protection against the shock of an earthquake.[40] A window on the western wall of this room provided light and air.

Further excavation revealed that the polythyron of Room 1 stood upon a solid partition wall in the room below, which was thus divided into two distinct areas. The southern part of this ground floor space became Room 1a, where two well-built stone pillars were uncovered. In addition to more than 400 vases, both local and imported, Room 1a contained a stone hearth near its western wall; close at hand was a basin, which must have held water used to control the fire on the hearth. Moreover, a pile of charcoal was stored in the room, perhaps in a net or sack that hung from the ceiling. The room thus appears to have served as a kitchen and storeroom, with access to light and fresh air provided by a window located above the hearth. A door in the northern wall led to the adjacent room, which also had a window on its western wall but which has not yet been fully explored. Finally, in the southern part of Room 1a were two doors that led into the complex of rooms lying to the west of Room 9 and labelled Rooms 9a–9e. Described by Spyridon Marinatos as a "labyrinth of corridors and narrow rooms,"[41] this complex contained enough pottery of various types to be characterized as a series of storerooms. There is, however, one highly unusual feature associated with these unimposing rooms: the so-called Pylon which fronted them on the west.

Best described as a covered entrance/porch to Complex Delta in the west, the Pylon was a late addition to the original structure in this area, possibly built after the earthquake early in LC I.[42] Its construction resulted in a division of the flow of traffic along the Telchines Road in this area: while traffic continued to pass freely to its west, more easterly traffic now had to pass through the southern and northern openings in the Pylon. Inside the Pylon, a doorway led into Room 9d, which provided access to the other narrow rooms of this complex. The Pylon itself was a massive structure with an upper storey of some elegance: its floor was a combination of stone slabs and sea pebbles, while its walls bore paintings of spirals and rosettes.

To the south of the Pylon and its associated rooms lay another architectural unit that appears to be focused around Room 16, which is separated from the Pylon rooms by a double wall. This ground floor room, only slightly smaller than Room 1 and having a ceiling supported by a central wooden column, was found to contain more than 450 artefacts, leading Marinatos to call it one of the storerooms in use after the earthquake that heralded the eruption. Another interpretation, advanced by Doumas, is that the room was actually a shop, with the window at street level on its western wall serving as a counter for transactions.[43] A religious function has also been proposed: given the presence of many vessels associated with cult, Room 16 could have served as a repository for ritual artefacts; through its large window such objects could have been handed out to people gathered in the street outside for ceremonial purposes.[44] Of these three suggestions (storage/safe-keeping; shop; cult storeroom), the first seems best to account for the number, variety and nature of the artefacts discovered: e.g., storage jars, remnants of a bronze scale, fragments of bronze tools, bronze vases, lead discs, a stone lamp, a steatite vase, a marble basin and chalice, an alabaster lid, a whet-stone, a schist writing tablet, silver rings, and a jasper gem depicting a griffin and a dolphin.

To the south of Room 16, with its door facing a courtyard/square, lay Room 15 (also known as the Mill House), which, like the Pylon, seems to have been a late addition to the complex.[45] Fronted by a doorway and window on its southern wall, the room contained a complete mill installation, including a stone slab bench opposite the door, a large container with smaller measuring bowls inside and three mill-stones. A stone staircase led from this area to an upper floor.

East of Rooms 15 and 16 lay Rooms 10–14, which may comprise a cohesive architectural unit with an entrance facing the east (now destroyed by the modern torrent). The contents of these rooms included pottery, an incense burner, a collection of loom weights, and some animal bones, tusks and teeth. Of somewhat greater interest were traces of painted plaster and a segment of a stone horn of consecration, ca. 55 centimeters high.

Towards the north are ground floor Rooms 9 and 9.1, the former of which was accessed by a door on its eastern facade; it contained more than 300 local and imported vessels, some of exceptional quality, such as a pitcher decorated with dolphins and an imported conical vessel (a rhyton) depicting crocuses.[46] To the south lay Room 9.1, divided in two by a flimsy wall; also serving as a storeroom, Room 9.1 contained numerous vessels stacked closely together, mainly along the southern and eastern walls. Again, both local and imported wares were represented, including a Syrian amphora.[47] A somewhat unexpected find was the skeleton of a medium-sized pig on the floor.

Also part of this complex was Room 20, to the east of Room 9.1 and communicating with it by a doorway. However, after the earthquake in early LC I this room was filled with debris. In fact, this entire complex of rooms affords ample evidence both of that earlier destruction and of the rebuilding that ensued. As a result of the piling up of debris, the ground level of the area changed, and what had been the first storey of 9.1 became the ground floor, while what had been the ground floor became the basement.[48]

Finally, to the north one reaches the most famous unit of Complex Delta, i.e., Rooms 18, 19 and 2. Room 18, being located directly in front of Room 2, may have served as an anteroom and had a mosaic floor made of sea pebbles. Excavations in 1993-1995 revealed, however, that Room 18 had been divided in two by a wall; this room has so far yielded the remains of a ceiling, evidence of furniture (thought to be tables or stools), and sealstones depicting griffins, chariots and bull-games. Even more important, however, was the discovery in this area of two broken clay tablets incised with the Linear A script, the first such tablets to be found at Akrotiri. Room 19, to the immediate south, has not yet been excavated but clearly had a door and window on its eastern facade. Given the fact that it appears to have been divided into two narrow corridor-like spaces, Room 19 most likely was the main entrance to this unit, with a staircase beyond the door leading to the upper storey.

The focal point of this area, however, was Room 2, whose extremely thick walls on three sides mark it as a later addition to the original Complex Delta. This ground floor room was only ca. 2.2 x 2.6 meters in size but contained a mosaic floor, furniture, a hoard of pottery and the best preserved wall-painting of the entire site. This two meter high "Spring Fresco" (as it is now generally called) was recovered *in situ* on three walls of the room (north, west, and south). Devoid of the human figures so common in the murals of Akrotiri, the Spring Fresco depicts a remarkable landscape with a colorfully rugged terrain that greatly resembles that of Thera itself. From red, blue and yellow rocks grow clusters of lilies with red flowers set off by leaves and stems of golden yellow.[49] The lilies are depicted in various stages of growth: some are merely buds, while others are fully open [see Plate VI].

Above the rocky landscape fly delicately drawn swallows, some in pairs, others depicted alone. The two pairs shown flying "bill to bill" have been interpreted as representing adults feeding their young.[50] Swallows in general have been seen as a native Theran motif with a history going back to the Middle Cycladic period. At Akrotiri not only Complex Delta but also Complex Beta, Xesté 3 and Complex Alpha have yielded examples of swallows in wall-paintings, and these birds are equally prominent in Theran pottery.

Room 2 is also remarkable in terms of its architecture. Already noted were its extremely thick walls on all but the eastern side. Secondly, its thick northern wall was fronted by a false wall made of wood and plaster, behind which was thus formed a tunnel-like space, with its own entrance on the east; this intramural space was found to be full of pottery and to communicate with Room 2 proper by means of a floor-level niche in the northwest corner of the latter. Thirdly, there was the so-called south window which stood in a projection of the southern wall of Room 2 towards the east, appearing to link that wall with the wall dividing Rooms 18 and 19. Finally, it appears possible that Room 2 was "originally built with a polythyron on the east wall. Subsequently, the polythyron was closed off in such a way that a door, window, and niche occupied the wall."[51]

The contents of Room 2 were many and often unusual. On the mosaic floor and in the northwest niche leading to the intramural "closet" were found more than 200 vessels, all crammed into a very small space. While some of these must have fallen from the wickerwork shelf that existed above the wall-painting on two sides of the room, most had the appearance of having been packed into the room as tightly as possible. In addition to this hoard of pottery there came to light traces of long-lost furniture: pouring gypsum plaster into the cavities left by the disintegrated wood, the excavators recovered the casts of a small stool and of a bed ca. 1.60 meters long and 68 centimeters wide. The position of the bed within the room indicated that it had been brought into Room 2 after the floor level had been raised by debris from a destruction, most likely that of the tectonic earthquake which preceded the eruption. The piles of vessels and a number of bulbous plants found underneath the bed seem to lead to an almost inescapable conclusion: as was apparently the case in Room 16, Room 2 served the restorers as a place for the safe-keeping of whatever goods they had been able to salvage. This re-use of the room makes it more difficult to determine its original function.

Nonetheless, most of those who have worked at the site have come to believe that Room 2 had a ceremonial/ritual function of some kind. Doumas, for example, finds evidence for a ritual use of Room 2 not only in the presence of the wall-painting but also in the open space beyond the eastern wall and in certain artefacts discovered in adjacent rooms (e.g., two tripod tables of offerings, two ritual vessels in the form of a boar's head, and even a horn of consecration found at the eastern facade created by Rooms 18 and 19; it was probably in that area that access to Room 2 was provided).[52] As for the Spring Fresco itself, Nanno Marinatos interprets its theme as related to cycles of vegetation, and its function as that of a scenic backdrop for a ritual involving grain. The space in front of the room is explained as having been used for grinding grain and enjoying communal meals.[53] All things considered, including the unique "closet" that looks very much like a treasury area, Room 2 must have had a ceremonial/ritual function at some point in its history.

Finally, Rooms 17 and 17a (north of Room 18) seem to have been storerooms. While a large bronze ewer was found in Room 17a, Room 17 to the south proved more interesting: small fragments of wall-paintings, probably fallen from the floor above, depicted osier branches, and a large quantity of pottery came to light as well as a 15 kilogram cylindrical piece of lead with a bronze handle attached. Despite the destruction of this region by the modern torrent, Room 17 still yielded over 80 vessels, including the two boar's head vessels mentioned above, a double-ewer decorated with dolphins, a cylindrical jar that had a perforated bottom and a removable door,[54] a table of offerings decorated with crocuses and an imported pitcher adorned with a heraldic bird.

The West House

The Pylon of Complex Delta juts out into Telchines Road and forms the southern boundary of the Triangular Square, a paved area that must have been one of the main squares of the settlement. Almost directly opposite the Pylon lies the House of the Anchor, named after the 65 kilogram black stone with a hole at the top found in the vicinity. The building is unexcavated except for its eastern facade, where a wide bipartite window, a door, and a second door-like opening have been located.

To the northeast of the House of the Anchor, and lying in a skewed orientation that creates the distinctive triangular shape of the square, is the

free-standing structure known as the West
House [see Figure 26]. With a history going
back to at least the Middle Cycladic period,
the West House was extensively rebuilt after
the earthquake in early LC I.[55] In its final
form, the building had two storeys in its
western part and apparently three storeys in
the east. Its southern wall, with a frontage of
over 15 meters, faced the Triangular Square
and provided access to the building at its
eastern end (Rooms 1 and 2), where a staircase led to the upper floor(s). As is common
at Akrotiri, the ground floor rooms constituted a general service area, while more
lavish quarters were located on the upper
level(s).

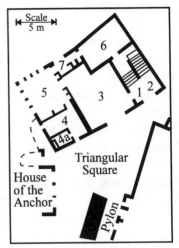

Figure 26: West House

The ground floor is thought to have contained areas for the storage and
preparation of food and for workshops. Some have postulated in particular the
existence of a metallurgical workshop in Room 4, whose contents included "a
stone mortar, pounder-grinders and other stone tools; a fragment possibly of
keroussite ore; a jar; two 'cooking pots', one of them containing a heavy
whitish substance; and a bowl caked with the same substance. The process is
tentatively interpreted as cupellation of silver."[56] That the "keroussite" has
now been reclassified as emery need not weaken the case for a metallurgical
work area as emery is useful for the polishing of finished products. It is more
difficult, however, to specify the precise functions of other ground floor
rooms, with the exceptions of the staircase area in Rooms 1 and 2 and the
kitchen area in Room 3a; the latter room contained a hearth by its western wall
as well as a basin to contain the water needed to control the fire.[57]

On the upper floor and to the west of the main staircase, the central and
largest area was occupied by Room 3, whose broad window (ca. 3.20 meters)
facing the Triangular Square is one of the most striking features of the West
House. Its interior was dominated by a central column and also featured a
stone trough beneath the window; a doorway in the northwest corner gave
access to Room 5. While storage jars and other vessels were found in Room 3,
the more than 450 loom weights uncovered provide the best evidence for the
function of the room: a large, well-lit space for weaving.

A study by Iris Tzachili argues that 20 to 30 weights would have been
needed by a warp-weighted loom and that Room 3 was large enough to hold

four or five such looms;[58] the large number of loom weights found suggests that different kinds of weights were used for different materials. This implies that Room 3 housed a weaving installation that specialized in several types of cloth. Supporting evidence for this thesis comes from the fact that loom weights are not found evenly distributed over the site: for example, none have been found in Xesté 3 (supporting its designation as a public building) or in the House of the Ladies; Complex Alpha, on the other hand, has yielded ca. 200. Weaving was thus a specialized trade at Akrotiri, the raw materials being wool, flax and possibly even silk. It is worthwhile to note that, in historical times, Thera was indeed famous for its textiles, which must have been a major export.[59]

As mentioned above, Room 3 provided access to Room 5, which, together with Rooms 4 and 4a to the south, formed a suite whose wall-paintings have been the subject of much speculative interpretation. Spyridon Marinatos believed that Room 5 had served as a living room, Room 4 as a bedroom and Room 4a as a lavatory, but others more recently have argued that these rooms had a religious function, perhaps serving as a shrine complex.[60] To take Room 5 first, its architecture is unusual in the degree to which the wall surfaces are broken by openings. No wall, in fact, presents a single solid surface: the northern and western walls each featured four large windows separated by thin wooden jambs; the southern and eastern walls were each broken by doors and niches/cupboards. Consequently, the only continuous space available for decoration was that on the uppermost level of the walls, above the various openings, and that at the lowest level, beneath the windows of the northern and western walls; the former accommodated long, narrow friezes, while the latter was painted to imitate marble panelling. There was additional space, however, for single panel decorations in the northeast and southwest corners. The mural decoration of the room was enhanced by a fine floor of schist slabs.

While Room 5 yielded a number of high quality vessels, including a painted stucco table of offerings with red floral designs, the most important finds were the four narrow friezes above the wall openings (collectively known as the "Miniature Frieze"). These were masterpieces on a small scale (ca. 43 centimeters tall on the northern and southern walls, only ca. 20 centimeters tall on the eastern and western walls), each extending the full four meters of its wall; of the original 16 meter frieze, however, only ca. 7.50 meters survive. Partly as a result of their fragmented state, these miniature compositions pose two major problems of interpretation: first, can we determine exactly what is being depicted on each wall; and second, are the friezes on each wall separate compositions, independent of each other, or were all four friezes linked in some way, perhaps as a progressive narrative?

A person entering Room 5 would pass through one of two doors in the eastern wall, one leading from Room 3, the other from Area 7. From either entrance, one would first see, directly ahead, the frieze atop the western wall, so badly damaged in the eruption that only a few fragments depicting part of a town (now called Town I) have come to light.[61] Roughly 40 fragments, however, survive from the frieze of the north wall, the first scene of which is generally called "The Meeting on the Hill." Here, a group of men, including several in long robes, meet on the crest of a hill. Very different interpretations have been offered for this scene: some believe that the men are engaged in a religious ceremony; others think that they may be holding a council of war in light of the scene that ensues.[62]

To the right of "The Meeting on the Hill" at least four men are depicted as looking towards the hill from the top of a building, while two women carrying water jugs walk towards a group of herdsmen and their animals. Below this pastoral tableau appear the ships of what has been called the "Shipwreck" scene: several ships appear alongside naked men in the water and, given the apparent damage to the vessels and the awkward positions of the bodies in the sea, Doumas writes confidently of shipwrecks and drowned men, perhaps the result of a naval battle.[63] Others attempt to be more specific, arguing, for example, that we are witnessing a pirate raid or the defeat of "non-Aegean" attackers. A few offer a very different interpretation: the men in the sea are not defeated warriors but swimmers, perhaps sponge divers, and the ships are simply pleasure boats.[64] Such a peaceful reading of this scene, however, crumbles under the weight of what is depicted directly above: a line of marching soldiers [see Plate VIIb].

This scene of the "Warriors" is set against the backdrop of a town (dubbed Town II) with a harbor to the left.[65] At least eight armed warriors move in a line to the right, towards the main part of the town. Most controversial has been the identity of these soldiers: Therans, Minoans and Mycenaeans have all been suggested. The core of the problem lies in the armor depicted: the soldiers carry rectangular body shields and long spears; on their heads are boar's tusk helmets. Thus, according to some, they must be Mycenaeans from the mainland, where such equipment is well documented. However, since the armor of the soldiers also finds parallels on Crete, the warriors could just as well be Minoans. There is also no *a priori* reason to reject them as Therans, especially if, as seems likely, the inhabitants of the Bronze Age Aegean shared a common type of armament.[66]

Why these soldiers are marching off to the right is even more contentious: they can be interpreted either as attackers or as defenders of the town. In support of the latter hypothesis, the fact that the townspeople go about their normal activities (i.e., getting water from a well and herding their animals) and do not appear to be alarmed by the marching soldiers suggests that these men posed no threat. Perhaps, then, they have restored peace and order after a sea-borne raid; indeed, the drowned men could easily be viewed as lightly-armed pirates.

Quite dissimilar is the frieze that adorns the eastern wall, which not only runs in a narrower band but also portrays an exotic, non-Aegean landscape painted on a different scale. Situated above the doors and niches of the wall, this so-called "Nilotic Landscape" [see Plate VIIIb] depicts a river running through a lush sub-tropical region which includes palms and papyrus, water fowl, a wild cat, a jackal-like beast and even a griffin. Although most of this frieze has been lost, Christina Televantou has recently identified eleven new fragments, two of which seem to feature a town by the river (now designated as Town III) and reportedly come from the northern half of the composition.[67]

The southern frieze, known variously as the "Ship Procession," the "Flotilla," or simply the "Fleet," is almost completely preserved. Extending above two niches and a door in the southern wall, the painting depicts two towns (Towns IV and V) and a fleet of seven elaborately adorned sailing ships, only one of which, however, is actually shown under sail. Two of the others have their masts upright, while the rest seem to have their masts stowed across the top of the canopy which shelters their male passengers. Curiously, the six ships not under sail seem to be propelled by men who are shown awkwardly bending over the sides of their ships with short paddles in hand. Since Aegean-style helmets are shown hanging from the canopies of some of the ships, the passengers appear to be soldiers, and it is thus reasonable to interpret the long poles which rest upon the uprights of the canopies as spears. Unlike its companions, however, the vessel under sail has its passengers' bodies obscured by a "side wall" that may be a device to protect them from the elements; in addition, there is no canopy above their heads and no sign of any helmets or spears. In common with the other ships, though, this sailing vessel has a rear cabin in which a single figure sits—generally thought to be the captain of the ship [see Plates VIIa and VIIIa].

The ships themselves are impressive vessels estimated to have been ca. 25–30 meters long. They are elaborately decorated, with most bearing heraldic motifs on both their sterns and prows. Moreover, their sides are adorned with abstract designs or with animal motifs (lions, dolphins, doves). One ship in fact has decorative bunting (festoons with crocus pendants) reaching from its mast to both ends; being the most lavishly decorated of all, this ship could lay claim to being the flagship of the fleet. The elaborate stern cabins (known as "ikria") on all the ships have been convincingly explained as litters that would have been carried onto the ships rather than being structurally integrated into them.[68] The stern projections above the water-line also look removable, being attached to the ships by straps/braces of some kind. But, whereas the stern cabin can be understood as a special place for the captain, the function of the stern projection is less obvious. The most logical hypothesis is that it served as a landing platform/gangway, since the vessel would have been beached stern first.[69]

The fleet is shown sailing to the right, away from the so-called Departure Town (Town IV) and towards the Arrival Town (Town V). The former town seems to have a river flowing by it, behind which the hinterland with its flora and fauna (including a lion) is depicted. The actual buildings of the town are close to the shore and some inhabitants are seen near or on them, watching the departure of the ships. Town V is also coastal and is approached by a rocky headland of variegated colors. There is a small structure (perhaps a watchtower) on a hill, to the right of which the town's harbor is depicted, followed by the buildings of the town itself. A large number of people watch the approaching ships, including a procession of men on the shore who appear to be leading an animal, most likely intended for sacrifice upon the arrival of the fleet. In addition, a small boat rowed by two men seems to be heading out to welcome the fleet.

Attempts to interpret this complex composition have been many and varied. The fact that Minoan horns of consecration are shown atop one structure of the Arrival Town has led many to set the entire scene of the southern frieze within the greater Aegean area and to argue that real places are being depicted. Indeed, the Arrival Town is often interpreted as Akrotiri itself, the most compelling evidence being that of topography: the rocky headland approached by the fleet looks very much like Cape Akrotiri today, and the harbor to the left of the Arrival Town appears to mirror the harbor of Bronze Age Akrotiri, almost certainly located to the west of the town between the ridges of Mavrorachidi and Mesovouna. Moreover, as Doumas has written, "the hilly landscape in the background is very reminiscent of the profile of the Mavro Rhachidhi ridge. The Late Bronze Age remains on the crest of Mavro Rhachidhi lend weight to the argument, for they could be identified with the watchtower illustrated in the wall-painting."[70]

Some who identify the Arrival Town as Akrotiri also argue that the

Departure Town should likewise be situated on Thera. By far the most cogent argument for placing *both* towns on Thera itself is the method of propulsion used by all but the ship under sail: paddling is a very strenuous and inefficient way of moving such large vessels and so it is difficult to envisage a long journey being represented. Moreover, given our new understanding of the topographical configuration of the island prior to the LBA eruption, it could be postulated that the fleet is travelling from a point on the western edge of the island, perhaps near the modern Aspronisi, across the Lower Pumice 2 caldera to the Akrotiri peninsula—a journey well within the limited range of paddlers. This thesis, however, faces at least two significant, if not fatal obstacles: first, the Departure Town is encircled by a large river for which there is no evidence on Thera or on any other Cycladic island, and second, the presence of a lion chasing deer in the background does not accord with what is known about the fauna on Thera in the Bronze Age. Indeed, the entire hinterland of the Departure Town looks far too lush to be Cycladic. In the end, it seems difficult to place the Departure Town either on Thera or anywhere else in the immediate Cycladic region.

The debate over the exact locations of both the Departure and the Arrival Towns has not, however, stifled more general theorizing about the nature of the narrative being depicted. One hypothesis, for example, argues that a marine festival celebrating a naval victory is being depicted.[71] A somewhat different interpretation has been advanced by Lyvia Morgan, who sees in the procession of the ships a nautical festival intended to celebrate the inauguration of a new sailing season in the spring.[72] This latter hypothesis, however, seems weakened by the clear depiction of soldiers with helmets and weapons on the ships: a military event of some kind almost seems demanded by the iconography.

If the exact "reading" of each of the miniature friezes remains elusive and contentious after many years of study, what can be said about the relationship among the friezes on each of the four walls? Are we looking at four independent scenes or are the friezes all part of a larger whole? Moreover, are the friezes historical narratives or traditional "genre" scenes of no relevance to any particular event(s)?

Many scholars have long viewed the Miniature Frieze as a "generic" tableau, full of conventional images and unrelated to specific historical events. For example, D.L. Page in 1976 had found it difficult to argue that an historical event (as opposed to a conventional or generic theme) was being represented in the northern frieze: "Military expeditions by a navy against a foreign coast with natives of exotic type are attested by the Town Mosaic from

Cnossos, the Siege-vase from Mycenae, and the battle-scene on a vase from Epidauros. How would one refute the opinion that the Acrotiri [sic] frescoes represent not an actual expedition but a traditional theme?"[73] Indeed, the argument on behalf of "genre scenes" is commonly bolstered by reference to similar artwork elsewhere. For example, Morgan pointed to fragments of a miniature fresco from the Northeast Bastion at Ayia Irini on Kea: in her opinion, this composition, which probably ran across all four walls of a large room, depicted a seaside festival that included ships, a rocky landscape with various types of plants, a river, buildings and men in procession. Moreover, the recent discoveries at Kabri of Minoan-style miniature fresco fragments depicting birds, houses, a rocky coast, a river and ships, and at Tell el-Dab'a of a fresco which apparently showed lions chasing deer were also seen to support the argument for the existence of a stock repertory of such scenes in the Aegean Bronze Age.[74]

The existence of such "stock" scenes, however, does not preclude their use in historical narratives. For example, if a victory in battle was to be celebrated in a wall-painting, the artist might select from his repertory the scenes/images that he deemed most appropriate for this particular composition. There is an obvious parallel here with Homeric poetry: the bard selects from a stock in trade of poetic formulae those best suited to the narration of his song. In short, the fact that scenes apparently similar to some found within the Miniature Frieze are now known to have existed elsewhere need not, and should not prevent us from seeing a particular narrative represented in Room 5 of the West House.[75] It is thus instructive to note that Spyridon Marinatos, the discoverer of the Miniature Frieze, had seen historical elements in the composition (e.g., a Theran expedition to Libya) and that the current excavator, Christos Doumas, believes the frieze as a whole tells the tale of a "major overseas voyage, in the course of which the fleet visited several harbours and cities, five in all;" Doumas adds that, whatever the frieze shows, "it must be connected with the master of the West House and concern an event significant for his status in Theran society."[76]

By far the most convincing and detailed argument that the Miniature Frieze represents one continuous historical narrative has been made by Christina Televantou. Because the west wall would be seen first by someone entering the room, Televantou believes the narrative began there and then proceeded to the north, east and south walls. The paucity of fragments from the west wall prohibits analysis, but on the north wall Televantou sees Aegean soldiers protecting a town by driving off attackers; ships carrying these soldiers then travel, on the eastern wall, to a small town elsewhere in the eastern Mediterranean. The south wall, finally, shows the homecoming of the fleet. Consequently, Televantou sees these paintings as a "unified representation in the narrative vein, consisting of one scene on each wall, *each scene being the narrative continuation of the other*" [emphasis mine]; the composition in her view is "a kind of geographical map, illustrating the countries and most important cities visited by the fleet," which included Theran ships under the leadership of the occupant of the West House.[77] The only troublesome aspect of this otherwise attractive reconstruction is the lush riverine landscape and exotic fauna of the eastern wall: looking far more Egyptian than Aegean, this scene suggests that what the artist has presented us with in Room 5 is not one continuous or unified narrative but rather sequential highlights of an extended voyage.

That the occupant(s) of the West House had a strong bond with the sea is also suggested by the other wall-paintings in Room 5: the two nude "Fishermen," one located in the northeast corner, the other in the southwest. Approximately two-thirds life-size, these paintings occupy the middle zone of their respective walls—the only paintings in Room 5 in that position because of the many openings in the walls. Each fisherman displays his catch: the west wall figure is depicted in profile, holding a string of fish with both hands; the north wall figure has a slightly more frontal stance and holds a string of fish in each hand.

In addition, the wall-paintings of the adjacent Room 4 also point to the presence of a seafarer in the West House. A person passing from Room 5 to Room 4 would, according to the most recent reconstructions, be met by the wall-painting of the "Priestess," a well preserved composition ca. 1.50 x 0.35 meters. Depicted here is a young woman with a snake-like lock on the top of her shaven head; a large yellow earring hangs from a red-painted ear, while red also highlights her lips. She is wearing a saffron-colored robe over her dress and moves to the left, carrying in her left hand what looks like a vase with a dark red object inside. With her right hand she appears to be sprinkling yellowish matter above the red object. A likely interpretation of her action is that she is sprinkling saffron over charcoal inside an incense burner [see Plate IX]. This elegant painting probably appeared on the eastern end of the northern wall that divides Room 4 from Room 5.[78]

Understanding the significance of the Priestess requires consideration of the other wall-paintings of Room 4. Divided by a partition wall into two unequal areas (called 4 and 4a), the room was thought by Spyridon Marinatos to have served as a bedroom (Room 4) with adjoining lavatory (Room 4a).[79] While there were no wall-paintings in the lavatory, Room 4 proper was decorated with at least eight life-size stern cabins (ikria) of the type seen on the ships of the Fleet in the Miniature Frieze; they may best be described as screens made of wooden frames covered in oxhide. The relevance of this ikria motif to the Priestess has been best explained by Lyvia Morgan: "Traditionally the stern has been considered the proper area for any form of preparatory ritual or thanksgiving worship connected with the welfare of a ship. The burning of incense near the stern was a feature of such rituals during the Classical period."[80] Thus, the Priestess would be engaged in a ritual ceremony involving the blessing of the ships *via* the dispersal of incense.

Room 4a is the best preserved example of a lavatory yet found at Akrotiri. It features two stone benches separated by a slit approximately 10 centimeters wide. Situated at the base of the slit is the drain, a cylindrical clay pipe that descends into a pit in the street outside, which, for obvious sanitary reasons, had a large slab-stone cover. (The pit was connected to the extensive drainage system of the town.) The lavatory also seems to have held a bath tub and a bronze tripod vessel, presumably used to prepare water for the bath. Unusual finds in Room 4a were two clay vessels containing fresh plaster and a bowl of what seems to be red pigment. The logical conclusion to be drawn is that painting was in progress just before the final abandonment of the site. However, it may not have been wall-painting: a stucco tripod table of offerings painted with figures of dolphins, rocks and seaweed was found on the window-sill of the room, where it was apparently set out to dry.

The suite formed by Rooms 5, 4 and 4a is best interpreted as a well-lit living room, bedroom and lavatory respectively, as was originally proposed by Spyridon Marinatos.[81] In the adjacent Room 3 existed, as mentioned above, a spacious weaving installation. Like it, the remaining rooms of the upper floor were all accessible from Room 5. Room 7 lies immediately to the east, roughly in the middle of the north wall of the West House. When excavated in 1982, it proved to be a corridor with two clay niches/cupboards that had been filled with over 200 vessels. Later excavation revealed a window, a stone bench, and a small internal staircase linking the upper and lower floors. Still further to the east lay Room 6, a large room that was also full of pottery, including over 100 small conical cups. Other finds included stone tools, a small stone lamp and 26 lead discs. In her study of these discs, A. Michailidou concluded that they constituted a set of balance weights.[82] Room 6 thus looks like it was used as a storeroom prior to its final destruction.

In sum, the West House was clearly an important building at Akrotiri, physically imposing and lavishly adorned with some of the finest wall-paintings of the Aegean Bronze Age. Thanks to these paintings, our knowledge of ships and seafaring in the Late Bronze Age has been vastly expanded; that the occupants of the West House had a close relationship with the sea seems certain. It is equally certain that they would have been members of the wealthy elite at Akrotiri.

The House of the Ladies

To the north of the West House and Complex Delta stands the structure known as the House of the Ladies [see Figure 27] after the wall-paintings found there in 1971. Although this area had been badly damaged by the modern torrent, there is evidence that the northern extension of the Telchines Road formed the eastern boundary of this complex, generally thought to be a single large building much like the West House.[83] It appears to have had three storeys, at least in the western section, and two staircases: the main one stood at the entrance to the building in the southwestern corner, while a secondary staircase lay roughly in the middle of the complex. This latter staircase was adjacent to what looks very much like a light well, the only one so far found at the site. This light well was surrounded by a corridor which provided access to the adjacent rooms.

In 1971, Spyridon Marinatos uncovered what was to become Room 1 of the upper storey. The central of three rooms along the northern wall of the house, Room 1 was accessed from the east through Room 2 and was sub-divided into two compartments by a north-south partition wall, with a connecting passageway at its southern end. A second internal partition wall seems to have existed in the eastern compartment of the divided room, running east-west and creating a northeastern cubicle that may have been a lavatory.[84] The southern section of the eastern compartment thus became corridor-like and led into the western compartment, whose northern, western and southern walls bore paintings of large plants identified as pancratium lilies.[85] These fragrant plants are shown growing on undulating reddish-brown ground. Forming an upper frame are simple horizontal bands of blue, black, white and red.

The eastern compartment of Room 1 was decorated with the wall-paintings which gave the house its name. At least three nearly life-size women were depicted, all positioned underneath wavy black and blue lines topped by a net-like pattern of four-pointed "stars" joined by red dots. This pattern is framed at the top of the wall by horizontal bands of black, white, red and yel-low. The Ladies themselves walk on an even dark ground line which forms the lower border of a unified composition that was spread over two walls.

The Lady of the south wall walks towards the east; she is elaborately adorned, with long, cascading black hair, red facial make-up, round golden earrings and a colorfully flounced skirt or apron over her long dress. The two Ladies of the north wall include one relatively well preserved figure who moves to the east and bends forward from the waist, allowing her ample breast to hang very unnaturally; she is as elaborately adorned as her counterpart on the south wall. She appears to be leaning towards the poorly preserved third Lady and holds a flounced apron in her right hand; her left hand is held higher, appearing to touch the arm of her otherwise lost companion [see Plates X and XI].

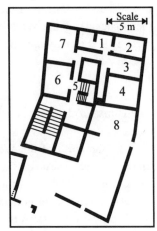

Figure 27:
House of the Ladies

The key to understanding this composition may lie in the flounced skirt/apron depicted to the right of the bending woman. As there are no feet visible below the apron, and her right hand appears to hold it out, it is reasonable to interpret the bending woman as offering the garment to the now missing woman. If so, the wall-painting depicts a ceremonial robing scene.[86] Similar scenes have been noted on Minoan seals and in the so-called "presentation scene" from the Pillar Crypt at Melos, where one woman is shown bending while another is seated and holds a piece of blue cloth in her hands. A parallel may even be found at Akrotiri itself, though here involving men: the male figures of Xesté 3, Room 3b, include one who holds a large swath of cloth in his hands. Since the Xesté 3 composition has been interpreted as a coming of age ceremony in which the assumption of a special garment played a prominent role,[87] a similar ritual may well be depicted in the House of the Ladies, i.e., a rite of passage in which a young woman assumes the flounced apron that signals her entrance into a new stage of life.

The net-like pattern noted above the heads of the Ladies in Room 1 should be relevant to the ritual. While some see here an attempt to represent the celestial arc, another interpretation better suits the context: S.A. Immerwahr has stated that "since a related diaper-net pattern occurs frequently as a textile pattern for women's garments at Thera (see *Thera* VII, pls. 59–62), it seems preferable to view the background here as a curtain, or pure decoration, rather than a stylized rendition of the star-studded sky."[88] Because a ritual robing ceremony might well take place behind a screening curtain, Immerwahr's first suggestion seems more probable.

How do the rooms themselves, as well as the other wall-paintings, fit into such an interpretation of the north wall? As noted above, both extant women face east, and the one on the southern wall actually walks to the east as if proceeding to another area. It thus seems plausible that, after the robing ceremony, the women would move into Room 2, where a large number of cups and cooking vessels were discovered, allowing the room to be characterized as a place for feasting.[89] Presumably, then, the conclusion of the ceremony would involve a celebratory feast held in Room 2.

This interpretation raises the question of the function of the western compartment of Room 1 with its larger-than-life pancratium lilies. Given that these plants have a strong fragrance, the initial preparations for the ceremony may have taken place here *via* the censing of the room and its occupants for reasons of purification; after this ritual, the initiate would be ready to move into the lavatory area to assume her special garment. Thus Room 1 as a whole could have served as a ceremonial area. This theory receives support from the presence of four repositories under the floor of Room 1. Covered by schist slabs, these compartments contained what are often interpreted as ritual vessels: e.g., libation jugs and painted pitchers.

An especially noteworthy architectural feature of the House of the Ladies is its light well, originally described by Spyridon Marinatos as "a square compartment with solid walls and no openings."[90] While there were indeed no doors giving access to this area, there did exist four interior openings or windows, one on each wall, to spread the light gathered by the well into the surrounding corridor. The windows on the northern, eastern and western walls were on line with each other, while that on the southern wall was lower, most likely because of the presence of the staircase to the immediate south.[91] To the west of the light well/staircase complex was Room 6, which has been called a lapidary's workshop because of the discovery there of a large, unfinished red marble jar, ca. 56 centimeters high. That the marble out of which this vase was being made may have been imported from Lakonia in mainland Greece provides us with additional data about Theran trade contacts.

While the rooms of the southern section of the House of the Ladies are only now being uncovered and studied, the area to the southwest has recently revealed some noteworthy structures, the most impressive of which is an apparently independent building that stood between the House of the Ladies and the West House. Some work has also been carried out on the building located to the east of the House of the Ladies, across the northern extension of the Telchines Road. While the existence of a building in this area had been known for some time, the identification of cross-walls has suggested where the now destroyed western wall of the building was. According to Doumas, wall-paintings of lilies and other flowers have been found in this structure.[92]

Complex Alpha

Discovered in the initial excavation season of 1967, Complex Alpha [see Figure 28] is best known for its basement magazines (Rooms 1, 2 and 3). These storerooms, however, are only one part of the complex, and the presence of a double wall suggests that Complex Alpha is in fact made up of two adjacent architectural units: a building with the magazines to the east and a building with a mill room to the west. The complex formed by the two buildings is demarcated by a narrow lane (called the South Corridor) to the south, and a roughly paved road (perhaps an extension of the Telchines Road) to the west.

To the eastern unit of the complex belongs the tripartite magazine area. Room 1, the southernmost of the three storerooms, was roughly square in shape and had a wide window (2.20 meters) on its eastern wall. Its contents provided evidence of the existence of an upper storey: in addition to vessels and loom weights precipitated from above, a stone column base had fallen into the storeroom, landing very close to a similar base still *in situ* on the magazine floor. Room 1 itself contained seven large storage jars standing in a row along the southern wall; traces of barley flour could still be detected in some of them. Also discovered was a rectangular clay hearth on the western side of the room; close by were a stone mortar and grinding stone, a tripod cooking pot and, south of the hearth, a stone basin embedded in the floor.

A door in the northern wall of Room 1 gave access to Room 2, which was slightly smaller than Room 1 but contained a larger and more varied deposit of artefacts. The room itself had two openings in its eastern wall, the more northern of which was a window; the other opening was either a second window or a door providing entry into the magazine area. In the western part of the room stood storage compartments separated by clay partition walls. Two especially noteworthy items were found in these compartments: a terracotta chest thought by Spyridon Marinatos to have served as a container for aromatic plants and/or incense[93] and weights that probably belonged to a pair of scales. But the mass of material uncovered was pottery, both local and imported, some of which appears to have fallen into the magazine from an upper floor. Stone tripods, grinders, lamps and bowls also came to light.

In Room 3 to the north lay heaps of vessels of various sizes, many of

which were still *in situ*. The most famous of
these was the brown jar decorated with white
lilies which now stands in the Fira Museum,
while the most interesting from an economic
point of view was the group of large stirrup-
jars that most likely bear witness to trade in
olive oil. To the north of this room there may
have existed another of the squares so typical
of Akrotiri.

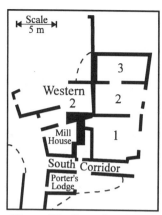

Figure 28: Complex Alpha

The so-called Western Rooms of Complex
Alpha are separated from the eastern magazines
by the aforementioned double wall.[94] The
southernmost of these is situated directly west
of Room 1 and, since it contained a mill-stone
in situ, has been named the Mill House. The room featured a paved floor and a
window in its western wall; it was accessed from a small anteroom located
immediately to the north. In addition to the fixed rectangular mill-stone by its
eastern wall, the Mill House yielded a slab to catch the milled grain, the
remains of a wicker basket and a clay bathtub with its interior decorated with
white reeds. The function of the tub, located in the southwest corner of the
room, is controversial, with some asserting that it was used for the storage of
grain and others connecting it with the lavatory that has been detected in the
southern part of the room.[95]

West of Room 2 of the magazines, but on the level of the upper storey,
lies what has been called Western Room 2. Both Spyridon and Nanno Marinatos came to regard this area as religious in nature on the basis of the ritual
vessels (including a table of offerings) stored there.[96] The argument for the
existence of a ceremonial area was strengthened when Spyridon Marinatos
began to excavate the basement below Western Room 2 and discovered a libation vessel in the shape of a bull, ca. 25 centimeters long.

Crucial to the cultic interpretation of at least part of Complex Alpha is
not only the pottery recovered but also the fragments of wall-paintings found
therein. In regard to the latter, the most famous fragment is the "African," so
named by Spyridon Marinatos, who discovered it early in the course of the
excavations. At present, most interpret the male face depicted as that of an
Aegean man who wears his hair short, has an earring in his left ear, and looks
towards a palm tree. Nanno Marinatos has argued that the man is most likely a
worshipper engaged in a ritual taking place within a sanctuary. That a sanctuary was indeed depicted is inferred from another fragment, which portrays at

least two blue monkeys near a columned structure crowned by multiple horns of consecration.[97] Other fragments of wall-paintings found included one with the head of a woman and three with birds.

It is not clear, however, whether these painted fragments actually come from Complex Alpha. Spyridon Marinatos claimed that the fragments were found at the western end of the South Corridor which borders Complex Alpha and had fallen there from an upper storey. This raises the possibility that these fragments might have originated in the structure to the south of Complex Alpha, where a small paved room, named the "Porter's Lodge," had yielded some pottery. Later soundings during the digging of pillar pit #28, south of the South Corridor and east of the Porter's Lodge, revealed not only more pottery but also walls and benches.[98] If, accordingly, the fragments of wall-paintings came from this unexplored building, the thesis that Complex Alpha contained a shrine complex is seriously weakened.

Looking at Complex Alpha as a whole, we find a mill room that produced flour to be stored in the adjacent magazines; a magazine with a hearth and utensils that could be used for cooking; loom weights and lead weights fallen from an upper storey which could have housed a work area for textile production;[99] stirrup-jars useful for trade in oil; and living quarters located as usual in the upper storey(s). Pending further excavation in this area, it seems reasonable to view Complex Alpha as a private residence with an adjacent storage area that may also have served as a shop.

Xestés 5 and 2

South of the large unexcavated area east of the House of the Ladies lie the barely investigated remains of two ashlar buildings called Xesté 5 and Xesté 2 [see Figure 29]. Very little is at present known of Xesté 5, as only segments of its western and southern walls have been located. It appears to have been a substantial structure that formed the northern boundary of a square or courtyard located to the east of Complex Delta and to the north of Xesté 2. Another unexcavated building is located southeast of Xesté 5 and would have formed the eastern boundary of this square, whose existence was first detected upon the opening of pillar pit #35. The construction of this square seems to have taken place after the early LC I earthquake, when the area was filled with debris, levelled and given retaining walls.[100]

Xesté 2 shows signs of having been a major building within the town. Its northwest corner had been found as early as 1967, and two years later Spyridon Marinatos characterized the building as "the most monumental structure hitherto discovered."[101] By 1973 it was apparent that Xesté 2 had three storeys, distinguished externally by projecting stone geisons on the exposed northern facade. It is the northern facade of Xesté 2 that most clearly bears witness to the spaciousness of this building: Marinatos traced it eastwards for about a dozen meters without reaching its northeastern corner; along its course appeared recesses, window openings, and vertical divisions that marked the existence of wooden framing. At present, the western wall of Xesté 2 has been found to extend more than 20 meters to the south and to possess at least two room-like additions to its facade. These small rooms were

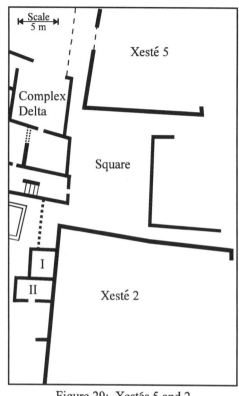

Figure 29: Xestés 5 and 2

located in 1978, and the northernmost was found to have been joined to Delta 19 to the north by a drywall. Once again, the earthquake of early LC I appears to have necessitated alterations in this part of the town: as Marisa Marthari has observed, "there is no doubt that the inhabitants gathered the debris from the destroyed buildings surrounding this area and contained them here with the drywall...[which] was constructed at a distance of 2 m. from the west wall of Xesté 2 so that it would not block either the door (or window) in this wall or the window in the N wall of room I." Marthari also postulates that, before the earthquake, a road had run along both the north and the west facades of Xesté 2, which implies that the western rooms of Xesté 2 had not existed at that time; the function of these rooms thus remains enigmatic.[102]

While the interior of Xesté 2 has not yet been excavated, two types of soundings have been carried out. First, the digging of pillar pits offered tantalizing glimpses of what lay inside: for example, pit #36 "revealed, at a depth of 6 to 7 m., great half-worked stones, a kind of slab-covered floor, and fragments of fine white stone, possibly marble. A worked stone, perhaps the base of a double-axe, was also found."[103] Pit #39 touched upon what seems to have been a storeroom: vessels discovered included an oil jar decorated with a rope pattern and medallions, a vase with incised Linear A symbols and an intact, sealed ewer. The last artefact was instructive both for the method of sealing and for its contents: "inside the neck was first put a handleless conical bowl, then a big lump of clay, which covered both the hollow space of the bowl and the broad lips of the ewer. The interior of the vase was full of little seeds...some of them had developed rootlets."[104] Finally, pit #64 turned up two stones with incised cross-like signs. The second type of sounding so far carried out in the interior of Xesté 2 has been that of ground-penetrating radar, which has attempted to locate interior walls with some success.

Xesté 4

South of Xesté 2 and situated at the southeastern extremity of the site is an imposing ashlar building called Xesté 4 [see Figure 30]. Although reached in 1972, excavation of Xesté 4 is still in progress. Nonetheless, this three-storey building had several outstanding features: first, it is the largest independent structure yet found; second, its exterior walls are built entirely of ashlar blocks; third, it had elaborate wall-paintings; and fourth, there was a poly-thyron complex in the eastern half of the building. Xesté 4 is thus the most palatial-looking structure yet to be unearthed.

The impressive exterior walls of Xesté 4 are best represented by the extremely well preserved northern facade: a massively constructed wall with no doorway or window opening along its entire course of ca. 25 meters. This straight-running wall is sharply contrasted on the southern side by a wall with projections and recesses. The shorter eastern and western walls also have this dentated style of construction, and a study of all the walls by Clairy Palyvou has revealed the mathematical precision employed by the builders: the facades show "a standard and well-calculated diminution of the height of each course from bottom to top." Such elaborate features led Palyvou to conclude that Xesté 4 may have been a completely new structure built after the early LC I earthquake.[105]

Excavation has now uncovered not only the entire outline of the building but also the main entrance in the west (marked by a grand staircase) and some of the interior rooms. These generally belonged to the upper floor and included the polythyra of Room 8. The third such room to be discovered (the others

being found in Com-
plex Delta and in Xes-
té 3), Room 8 was
surrounded on three
sides (east, south and
west) by pier-and-door
partitions. During the
clearing of this area
the excavators came
across poorly preserv-
ed walls to the west;
here were recovered
fragments of paintings
which Spyridon Mari-
natos attributed to the
walls of a fallen stair-
case. These frescoes
depicted two calyxes
akin to lotus, leaves
from reed-like plants,
and zig-zag bands. By

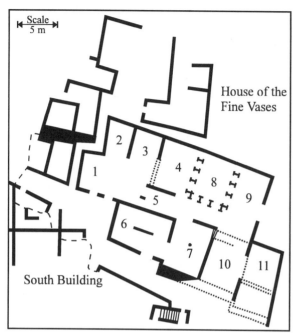

Figure 30: Xesté 4

1975, Doumas could write of eleven boxes of fragments found in various parts
of the building, and in 1977 came some fragments depicting nearly life-size
men apparently wearing kilts.[106] These figures are now thought to have
adorned the walls flanking the grand staircase in the west; in a case of art
imitating life, these dark-haired men seem to be part of a procession ascending
a flight of stairs.[107]

Other significant discoveries included a column base found during the
digging of pillar pit #43, to the immediate south of the polythyron complex;
this column base is now attributed to the upper floor of Room 7. Also
uncovered were fragments of fluted plaster that may have come from plaster-
coated cupboards or shelves made of rods or reeds, elaborate pottery and
mason's marks (including a double-axe) on the stonework. Such features, taken
in conjunction with the size and quality of the construction, the polythyra and
the mural composition(s), have led more than one scholar to view Xesté 4 as a
public building approaching Minoan palatial standards and probably serving as
a ceremonial center.[108] Indeed, the very location of Xesté 4 hints at a special
function: it has long been obvious that the eastern and southeastern parts of the
excavation site are dominated by a series of large, impressive structures. In

addition to Xesté 5, Xesté 2 and Xesté 4, there are the so-called "House of the Fine Vases" and the "South Building;" the former stands to the north and the latter to the south of Xesté 4. Although barely investigated, both show the dentated facades associated with important structures. Finally, a major street, running roughly east-west, passed between the southern facade of Xesté 4 and the northern facade of the South Building.[109] As the initial seed of the Akrotiri settlement had been sown in the Neolithic and Early Bronze Age in the area now containing Xesté 3, and given the recent discovery of the "House of the Benches" to the southwest of Xesté 3, it seems safe to postulate that the entire southern region of the present excavation site played an important role in the lives of the Late Bronze Age inhabitants of Akrotiri.

CHAPTER FIVE

THE LATE BRONZE AGE SOCIETY OF THERA

Reconstructing a society on the basis of archaeological evidence alone is a daunting task. There are no written records to consult—only the often enigmatic data provided by artefacts such as pottery and wall-paintings. The field is therefore open to many divergent and extremely speculative interpretations, any one of which may be tossed aside unceremoniously as a result of the next season's finds. The ensuing reconstruction of society in Late Bronze Age Thera must be read in this light and regarded as no more than an attempt, based on presently known data, to interpret what was clearly a very complex social system.

Theran society originally had a strong agricultural foundation, for no Neolithic immigrants were likely to settle in a land incapable of providing them with basic foodstuffs. That the earliest signs of human settlement on Thera come from the Akrotiri peninsula reinforces this point: here was the most fertile land to be found on the entire island. Indeed, both the actual remains and pictorial evidence from Akrotiri now allow us to determine the basic food crops grown: barley, wheat, olives, grapes, figs, nuts, beans, lentils and peas.[1] Various herbs and spices were also cultivated and, as suggested earlier, saffron may have been an important crop on Thera not only as a spice but also as a dye and a medicine. To supplement this primary diet, Theran farmers practiced animal husbandry, rearing sheep and goats in large numbers, and pigs and cattle on a smaller scale.[2] Thus, mixed farming was the norm on Thera as it was in Crete and elsewhere in the Aegean.

More intangible in the archaeological record are such data as the size of Theran farms, farming practices, the lives of the farmers themselves or the existence of a land-owning elite. The identification of farmsteads at Balos, Ftellos and the Alaphouzos Quarry on Therasia suggests that farmers lived on or close to the land they cultivated at least for some part of the year; each farmer may well have had more than one field under cultivation annually in order to accommodate diverse crops and guard against total crop failure in any single year. Given the size and general topography of Bronze Age Thera it is probable that individual fields tended to be small and were worked intensively with only a summer fallow.[3] The farmer's plow would have been made of wood, while basic tools such as grindstones, sickles and blades were stone, bronze or obsidian.

The existence of mill installations in several buildings at Akrotiri indicates that at least the final stages of crop processing took place in the town. This raises the difficult question of the relationship of the farmer to the town:

for example, did a central authority within the town control the produce of local farms? Did a land-owning elite resident in the town collect produce from tenant farmers? Or were farmers independent producers who exchanged any surplus crops for items obtainable only from the town? An important step towards our understanding of this economic relationship has been taken by Anaya Sarpaki, who postulates, on the basis of her botanical studies of material from the West House, that this building had its own self-contained economy, a phenomenon she finds reflected at other buildings on the site.[4] The existence of at least some economically independent structures at Akrotiri would suggest strongly that there existed a land-owning elite residing in the town but controlling the produce of the rural hinterland. Such a thesis is supported by the variations in the size and opulence of the excavated buildings at Akrotiri, by the existence of substantial storage facilities in many structures on the site and, conversely, by the absence (at least so far) of a "palatial" building with storage magazines extensive enough to imply centralized control of a regional redistribution system. If the theory of a land-owning elite existing on Thera is correct, there would be important ramifications in political as well as economic terms.

Nonetheless, the basic fact remains that Bronze Age Thera was not fertile enough to support a growing population and other sources of foodstuffs were required. An obvious additional source of food was the sea which surrounded the island: the two Fishermen depicted in the West House clearly prove that seafood was part of the Theran diet. The sea, however, rapidly became even more important as a highway by which imported foodstuffs could be introduced into the local supply. Moreover, sea-borne trade became increasingly employed not only for those necessities of life that Thera itself could not supply in sufficient quantities but also for access to highly prestigious foreign luxury items, the demand for which would come largely from the wealthy, land-owning elite postulated above. Indeed, their possession of such exotica would further enhance the position of the members of this elite class within Theran society. The resultant elite-driven growth of trade transformed Theran society by re-establishing the island's economy on the twin foundations of farming and trade. By the Late Bronze Age, it would even appear that trade had become the dominant partner and was ultimately responsible for the great wealth and general prosperity of Thera, seen so vividly at Akrotiri that Christos Doumas has proclaimed that "it is...beyond doubt that the wealth of this city is the product of the seafaring and trading activities of its inhabitants."[5]

The growing importance of trade had another significant effect on Theran society: it fostered the rise of skilled local artisans whose products would be highly prized in an expanding exchange network. An illustrative example is furnished by the Theran stone-working industry so thoroughly investigated by Peter Warren: specialist craftsmen used local and at times imported stone to create such articles as vases, mill-stones, lamps and tripod mortars, the last of which were widely exported.[6] Similarly, there existed a large-scale pottery industry of great sophistication: over 50 different types of vessels were locally made and display such a high degree of standardization in both types and sizes that one is tempted to envisage production on an industrial scale.[7] Elizabeth Schofield, in fact, has written of "more or less full-time potters equipped with kilns, located presumably at the extremities of or outside the towns," while others have postulated the existence of major industries in obsidian, wine, perfumed oils and saffron, as well as specialist metal-workers, masons and painters.[8] In this regard, it is important to note that not only products but also people could be exported: in the Near East at this time various royal courts are known to have exchanged such skilled workers as diviners, sculptors and physicians. Moreover, the recent discoveries of Minoan-like frescoes at Kabri and Tell el-Dab'a have been interpreted as proof that specialist Minoan painters plied their trade far beyond the confines of Crete itself.[9] The emergence of a class of highly skilled specialists, separate from the wealthy elite, served to change the very nature of Theran society.

Alongside the large-scale specialized industries there existed smaller household industries whose products might also find their way into the exchange network, for Schofield has found enough evidence at Akrotiri to suggest that virtually every house contained one or more types of craft and/or industrial activity.[10] An obvious example would be the textile production believed to have taken place in the West House and possibly in Complex Alpha; the uniquely transparent garments and the elaborately colored flounced skirts seen in the Theran wall-paintings would almost certainly have been highly prized as exotic luxury items in other lands. Their perishable nature, however, has rendered such exports invisible to the archaeologist.

Given that trade was crucial to the prosperity of Thera in the Late Bronze Age, what do we know about the Theran traders themselves or of their status in Theran society? Two models have been widely debated: (1) that of a merchant class under the direct control of a central authority or ruler, and (2) that of free-lance entrepreneurial merchants acting independently for their own profit.[11] In truth, the two models are not mutually exclusive and both types of merchants are likely to have existed on Thera, as they did in Egypt and the Near East. This does not necessarily mean that there were two separate classes of traders, i.e., royal merchants and private commercial entrepreneurs. In reality, an individual trader might at one time act on behalf of a central authority or ruler, and at another time act only on his own behalf; his cargo might contain prestige goods specifically intended for elite exchange as well as other goods intended for anyone with the means to purchase them.[12] As for the social status of these traders, the major role played by trade within the Theran economy makes it probable that successful merchants were highly regarded members of society.

These Theran merchants, however, also need to be seen in the context of seafaring in the eastern Mediterranean as a whole: simply put, how far afield did Theran ships venture? Perhaps due to the dominant position of Crete as general gatekeeper of the Aegean, there is as yet no compelling evidence that large numbers of traders from Thera regularly ventured far from their home waters. Instead, Theran merchants should be viewed as but one of many peoples engaged in regional trade networks that had, over time, established inter-regional links.[13] Nonetheless, in view of the long-lived Cycladic tradition of seafaring, the non-Aegean scenes and/or creatures found on Theran wall-paintings, and the Near Eastern paintings (both from Kabri and Tell el-Dab'a) that find their closest stylistic parallels on Thera,[14] it seems somewhat perverse to limit Theran seafarers *en masse* strictly to the Aegean: a few must have ventured farther afield, though whether as merchants, pirates or soldiers is difficult to determine. The master of the West House in particular stands out as a prime candidate for a Theran who sailed far from home: not only the Nilotic landscape of Room 5 but also two recent and unexpected archaeological discoveries provide tantalizing hints of the possible scope of his travels. First, entomological research has revealed the presence of insects apparently foreign to the Aegean in the West House, and, second, the Bronze Age site of Nami in Israel has yielded evidence of an Aegean pulse known as *Lathyrus clymenum* or Spanish vetchling; this pulse had been stored in large quantities in the West House but was apparently unknown outside the southern Aegean. Even today it is only cultivated on the islands of Thera, Anaphe and Karpathos.[15] At the very least, the presence of Spanish vetchling at Nami offers strong evidence of contact between Thera and the Levant.

Accordingly, some Theran seafarers as well as Theran ships may have participated in the inter-regional "tramp routes" which connected the major gateways in Crete, mainland Greece, Egypt, the Levant, Cyprus and Asia Minor. While it belongs to a slightly later stage of the Late Bronze Age, the Ulu Burun ship, with its multifaceted and multinational cargo of luxury and everyday items, looks very much like a merchant vessel that navigated the eastern Mediterranean in a loop that followed natural winds and currents; its crew may well have been as multinational as its cargo.[16] Such vessels would make calls at numerous major ports, bringing "luxury goods and prestige items to ruling elites; metals, precious and semi-precious stones and other raw materials...to craftspeople; subsistence supplies and basic commodities to rural peasants."[17]

Given the strategic geographical position of Thera, the harbor of Akrotiri must have been one of the busiest in the Aegean regional network. Not only Theran and other Cycladic ships but also those of Crete would have regularly used its facilities, so that Akrotiri became a convenient trans-shipment center between Crete and the islands/mainland to the north; this would have necessitated the Theran adoption of both the Minoan Linear A script and Minoan weights and measures. Even occasional visits from ships of the Near East and Egypt cannot be categorically ruled out, though Egyptian and Near Eastern artefacts found at Akrotiri (such as ostrich eggs and gypsum vases) may have reached the island through Crete.

The intensive trade networks of the Late Bronze Age also provided a source of wealth for those who were not simply peaceful merchants, since a by-product of sea trade has commonly been piracy. Indeed, from historical antiquity to the nineteenth century A.D. the Cycladic islanders were famous for piratical activities and there must have been Theran pirates plying the waters of the Bronze Age, preying upon merchant vessels and coastal settlements alike. The archaeological record, however, does not allow us to distinguish between goods imported to the island by bona fide merchants (Theran or foreign) and those brought in by less peaceful means. In fact, the only archaeological evidence at Akrotiri that might possibly reflect a pirate raid is the Miniature Frieze on the north wall of Room 5 in the West House. Nonetheless, one can still speculate that some of the wealth seen at Akrotiri was gained in a less than savory manner.

The foregoing analysis (as well as the very existence of a highly developed town such as Akrotiri) certainly points to a complex hierarchical social organization with clear-cut divisions of labor on Late Bronze Age Thera. On the basis of the present evidence, however, it is difficult to discern exactly how this sophisticated society was organized and governed. At the moment, Akrotiri remains the only candidate for what may be called a capital city, i.e., the headquarters of those who formed the central authority that ruled the island. That there were "rulers" of some sort seems certain given the general political patterns of the time both in the rest of the Aegean and in the Near East.[18] Yet no indisputable image of a King or a Queen has so far been identified among all the varied wall-paintings of Akrotiri, nor have artefacts come to light that cry out to be interpreted as "royal." It would thus appear that there was no ruler iconography of the type so well represented in contemporary Egyptian and Near Eastern art and architecture.

One explanation for this phenomenon has been strongly advocated by Nanno Marinatos, who believes that priests or priestesses controlled all aspects of society on Bronze Age Thera.[19] In such a theocratic polity what mattered most were the divinities worshipped, and their images, or perhaps those of the priests/priestesses who represented or even impersonated them, should be sought in the archaeological record. At Akrotiri, one immediately thinks of the goddess depicted in the wall-paintings above the adyton of Xesté 3, of the robing scene in the House of the Ladies or of the Priestess of the West House. Moreover, as seen in Chapter 4, many other wall-paintings at Akrotiri seem to have had a religious dimension or implication. These paintings are complemented by other artefacts that must have had religious functions (e.g., horns of consecration, libation vessels, tables of offerings) and that were widely discovered throughout the town. Consequently, there can be no doubt that religion played a vital role in the lives of the inhabitants of Bronze Age Akrotiri.

But was Theran society 'god-haunted' to the extent that religious officials, whatever their gender, wielded political, social and economic power in the name of their divinities? In the absence of written evidence and of a ruler iconography, one can only speculate while bearing in mind contemporary Aegean and Near Eastern cultures, in which there is a tendency to invest the ruler with priestly functions or attributes, if not to identify him/her openly with a divinity. In the particular case of Minoan Crete, a society which obviously had much in common with that of Thera, there is a strikingly similar absence of a ruler iconography in favor of one which concentrates on depicting rituals, gods and goddesses. As Ellen Davis has stated, the ideological message of Minoan art "is not a proclamation of the supreme status or of the divine sanction of a ruler, but rather of the status and divine sanction of the cult."[20] Nanno Marinatos has consequently viewed Minoan rulers as earthly representatives of divinities; this construct leads her to speak of "Priestess Queens" and "Priest Kings" on Crete, echoing the often maligned Sir Arthur Evans, who first used the term Priest-King in relation to the governing of Minoan palaces.[21] In short, it would now appear that those who controlled the cult also controlled the state, resulting in our present difficulty in trying to separate the spheres of economics, religion and politics in Bronze Age Crete.[22] Marinatos concludes that this integration of what we today might call the sacred and the secular in Minoan culture "can only mean one thing. Minoan society was theocratic and had a sacred economy...[and the] Minoan economy was under the control of the sanctuaries and their priests."[23]

Returning to Thera with such analogies in mind, a theocratic state seems at least possible if not probable. One can indeed imagine the early emergence of certain individuals from the ranks of the elite who were thought to have special powers and hence to be representatives of the gods who ensured the survival of all those on the island. To these men and/or women would naturally be entrusted the running of the state as well as the duty of representing or impersonating the gods as occasion demanded. Their own human identities would be subsumed by their divine roles, resulting in the absence of any ruler iconography as such. This state of affairs, however, need not exclude others from assuming priestly functions from time to time, just as it need not exclude others from participating in the affairs of state. Nonetheless, there is no evidence to suggest a broad sharing of power: ultimate control over Theran society must have remained in the hands of the few rather than the many.

In this highly speculative atmosphere, we cannot afford to be dogmatic about the exact amount or type of political and economic power wielded by priests or priestesses in Theran society. We can, however, say something more substantial about the religious beliefs and practices of these islanders since, in this realm at least, the archaeological evidence is somewhat more illuminating. In addition, this same archaeological evidence demonstrates clearly that the religion of Thera was very similar to that of Minoan Crete, so much so that Nanno Marinatos has spoken of a Minoan-Cycladic syncretism. Thus, we may look to Minoan cult as an additional resource to help us reconstruct religious practices and beliefs on Thera.[24]

First of all we need to understand the nature of the divinities worshipped. While there is general agreement that Theran religion was polytheistic, there is less agreement on how many divinities were thought to exist. A minimalist position would be that there was one dominant goddess who may have been worshipped under different aspects, as well as one male god whose status *vis-à-vis* the goddess is unclear: he may have been her equal or her subordinate. These divinities were conceived anthropomorphically, as clearly seen in the goddess from Xesté 3, and appear to have been connected with nature in general and with fertility in particular. The goddess was initially invoked to ensure the fertility of the land, something extremely crucial on a small and generally barren island such as Thera, but in time she might also come to be associated with the sea. To encourage her beneficence, the Therans would honor their goddess with offerings (including animal sacrifices) and with rituals or ceremonies of various types, each tied to the kind of protection or blessing being sought. For example, it has been suggested that a crop festival of some sort was celebrated in front of the frescoed backdrop of Delta 2. At such ceremonial occasions, a priestess might have assumed the role of the goddess being invoked.[25]

The goddess was believed to be served and attended by what may be called her familiars or totem animals. In Xesté 3 she was flanked by a monkey on one side and a griffin on the other; similar scenes are depicted on Minoan seals and frescoes, with the griffin an especially common figure.[26] These animals may be interpreted as intermediaries between the goddess and the humans who worship her. For example, in the wall-painting of the Crocus Gatherers, the women who collect the crocus do not directly offer their harvest to the goddess; instead, the actual presentation is carried out by the monkey attendant on the divinity. It is likely that these totem animals were themselves considered sacred in light of their special relationship with the goddess.[27]

The wall-paintings of Xesté 3 are, of course, of major importance in reconstructing Theran cult. As stated in Chapter 4, Xesté 3, with its unique adyton, looks very much like a ceremonial building used mainly for initiation rites. Its wall-paintings seem to reflect an actual ritual in which a priestess either impersonating or representing the goddess would oversee a rite of passage designed to admit a young woman into adulthood by uniting her with the goddess herself. The essential act of this initiation would appear to have been the shedding of blood: blood not only drips from the foot of the so-called Wounded Woman but also flows over the shrine on the adjacent wall. The offering of blood to a divinity is well attested in Minoan Crete: animal blood was usually presented but at special times, such as an initiation, human blood could have been deemed more appropriate.[28]

Also of relevance to the initiation ritual is the fact that some of the figures in Xesté 3 have partially shaved heads. When wall-paintings depicting figures with shaved heads began to turn up in the course of the excavation, they presented an enigma, but our increasing understanding of the Aegean Bronze Age now allows us to decipher the iconography of Theran hairstyles with greater confidence. Ellen Davis convincingly articulated the significance of the shaved heads in 1986, arguing that the hairstyles varied according to the age of the figures depicted. In her view, young children would have their heads shaved except for two reserved locks; somewhat older children would still display shaved heads but with additional and longer reserved locks. When approaching maturity both men and women would stop shaving their heads and would appear with full heads of short hair. Once fully mature, women would allow their hair to grow freely, adopting long, flowing hairstyles; older women would have their long hair bound up in snoods.[29] Similar practices are known in both Minoan Crete and Egypt, and cutting off the reserved locks of childhood must have been an important rite of passage in the lives of young Therans.[30] These locks, once ceremonially removed, would probably have been offered up to the divinity.

If blood and hair can be understood as appropriate offerings to the gods, designed to ensure divine favor, so too was saffron, as the wall-paintings in Xesté 3 make abundantly clear. The many properties of saffron have already been noted but in the specific context of the initiation ritual of Xesté 3 its usefulness in alleviating the feminine pain of menstruation and childbirth, both obviously connected with blood, is most relevant. The relief afforded Theran women by this medicinal plant would be viewed as a gift from the goddess, who would be asked to ensure the continued growth of such a magical plant by presenting her with offerings of it. As Peter Warren has written, "When...a flower or plant...is offered to a goddess it is because the goddess was believed...to influence or affect its usefulness;" Warren then cites as evidence the Cretan plant dittany, which "was considered helpful to childbirth and was offered to Eileithyia [the Minoan goddess of birth], and she in turn was believed to assist birth."[31]

The actual existence or the artistic depiction of altars and tables of offerings attest to the importance of offerings in general to Theran cult. The wall-painting of the Fleet in the West House includes a procession of men leading what looks very much like a sacrificial animal. The ritual killing of bulls, sheep and goats is well known from Crete, and the procedure involved (1) collecting the animal's blood in a container so that it could be poured out as a libation to the divinity, and (2) dismembering the animal so that its flesh could be cooked and consumed by the participants. Remains of the ritual meal would then be burned and buried; relevant to this practice may be a Middle Cycladic pit found at Akrotiri "which contained animal bones, horns and ashes mixed with organic substances, fragments of burned pots and remnants of fava beans."[32] The more grisly skeletal remains of apparently sacrificed children found by Peter Warren in a building to the west of the palace at Knossos show signs of having been cut for the removal of flesh, and Warren postulates the cooking and consumption of this human flesh in order to effect a communion with the divinity.[33] Other foodstuffs, however, would also be suitable for offering, such as grain, honey, wine and perhaps even beer.[34]

Clearly, an important aspect of sacrifice was the meal that ensued. These cult meals would probably be communal and highly ceremonial, making use of specially consecrated vessels. Many vessels of this type have come to light at

Akrotiri, two of which seem native to Thera: the nippled ewer (a libation vessel with prominent nipples that suggest an association with fertility) and the so-called kymbe, an oblong vessel that may have been used for cooking or as dishes for meals and/or offerings.[35] Other cult vessels found at Akrotiri are also known from Crete: tables of offerings, the libation vessels known as rhyta (including one in the shape of a bull and two made from ostrich eggs), conical cups, triton shells and an alabaster chalice. Minoan religious influence is also demonstrated by the discovery of a cooking vessel with a Cretan double axe engraved on its bottom, comparable to a vessel discovered in a shrine at Mallia.[36] Also related to the double axe symbol are the very Minoan-looking horns of consecration found in Complex Delta: a hole in the middle would have accommodated the shaft of a double axe, thereby imitating a common practice on Crete. Horns of consecration were also depicted in wall-paintings in the West House, Xesté 3 and Complex Alpha.

Formal processions would also be part of ritual activity. As mentioned above, the Fleet fresco from the West House depicts a procession of men leading a sacrificial animal. Such processions are well known from Crete and even turn up elsewhere in the Theran wall-paintings, e.g., the procession of men along the staircase of Xesté 4, the older women with bound-up hair depicted in Xesté 3 and, possibly, the women of the House of the Ladies. As processions were important for the conveyance of offerings to the gods, it would seem that the objects associated with these figures (such as flowers and robes) were also intended as offerings.[37] Especially interesting is the offering of a sacred garment or cloth to a divinity, a practice that endured in Greece into historical antiquity. Warren has reconstructed the basic stages of this ritual: first the robe would be made and dyed (perhaps with saffron), then would come the procession to a sacred place, where the actual presentation of the garment/cloth to the divinity would occur.[38] The pieces of clothing shown being carried in the wall-paintings of the House of the Ladies and Xesté 3 (where one of the male figures holds a long piece of cloth) thus probably had sacred connotations.

Religious processions tend to move towards special cult places and it is possible that a sacred space well known from Minoan Crete also existed on Thera in a modified form: the peak sanctuary. The main evidence comes from the scene of the Meeting on the Hill from Room 5 of the West House, where "a ritual is indicated by the processional grouping of the figures, their votive gestures and their long garments."[39] In addition, the rugged landscape of the wall-paintings of the adyton area in Xesté 3 may set the shrine depicted therein on a hill-top. So far no Minoan-like peak sanctuary has been conclusively identified on Thera but a much simpler version of such a sacred space may have once existed on Mount Archangelos to the west of the excavation site. Not only has its summit yielded unusually large quantities of Bronze Age pottery sherds but also the modern presence of a small Christian church on the site may well reflect an entrenched belief in the sanctity of this hill that stretches back into prehistory.

As has now become obvious, Theran cult shared many features in common with Minoan cult, including, for example, sacred architecture (e.g., polythyra, adyta, shrines); ritual vessels (e.g., libation jars, tables of offerings, conical cups); and iconography, especially as seen in the wall-paintings (e.g., horns of consecration, altars, monkeys, priestly clothing, flounced skirts). Some have seen in this phenomenon evidence of Minoan control of Thera but there is a more likely explanation, one advocated especially by Nanno Marinatos: a kindred system of religious beliefs and practices existing on both islands even before the "Minoanization" of Thera.[40] Indeed, Marinatos writes of a Minoan-Cycladic syncretism in which "the Theran upper classes adopted Minoan paraphernalia of the cult, they employed artists schooled in the Minoan iconographical tradition, and they made use of those symbols which carried emblematic and ideological meaning...And yet the people of Thera must have carried on their age-long traditions of local fertility cults, practising their libations with their local nippled ewers."[41] What is postulated here, then, is a common religious foundation: both cultures worshipped a female divinity especially connected with fertility, both cultures practiced similar rites of passage, and both cultures integrated religion into the very fabric of their lives. This kinship naturally made it easier for Therans to adopt Minoan cult forms and iconography as their powerful neighbor to the south exerted more and more cultural influence; nonetheless, these Cycladic people did not abandon their own age-old religious beliefs.

Finally, it is tempting to speculate on a reverse influence in the religious sphere. From the point of view of the Minoans on Crete, Thera must have seemed a strange, even foreboding place, smelling of volcanic gases, having expanses of barren lava shields on which little grew, and possessing rocks of the most peculiar colors and compositions. It would be natural to invest such a mysterious place with unique powers and to consider it a place special to the divinities. Perhaps, then, future researchers might attempt to investigate more carefully whether some features of Minoan cult were in fact influenced by Thera; for example, was there a goddess named Qe-Ra-Si-Ja (a name mentioned in the Linear B tablets found at Knossos and translatable as the "Theran one") or a "pumice cult" on Crete even *before* the LBA eruption of Thera?[42]

In the end, reconstructing the society of Late Bronze Age Thera must be viewed as a work in progress, with large gaps in our knowledge that prevent us from drawing any definitive conclusions about the nature of its ideologies, its political and religious authorities, its various types of social interaction and other such complexities. Even when all the evidence is found and studied there may still be no absolute certainties. Still, after more than 30 years of excavation at Akrotiri, enough has now been uncovered to allow us to embark on this long journey of exploration and rediscovery.

CHAPTER SIX

APOCALYPSE

Tragically for the inhabitants of Thera, the earthquake that struck the island near the beginning of Late Cycladic I was only a harbinger of still greater destruction to come: towards the end of LC I (in the Cretan ceramic phase known as Late Minoan IA) another earthquake not only devastated the island but also signalled the start of explosive volcanic activity that would forever change the face of Thera. The evidence for this so-called tectonic earthquake is best seen at Akrotiri itself, where almost every building shows signs of serious damage; so great were the forces unleashed by this earthquake that even solidly built stone staircases were shattered as if made of clay. Yet the Therans had experienced and survived such extensive destruction before, and after the tremor had ended they began to rebuild their town. First of all they cleared the streets of obstructive debris, as evidenced in the Telchines Road, where rubble was gathered together in piles so that workers could move more freely through the street.

The restorers also turned their attention to the badly damaged buildings of the town, especially those whose contents could be at least partially salvaged. For example, workers placed a still serviceable bed in Delta 2; this bed was in turn used as a canopy to shelter numerous vessels placed beneath it. In Delta 16 more than 450 artefacts of various types were gathered together for apparent safe-keeping. Finally, recent excavations west of Delta 15 and 16 have revealed the impressions of three small beds which had been placed outdoors and (as in Delta 2) used to protect vessels that had been carefully gathered from the vicinity. It was especially important to salvage such useful items from those buildings with walls so badly ruined that they were now unsafe and had to be razed; as Christos Doumas has noted, "parts of the walls which were heavily shaken and were ready to collapse had been deliberately demolished and cleared."[1] Accordingly, there can be no doubt that the restorers intended to clear and rebuild their city, a process that must have included the removal of the bodies of those inhabitants who had been killed in the earthquake.

Restoration work was still in progress when the explosive eruption apparently triggered by the earthquake began. The interval between the earthquake and the start of eruptive activity was, in all probability, short—perhaps no more than a few months. While the inhabitants of Thera certainly did have some familiarity with earthquakes (and the ability to rebound from them), they were most likely terrified by the unusual phenomena that marked the beginning of the eruption. A mass exodus from the island would have begun, although the often expressed belief that everyone eventually escaped seems ill-founded: further excavation could easily bring to light the remains of hundreds or even thousands of victims, especially in the vicinity of the harbor at Akrotiri (as was the case at the harbor of Herculaneum in Italy).

The eruption itself was a complex geological process that began with a precursory ash fall probably vented from the Skaros volcano and carried south-southeast by the prevailing winds.[2] During this earliest stage, some interaction between the rising magma and ground or surface water took place, generating explosive steam blasts. It is indicative of the complexity of the eruption that, although this precursor ash deposit is generally thin (at most 10–15 centimeters thick), it is nonetheless composed of four distinct layers, suggesting that there were brief pauses between each blast.[3] These explosions and the resultant ash fall at Akrotiri, estimated to have been roughly about 2 centimeters, would have encouraged the general abandonment of the settlement.

Some time, perhaps even several weeks, may then have passed between the precursor ash fall and the onset of the main eruption. Phase 1 of the latter began with the generation of a tall eruption column at a vent located on the Skaros volcano, 1 or 2 kilometers to the southwest of modern Fira. Rising 30 to 40 kilometers into the atmosphere, this eruption column deposited as much as 6 meters of airfall debris in the form of pumice, ash and lithic fragments. While the duration of this hot blast is uncertain (estimates range from 1 to 24 hours), it most likely followed the pattern of similar eruptions in increasing its intensity over time. Blown by high velocity winds mainly to the east and southeast, the volcanic debris buried most of the settlement at Akrotiri, leaving only the uppermost walls of its buildings exposed. This accounts for the relatively well preserved state of most of the buildings, since the later, even more violent phases of the eruption only affected those walls which were still exposed to the elements.

Phase 2 of the eruption began when the eruption column collapsed as the vent widened and magma came into contact with sea water. This interaction led to the phenomenon known today as base surge, in which clouds of hot gas expand horizontally outward from the base of the eruptive column and generate dune-like deposits of pumice and ash that flow across the landscape at a high velocity and with great destructive power.[4] At Akrotiri the base surge was powerful enough to blast away any walls that had not yet been afforded protection by the earlier ash fall. Easily identified today by its well-bedded, cross-stratified deposits, which in places reach a thickness of 8 to 12 meters, the base surge phase of the eruption generally saw the deposition of a finer grained (and whiter) pumice than that produced in the preceding phase.

After the scouring action of the base surge phase came lower temperature pyroclastic flows. Laying down the thickest deposits of the entire eruption (up to 55 meters in places), this third phase reflected a further opening of the vent to sea water. R.S.J. Sparks and C.J.N. Wilson in fact describe the vent as now having evolved into "a large funnel full of a slurry of ash, pumice, steam and water."[5] It would even appear that the expanding vent had breached the relatively shallow waters of the old Cape Riva caldera, since the pyroclastic flows now contained the stromatolitic blocks associated with that formation as well as large amounts of other lithics.[6] Indeed, the abundance of large lithic blocks is one of the most characteristic features of this phase. The emplacement mechanism is thought to have been not one but probably four extremely violent explosions that generated successive pyroclastic flows moving with high viscosity across the landscape. Whether this high energy, lithic-rich phase of the eruption marked the initiation of caldera collapse is still unclear, although Heiken and McCoy have championed the theory that the huge amount of lithic material expelled at this time must be linked to the start of such collapse.[7]

The fourth phase of the eruption witnessed massive gas-rich and highly fluid pyroclastic flows of pumice, ash and small lithics that fanned out to incorporate the previously independent islet of Monolithos and thus created the present coastal plains of Thera, e.g., those stretching from Cape Koloumvos to Monolithos and from Exomiti to Akrotiri. This deposit seems to have been the product of a large number of episodic flow units and hence is very thick (40 to 50 meters in places). Had caldera collapse already begun, this phase would have seen its continuation through increased slumping of the caldera walls.

Phase 4 brought about the total depletion of the magma chamber of the volcano, which in turn ended the actual eruption and led to the final stage of caldera collapse. This featured the destruction of the Skaros-Therasia volcanic complex and the flooding of this northern region of the island.[8] Geologists have in fact discovered flood deposits and accompanying evidence of erosion at this time, leading Sparks and Wilson to postulate that these floods were "related to subsidence and post-eruption instability of the caldera walls." They go on to suggest that "sudden floods were generated by repeated avalanches of the unstable walls of the new caldera."[9]

While the volcanic phases of the eruption are now generally agreed upon, a number of questions still remain. One of these concerns the duration of the main (i.e., post-precursor phase) eruption, which some researchers had once believed covered a lengthy period, perhaps many years. However, there is now a growing consensus that the duration of the main eruption was more likely a matter of days than of weeks or months, with three or four days being most commonly suggested.[10] A second question pertains to the total volume of magma erupted. As noted in Chapter 1, the determination of the volume of ejecta is extremely important in formulating how much of the present-day Theran caldera is the product of the Late Bronze Age eruption. The modern caldera as a whole would require approximately 60 cubic kilometers of Dense Rock Equivalent ejecta,[11] whereas the volume of the modern northern caldera basin alone closely corresponds to the recent 30 to 40 cubic kilometer estimate for the amount of magma ejected.[12] This accords well with the belief, expressed in Chapter 1, that LBA Thera already featured at least one or two calderas, and that the LBA event was primarily responsible for the enlargement of the caldera(s) to the north. Other issues pertaining to the eruption, however, remain much more contentious, especially (1) the actual date of the eruption and (2) the effects of the eruption in the eastern Mediterranean.

The Date of the LBA Eruption

No question has created more controversy than that of when the eruption took place. Based on the pottery found in the Volcanic Destruction Level (VDL) at Akrotiri, there is general agreement that the disaster occurred at a time when mature Late Minoan IA (LM IA) pottery was arriving in Thera from Crete. The problem that has come to haunt both archaeologists and geoscientists alike is the determination of the calendrical dates to be assigned to the LM IA period. On the evidence of Egyptian synchronisms (i.e., datable objects of Egyptian manufacture found on Crete and of Minoan manufacture found in Egypt), archaeologists have traditionally dated LM IA to the sixteenth century B.C. and have placed the Theran eruption at the middle or end of that century—namely, between 1550 and 1500 B.C. The development and increasing refinement of scientific dating techniques, however, have thrown this traditional archaeological chronology into question.

The first indication that something could be amiss with the traditional sixteenth century date came by way of radiocarbon (C14) dating. As short-lived organic material from the VDL at Akrotiri began to be tested by independent laboratories, it became clear that the results did not confirm the traditional chronology: while the tested material provided a wide "scatter" of dates (i.e., different samples tested by the same laboratory were yielding not an internally consistent date but rather a range of different dates), a large percentage seemed to indicate that the eruption took place about a century earlier. At first, these C14 results were greeted with skepticism: critics focused on the large degree of scatter in the dated remains and suggested that the samples themselves might even be contaminated by the volcanic gases presumed to have existed on the island prior to the eruption. There were also questions raised about the accuracy of the calibration curves that are used to translate C14 results into calendrical dates. In sum, many archaeologists expressed no confidence in the radiocarbon dating process itself.

As time passed, however, the number of short-lived samples subjected to radiocarbon dating increased and significant improvements were made to the techniques of C14 testing and calibration (e.g., the use of Accelerator Mass Spectrometry [AMS] and the development of a high precision calibration curve). Nonetheless, the resulting data still seemed to show a distinct clustering of dates within the seventeenth century B.C. In addition, the theory that volcanic gases on Thera were distorting the C14 results was generally rejected: by 1990, "all laboratories were certain that previous fears of contamination from volcanic carbon dioxide were unjustified and could have affected very few samples."[13]

The mounting radiocarbon evidence for a so-called "high chronology" for the LM IA period resulted in the creation of an academic battlefield. The adherents of the traditional "low chronology" (i.e., the sixteenth century B.C.) marshalled their arguments for rejecting the C14 data, pointing to the continued questioning of the calibration curves, the imprecision inherent in standard deviation ranges, the different results obtained by different laboratories on identical samples, the tendency to downplay "deviant" results, the small size of the data base itself, and the suggestion that some of the organic material tested may have been contaminated by preservatives applied after their excavation.[14] Their preference for the traditional low chronology, moreover, was sustained by high-precision calibration curves that placed the eruption between 1620 and 1525 B.C. at the 68% level of confidence and between 1670 and 1520 B.C. at the 95% level of confidence. This large spread of dates would obviously support *both* the traditional and the high chronology, leading some scholars to discount entirely the usefulness of the C14 data in dating the eruption.

In response, those who advocated the adoption of the new "high chronology" resorted to statistical analyses of the existing C14 data. For example, in 1988 S.W. Manning published the results of a computer-assisted statistical analysis of the Theran C14 results which, in his opinion, proved that the "short-life destruction level Akrotiri radiocarbon dates [yield] a precise range, strongly supporting a mid–later 17th century BC dating for the late LMIA destruction of Akrotiri, and the ensuing eruption of Thera."[15] That same year also saw the publication of a study by H.N. Michael and P.P. Betancourt which concluded that the most probable date for the eruption lay between 1639 and 1600 B.C.; they asserted that the traditional low chronology had less than a 25% probability of being correct.[16] A very similar conclusion was reached in 1990 by researchers using the Oxford AMS facility: they postulated a 70% probability for a seventeenth century eruption and only a 30% probability for a sixteenth century eruption.[17] Thus, while a sixteenth century eruption could not be ruled out, the cumulative radiocarbon evidence in 1990 pointed rather to the seventeenth century B.C. Even Peter Warren, a staunch defender of the traditional low chronology, acknowledged in 1988 that there was "a distinct clustering in the last quarter of the seventeenth century B.C. (1628–1606 B.C.)."[18]

In 1993, however, a new calibration curve served to add fuel to the controversy, as it suggested an almost equal 50% probability for both the seventeenth and sixteenth centuries as the dates of the eruption. This has led Michael Baillie, one of the leading researchers in precision dating, to remark that, at present, "radiocarbon cannot resolve satisfactorily between the seventeenth and the sixteenth century archaeological options."[19] Three things now seem vital in order to resolve this impasse: the continued refinement of the C14 testing method itself, additional collection and C14 testing of short-lived samples from Thera, and the construction of a C14 chronology for the entire period from Middle Minoan through Late Minoan that would allow LM IA to be "bracketed" in time.

Meanwhile, Philip Betancourt has attempted to reconcile the high and low chronologies by a re-examination of the archaeological data. In 1987, Betancourt published a new analysis of the Egyptian correlations that have formed the basis of the traditional chronology; he concluded that, radiocarbon dating aside, there was in fact evidence to suggest that the traditional chronology was too low by about 100 years. He proposed a revised chronology for the Aegean that placed LM IA between 1700 and 1610 B.C. (roughly contemporary with the Hyksos period in Egypt), thereby making the radiocarbon results compatible.[20]

Archaeological evidence that would seem to support Betancourt's upward revision of Aegean chronology was presented at the Third International Congress in 1989. The source of this new evidence was Tel Kabri in Western Galilee, the site of a large fortified city that met its end around 1600 B.C. The site had yielded some Canaanite jars that were very similar to a Canaanite jar discovered at Akrotiri in 1973. In addition, in 1987 the palace at Kabri proved to have had a painted threshold without parallel in the Near East but akin in design and technique to work being done in the Aegean. Two years later, the excavators cleared the room behind this threshold (Room 611) and found an entire floor plastered and painted in the true fresco technique and featuring a grid-like pattern of squares, some of which were decorated with rockwork and floral motifs in the LM IA style. Even more significantly, in 1990 fragments of wall-paintings came to light which resembled both LM IA Minoan and LC I Theran miniature wall-paintings; these fragments were apparently part of a composition that depicted a rocky landscape adorned with plants and flowers. The excavators soon became convinced that the source of these motifs and techniques was unlikely to be local, and they even suggested that a Minoan artist was responsible for the decoration.[21] In terms of chronology, W.-D. Niemeier has stated that "the palace and town of Kabri were abandoned around 1600 BC. Since the painted floor in the palace with its distinct stylistic LM IA affinities shows clear signs of wear, it must have been painted some time before *c.* 1600 BC." He concludes that this new archaeological evidence from Kabri would support the higher, seventeenth century date proposed for the eruption of Thera.[22]

Additional, though controversial, evidence in favor of a seventeenth century date for the Theran eruption has come from the fields of dendro-chronology and ice-core studies. The advantage this evidence has over both radiocarbon dating and conventional archaeological relative dating is that it is much more precise; the study of tree-rings and ice-cores can, in fact, produce specific dates for major events that have had an impact on climate world-wide, such as large volcanic eruptions. Accordingly, as early as 1984, evidence from these scientific disciplines began to filter into the debate on the date of the eruption of Thera.

Dendrochronologists rely on the annual growth rings of trees to provide them with information about climate and general growing conditions. It has long been recognized that volcanic aerosols, especially those with a high concentration of sulphur, will, when ejected high into the stratosphere, exert a cooling effect on the surface of the earth. This cooling will often be manifested as frost-damaged zones in the tree-ring record. In a landmark study published in 1984, V.C. LaMarche, Jr. and K.K. Hirschboeck presented data from long-lived bristlecone pines from seven sites in the western United States and argued that a "frost event" dated between 1628 and 1626 B.C. could be attributed to the eruption of Thera.[23] It was also significant that no evidence of frost damage was found in tree-rings datable to the sixteenth century B.C. Indeed, the 1628–1626 event appeared to be the only serious "frost event" recorded in the entire second millennium B.C.[24]

This North American work was supplemented significantly by the efforts of European researchers, who managed to construct a European tree-ring chronology over 7200 years old. In Ireland, Michael Baillie was able to use Irish bog oaks to create a continuous chronology beginning in 5289 B.C. (the so-called Belfast Chronology); meanwhile, other scientists working in England and on the European continent had likewise succeeded in establishing lengthy tree-ring chronologies which harmonized well with the Irish evidence.[25] Baillie reported at the Third International Congress that the Irish tree-rings record a "narrow ring" event (i.e., a period of minimum growth) in 1628 B.C., an event which obviously echoes the "frost event" isolated by LaMarche and Hirschboeck.[26] Moreover, this low-growth event in Ireland is matched by a similar event recorded in trees growing in England and Germany at the same time. As a result, there can be no doubt that the period around 1628 B.C. saw tree growth in both North America and Europe adversely affected by some global climatic event, and Baillie and others are convinced that a volcanic eruption, probably that of Thera, was the culprit.[27]

In 1996, an important new source of dendrochronological data entered the picture: a tree-ring sequence of ca. 1500 years from Asia Minor, the result of years of work by the Aegean Dendrochronology Project.[28] Dated as running from 2220–718 B.C., this sequence records a highly unusual "growth event" in ring 854, thought to correlate with the 1628 B.C. event in North America and Europe. The project's researchers suggest that "such an exceptional growth event must be due to unusually high and sustained soil moisture content and a sharp reduction in midsummer evapotranspiration; that is, for a short time there was unusually cool and wet weather." They then propose that the eruption of Thera was the cause of this Anatolian climatic event.[29]

All such dendrochronological evidence for a Theran eruption ca. 1628 B.C., however, suffers from at least one obvious drawback: there is no "smoking gun" to prove that the tree-ring anomalies record the eruption of Thera rather than that of some other volcano. Moreover, there are other viable candidates: the Avellino eruption of Vesuvius, for example, has been re-dated to sometime between 1703 and 1617 B.C. on the basis of radiocarbon test using AMS.[30] Likewise, one cannot rule out the Mount St. Helens Y eruption or the Aniakchak II eruption, both dated by C14 to around the seventeenth century B.C. A second problem with the dendrochronological evidence also exists: the tree-ring records do not in fact reflect the impact of every large volcanic eruption. It would appear that only a select few leave an indelible impression in the wood—namely, those with a high sulphur content. Whether the eruption of Thera produced enough sulphuric aerosols to have had a impact on the global climate, and hence on tree development, remains unclear.[31]

The question of sulphur content, however, leads to another scientific dating method of relevance to the eruption of Thera: the dating of acidity layers in ice-cores. When a volcanic eruption injects a significant amount of sulphur dioxide into the stratosphere, sulphuric acid will be precipitated back to the surface; this sulphuric acid can then be deposited on icecaps, where it will become incorporated into the distinct layers of ice created each year by seasonal variations in temperature. Like annual growth rings in trees, these ice layers can be identified and dated by a relatively straightforward stratigraphic counting method. A specific annual layer displaying what has been termed an acidity peak can in theory be synchronized with a specific volcanic eruption. One of the best places on earth at which to discover such acidity peaks in ice is Greenland.[32]

In 1987, Danish scientists reported that their analysis of acidity peaks in the annual ice layers of a core obtained from the so-called Dye 3 site in southern Greenland suggested that the eruption of Thera took place ca. 1645 B.C., with an error margin of ± 20 years.[33] The resultant range of ca. 1665 to 1625 would agree with the dendrochronological evidence for a major event that affected the global climate around 1628 B.C. But one is again faced with the obvious question: how can it be proved beyond doubt that the event being recorded in the ice-cores is the Theran eruption as opposed to other volcanic explosions that took place in the seventeenth century B.C.?

As in the case of the tree-ring data, the likelihood that the Theran eruption was responsible for the ca. 1645 B.C. acidity peak depends on how much sulphur it injected into the stratosphere. Not long after the Danish results were published, several researchers argued that the magma of the Theran eruption was rich in silica and poor in sulphur; hence, the Theran event was unlikely to have left any record either in tree-ring growth or in acidity peaks in ice-cores. D.M. Pyle, for example, estimated that the sulphur yield of the eruption was approximately 3 megatonnes and hence too small, in his opinion, to create the Greenland acidity spike.[34] This view found substantial support at the Third International Congress but, in 1992, Sturt Manning argued that recent eruptions, such as the 1991 Mount Pinatubo event, demonstrate that "sulphur emissions from silicic-rich volcanoes (like Thera) were considerably greater than expected according to the conventional wisdom." Manning thus sees the Theran eruption as a strong candidate for the seventeenth century B.C. anomalies witnessed in the tree-rings and ice-cores.[35] Still, the hypothesis that the real culprit/culprits were the Avellino eruption of Vesuvius, Mount St.

Helens Y, Aniakchak II, or even some presently unknown seventeenth century eruption cannot be dismissed. On the other hand, the theory that the Theran event was one of a series of eruptions that clustered in the seventeenth century, causing severe climatic effects globally, also cannot be dismissed.[36]

Clearly, what is needed is the proverbial "smoking gun" that would unquestionably link the seventeenth century anomalies with Thera, and some scientists have looked eagerly at sulphur isotope ratios or micro-shard comparisons as ways of settling the Theran controversy. A breakthrough in this area may yet come from the Greenland Ice Sheet Project Two (GISP2) at Summit, Greenland, where a group of researchers have used their analyses of sulphur concentrations in ice-cores to reconstruct a record of volcanism from 7000 B.C. to the present. They have suggested that a high sulphate residual at 1623 B.C. may come from the eruption of Thera.[37] This by itself still fails to supply the needed smoking gun, but the GISP2 researchers are searching this crucial layer for microparticles of tephra that can be subjected to chemical analysis to ascertain whether they came from the Theran eruption. The discovery of undeniably Theran tephra in a datable ice layer should resolve the issue of the calendrical date of the eruption once and for all.[38]

If this quest for Theran tephra fails, the argument for the seventeenth century B.C. will remain grounded in what may be called converging lines of evidence. As Baillie once wrote, "Three lines of evidence—ice cores, bristlecone frost rings and an Irish oak minimum-growth event—combine to make it virtually certain that there was a large volcanic dust-veil event in 1628 BC. None of these lines of evidence is capable of specifying the volcano involved...[but] none of these continuous records...indicate any other consistent event between 1628 BC and 1159 BC."[39] Now a fourth line of evidence may be added: the Anatolian growth event. Thus, either the eruption took place in the seventeenth century and was large enough to affect the global climate or it took place later (in the sixteenth century) but was not large enough to leave any record in ice-cores or tree-rings. If the latter is indeed the case, determining credible radiocarbon dates for material from the Volcanic Destruction Level at Akrotiri becomes the only key to the chronological mystery.

Needless to say, if the seventeenth century B.C. date is eventually upheld, the traditional chronology of the entire Bronze Age in the eastern Mediterranean will have to be rethought. That a chronological revolution is on the horizon may account for the general reluctance of many archaeologists to accept the proxy data provided by dendrochronology and ice-core studies.[40] And yet, even some archaeologists have admitted that the foundation on which the traditional Aegean chronology has been built is not all that firm. For example, Peter Warren, who dates Late Minoan IA from 1600/1580 to "pre-1504/1480 BC" and rejects Betancourt's recent high chronology,[41] nevertheless admits that his dates are "derived from...fewer cross links to the historical chronology of Egypt than one would prefer," and that "absolute dating of [the] ceramic periods from artefactual evidence is far less precise than we would like."[42] Critics of the conventional chronology are predictably harsher: Manning, for example, writes of "the flimsy nature of accepted Bronze Age absolute ceramic correlation chronologies," noting that "each conventional archaeological datum at issue is contestable to varying degrees."[43] Indeed, the very presumption that a foreign object found in a datable context must date that object to the same time as the context need not be true: the context provides only a *terminus ante quem* and the object itself could well have been manufactured earlier. As R.S. Merrillees once noted, "There are certain tomb groups [in Egypt] which demonstrate beyond doubt that funerary objects could and did cover a wide range in time, even though they were all deposited at the same moment in their final resting place."[44] In sum, the traditional archaeological chronology, based on alleged Egyptian/Minoan synchronisms, is not firm enough to rule out a seventeenth century date for the eruption of Thera.

The Local Effects of the LBA Eruption of Thera

The magnitude of the Theran eruption makes it likely that not only Thera itself but also other regions suffered serious consequences. If the late seventeenth century B.C. date for the eruption becomes established beyond doubt, the dendrochronological and ice-core evidence strongly suggests that the Theran event affected the global climate by releasing substantial amounts of volcanic aerosols into the stratosphere. Geoscientists now recognize that such volcanic aerosols exert a cooling effect on the climate by preventing solar radiation from reaching the surface of the earth. If there were also other eruptions taking place around this time, it is possible that their cumulative aerosols created severe climatic disturbances on a global scale.

That the eruption of Thera had an impact upon the eastern Mediterranean region seems undeniable. The wind currents in force at the time of the eruption dispersed Theran tephra in an arc extending east, northeast and southeast, as demonstrated by Theran fall-out discovered in Turkey, Kos, Rhodes, eastern Crete and Egypt. In Turkey, a core from Lake Gölcük, located 90 kilometers east of Izmir, revealed a 12 centimeter thick layer of tephra chemically traced to the eruption of Thera; as Lake Gölcük is approximately 320 kilometers northeast of Thera, this discovery put an end to the earlier belief that debris from the eruption fell mainly to the east and southeast. Later work in Turkey turned up additional evidence of Theran fall-out in the form of a 9 centimeter deposit in a sediment core obtained from Lake Köycegiz, south of Gölcük. Given that the minimum fresh-fall equivalent at Gölcük has been estimated at ca. 24 centimeters, the Theran eruption had the potential not only to damage buildings but also, more importantly, to disrupt agriculture.[45] Off the coast of Turkey, the islands of Kos and Rhodes seem to have experienced an earthquake followed by ash-fall. On Kos the tephra layer measures from 10–20 centimeters thick, while on Rhodes a more substantial deposit has come to light at Trianda, ranging from 10 centimeters to 3 meters in thickness. It even appears that the fall-out at Trianda was severe enough to force the abandonment of the southern sector of the town.[46] An almost equally impressive tephra deposit, in places in excess of 50 centimeters, was discovered in 1985 in the course of ditch digging operations at the international airport on Rhodes.[47]

In Egypt, volcanic glass shards have been discovered in sediment cores taken in the eastern Nile Delta around Lake Manzala, confirming earlier suspicions that the Egyptians would have experienced the effects of the eruption.[48] In light of the extensive records left by the Egyptians, scholars have long tried to find some reference to the Theran event in Egyptian writings, even to the point of connecting the myth of Atlantis to Egyptian records allegedly seen by Solon but not recognized by either that poet or Plato as pertaining to a volcanic eruption on a Cycladic island.[49] At the Third International Congress, E.N. Davis drew attention to an inscribed stele from Thebes, dated to the reign of Ahmose (on the high Egyptian chronology ca. 1550–1525; on the low Egyptian chronology ca. 1539–1514),[50] and, more recently, K.P. Foster and R.K. Ritner have also suggested that this inscription records the eruption of Thera.[51] According to this "Tempest Stele," a fierce storm brought darkness and flooding to Thebes and the area to the north. There is, however, no firm correlation between this event and the Theran eruption; the storm in Egypt may have had a totally different, even local, cause.[52]

Egypt has, however, recently yielded pieces of Theran pumice at the excavation of Tell el-Dab'a (Avaris) in the eastern Nile Delta. Some have attempted to date the eruption on the basis of this pumice, which came to light in a New Kingdom stratum. Leaving aside entirely the vexing question of whether the traditional dates for the New Kingdom are historically secure, it should be pointed out that, according to the excavator, these lumps of pumice were sea-borne and were discovered in workshops.[53] Thus, they may have arrived in the Delta long after the eruption and been occasionally collected for industrial use; floating pumice from the Theran eruption can still be found in the Aegean and is worthless for chronological purposes.

The effect of the eruption on Minoan Crete has been the subject of much contentious debate since the publication, in 1939, of an article by Spyridon Marinatos connecting the fall of the Minoan civilization to the eruption of Thera; this hypothesis received endorsement in 1969 from such eminent scholars as J.V. Luce.[54] In recent years, however, a major impediment to this linkage has emerged: while the ceramic remains from Akrotiri indicate that its demise took place in mature Late Minoan IA, the ceramic evidence from the destruction levels on Crete dates the Minoan collapse to Late Minoan IB. There is consequently a general consensus at present that the eruption of Thera and the general destructions on Minoan Crete were two separate events.[55] The eruption did, however, affect Crete: an estimated 1 to 5 centimeters of tephra fell on the eastern part of the island, enough to have disrupted agriculture for a short period of time.[56]

Other after-effects of the eruption on Crete are perhaps more noteworthy. Sea-borne pumice from Thera certainly reached the shores of Crete as well as Egypt,[57] and such a phenomenon might have given rise to a "pumice cult" and a related goddess named on Linear B tablets as "QE-RA-SI-JA" (see Chapter 5).[58] But pumice may not have been the only Theran "export" at this time: refugees from the eruption might have ended up on Crete. Indeed, the movement of Therans from their island to Crete could explain the presence of nippled ewers of the Theran type found in an LM IB context at Pyrgos on Crete. What the general psychological effects of the Theran eruption and its associated phenomena on the Minoans would have been is a matter of speculation, but it seems likely that the Minoans experienced fear and anxiety for some time afterward.

The eruption would also have made an impression on the mainland of Greece. Sea-borne pumice apparently reached the Gulf of Messenia and was carried to the site of Nichoria.[59] Moreover, some Theran refugees may well have headed north to the mainland: artefacts found in the Shaft Graves at Mycenae have styles and techniques that share much with Theran counterparts.[60] Such a migration of Therans to the north would not be unexpected in light of the existing trade relations between the island and the Greek mainland.

Finally, the recent discoveries of Minoan-style wall-paintings not only at Kabri but also at Alalakh, Tell el-Dab'a and Miletus even raise the intriguing possibility that refugees from Thera moved eastward and gained employment as artists at major Egyptian and Near Eastern sites. But, wherever surviving Therans went, they left behind an island that would be uninhabitable for centuries. Only in Mycenaean Late Helladic IIIA/B (or Late Cycladic III), presently dated to the 13th/12th centuries B.C., do archaeologists find any evidence of a renewed human presence on Thera, and then only in the form of a few surface finds of Mycenaean pottery sherds near Monolithos.[61] While some have postulated an actual Late Cycladic III settlement around Monolithos on the basis of these finds, it is equally possible that the sherds represent only the occasional presence of traders carrying Mycenaean ceramics. The newly-created plain and beach around Monolithos would have attracted seafarers looking for safe landing places as stop-overs along their wide-ranging routes. Thus, permanent re-occupation of Thera might well have awaited the ninth century B.C., when the city today called Ancient Thera was founded on Mesa Vouno.

LIST OF ABBREVIATIONS

Congress Proceedings:

Acta   *Acta of the 1st International Scientific Congress on the Volcano of Thera.* Ed. A. Kaloyeropoulou. Athens: Archaeological Services of Greece, 1971.

T & AW I   *Thera and the Aegean World I.* Ed. C. Doumas. London: Thera and the Aegean World, 1978.

T & AW II   *Thera and the Aegean World II.* Ed. C. Doumas. London: Thera and the Aegean World, 1980.

T & AW III: Arch   *Thera and the Aegean World III. Volume One: Archaeology.* Ed. D.A. Hardy, with C.G. Doumas, J.A. Sakellarakis and P.M. Warren. London: The Thera Foundation, 1990.

T & AW III: ES   *Thera and the Aegean World III. Volume Two: Earth Sciences.* Ed. D.A. Hardy, with J. Keller, V.P. Galanopoulos, N.C. Flemming and T.H. Druitt. London: The Thera Foundation, 1990.

T & AW III: Chron   *Thera and the Aegean World III. Volume Three: Chronology.* Ed. D.A. Hardy, with A.C. Renfrew. London: The Thera Foundation, 1990.

Journals/Periodicals:

AA   *Archäologischer Anzeiger*
AAA   *᾽Αρχαιολογικὰ ᾽ανάλεκτα ᾽εξ ᾽Αθηνῶν*
ADeltion   *᾽Αρχαιολογικὸν Δελτίον*
AE   *᾽Αρχαιολογικὴ ᾽Εφημερίς*
AJA   *American Journal of Archaeology*
AM   *Mitteilungen des Deutschen Archäologischen Instituts. Athenische Abteilung*
BICS   *Bulletin of the Institute of Classical Studies of the University of London*
BSA   *The Annual of the British School at Athens*

IJNA	*International Journal of Nautical Archaeology and Underwater Exploration*
JHS	*Journal of Hellenic Studies*
JMA	*Journal of Mediterranean Archaeology*
PAA	Πρακτικὰ τῆς ᾿Ακαδημίας ᾿Αθηνῶν
PAE	Πρακτικὰ τῆς ᾿εν ᾿Αθήναις ᾿Αρχαιολογικῆς ῾Εταιρείας
TUAS	*Temple University Aegean Symposium*

BREVARD COMMUNITY COLLEGE
MELBOURNE CAMPUS LIBRARY
3865 N. WICKHAM ROAD
MELBOURNE, FL 32935

NOTES

Chapter One: Genesis: Birth of an Island

1 J. Keller, Th. Rehren and E. Stadlbauer, "Explosive Volcanism in the Hellenic Arc: a Summary and Review," *T & AW III: ES*, 15; see also S. Kalogeropoulos and S. Paritsis, "Geological and Geochemical Evolution of the Santorini Volcano: a Review," *T & AW III: ES*, 164 [hereafter Kalogeropoulos and Paritsis:1990].

2 G. Heiken and F. McCoy, Jr., "Caldera Development during the Minoan Eruption, Thira, Cyclades, Greece," *Journal of Geophysical Research* 89 (1984) 8442 [hereafter Heiken and McCoy:1984].

3 For a comprehensive account of volcanism in the Santorini complex, see T.H. Druitt, R.A. Mellors, D.M. Pyle and R.S.J. Sparks, "Explosive Volcanism on Santorini, Greece," *Geological Magazine* 126 (1989) 95–126 [hereafter Druitt et al:1989].

4 Heiken and McCoy:1984:8447–8450; also Druitt et al:1989:110.

5 Druitt et al:1989:100.

6 Druitt et al:1989:123–124.

7 H. Pichler and S. Kussmaul, "Comments on the Geological Map of the Santorini Islands," *T & AW II*, 420 [hereafter Pichler and Kussmaul: 1980]. It should be noted, however, that the precise date of the Skaros caldera remains in dispute: see Druitt et al:1989:114.

8 Heiken and McCoy:1984:8446.

9 Pichler and Kussmaul:1980:420.

10 Druitt et al:1989:114.

11 T.H. Druitt, "Vent Evolution and Lag Breccia Formation during the Cape Riva Eruption of Santorini, Greece," *Journal of Geology* 93 (1985) 439–454.

12 Evidence for the existence of a shallow caldera in the region of northern Therasia and Thera takes the form of stromatolites (blocks of algal lime-stone formed under shallow marine conditions) found in the volcanic debris deposited in this area by the Late Bronze Age eruption and carbon-dated to ca. 17,000 years ago. See W.L. Friedrich, U. Eriksen, H. Tau-ber, J. Heinemeier, N. Rud, M.S. Thomsen and B. Buchardt, "Existence of a Water-Filled Caldera Prior to the Minoan Eruption of Santorini, Greece," *Naturwissenschaften* 75 (1988) 567–569 [hereafter Friedrich et al:1988].

13 Kalogeropoulos and Paritsis:1990:166.

14 N.D. Watkins, R.S.J. Sparks, H. Sigurdsson, T.C. Huang, A. Feder-man, S. Carey and D. Ninkovich, "Volume and Extent of the Minoan

Tephra from Santorini Volcano: New Evidence from the Deep-sea Sediment Cores," *Nature* 271 (1978) 122–126 [hereafter Watkins et al:1978].

15 Heiken and McCoy:1984:8441.

16 Heiken and McCoy:1984:8448.

17 Heiken and McCoy:1984:8448–8450.

18 Heiken and McCoy:1984:8450.

19 Friedrich et al:1988:568.

20 G. Heiken, F. McCoy and M. Sheridan, "Palaeotopographic and Palaeogeologic Reconstruction of Minoan Thera," *T & AW III: ES*, 370.

21 T.H. Druitt and V. Francaviglia, "An Ancient Caldera Cliff Line at Phira, and its Significance for the Topography and Geology of Pre-Minoan Santorini," *T & AW III: ES*, 362 [hereafter Druitt and Francaviglia:1990].

22 U. Eriksen, W.L. Friedrich, B. Buchardt, H. Tauber and M.S. Thomsen, "The Stronghyle Caldera: Geological, Palaeontological and Stable Isotope Evidence from Radiocarbon Dated Stromatolites from Santorini," *T & AW III: ES*, 139–150 [hereafter Eriksen et al:1990].

23 McCoy, in Druitt and Francaviglia:1990:369.

24 D.M. Pyle, "New Estimates for the Volume of the Minoan Eruption," *T & AW III: ES*, 113–121 [hereafter Pyle:1990].

25 Druitt and Francaviglia stated at the Congress that "the possibility that the west or north-west channels were already breached prior to the Minoan eruption cannot be disproved;" see Druitt and Francaviglia: 1990:368.

26 For the soil, see S. Limbrey, "Soil Studies at Akrotiri," *T & AW III: ES*, 377–383; for the water supply, see N. Kourmoulis, "The Consequences of Volcanic Activity of the Minoan Period on the Hydrogeological Conditions of the Island of Thera," *T & AW III: ES*, 237–240 [hereafter Kourmoulis:1990].

27 M.A. Aston and P.G. Hardy, "The Pre-Minoan Landscape of Thera: a Preliminary Statement," *T & AW III: ES*, 348–361 [hereafter Aston and Hardy:1990]; and J.P.P. Huijsmans and M. Barton, "New Stratigraphic and Geochemical Data for the Megalo Vouno Complex: a Dominating Volcanic Landform in Minoan Times," *T & AW III: ES*, 440 [hereafter Huijsmans and Barton:1990].

28 Aston and Hardy:1990:355.

29 O. Rackham, "Observations on the Historical Ecology of Santorini," *T & AW III: ES*, 388 [hereafter Rackham:1990].

30 Rackham:1990:388–389.

31 T.H. Van Andel and C.N. Runnels, "An Essay on the 'Emergence of Civilization' in the Aegean World," *Antiquity* 62 (1988) 237 [hereafter Van Andel and Runnels:1988]; also J.F. Cherry, "Islands out of the Stream: Isolation and Interaction in Early East Mediterranean Insular Prehistory," in A.B. Knapp and T. Stech (eds.), *Prehistoric Production and Exchange: The Aegean and Eastern Mediterranean* (Los Angeles, 1985) 15 [hereafter Cherry:1985]. R.L.N. Barber, in *The Cyclades in the Bronze Age* (London, 1987) 118 [hereafter Barber:1987], thinks it possible that obsidian from Melos was reaching the mainland as early as the 11th millennium B.C.

32 Cherry:1985:15.

33 J.E. Coleman, "The Chronology and Interconnections of the Cycladic Islands in the Neolithic and the Early Bronze Age," *AJA* 78 (1974) 333 [hereafter Coleman:1974]; and J.F. Cherry, "Pattern and Process in the Earliest Colonization of the Mediterranean Islands," *Proceedings of the Prehistoric Society* 47 (1981) 45 [hereafter Cherry:1981].

34 J.L. Davis, "Review of Aegean Prehistory I: The Islands of the Aegean," *AJA* 96 (1992) 704 [hereafter J.L. Davis:1992]. See also A.B. Knapp, "Bronze Age Mediterranean Island Cultures and the Ancient Near East, Part 1," *Biblical Archaeologist* 55 (1992) 62 [hereafter Knapp:1992a].

35 J.F. Cherry, "Island Origins: The Early Prehistoric Cyclades," in B. Cunliffe (ed.), *Origins: The Roots of European Civilisation* (Chicago, 1988; hereafter Cunliffe:1988) 26 [hereafter Cherry:1988].

36 B. Cunliffe, "Aegean Civilisation and Barbarian Europe," in Cunliffe: 1988:8; and C. Lambrou-Phillipson, *Hellenorientalia: The Near Eastern Presence in the Bronze Age Aegean, ca. 3000–1100 B.C.* (Göteborg, 1990) 152–153 [hereafter:Lambrou-Phillipson:1990].

37 C. Renfrew, "Saliagos—A Neolithic Settlement in the Cyclades," in J. Filip (ed.), *Actes du VII Congrès International des Sciences Préhistoriques et Protohistoriques*, 1 (Prague, 1970) 393; Renfrew believes the sea level during the Neolithic was about 6 meters lower than at present.

38 C. Doumas, "The Transition from Late Neolithic to Early Bronze Age: The Evidence from the Islands," in Y. Maniatis (ed.), *Archaeometry: Proceedings of the 25th International Symposium* (Amsterdam, 1989; hereafter Maniatis:1989) 706.

39 Cherry:1985:24.

40 O. Hadjianastasiou, "A Late Neolithic Settlement at Grotta, Naxos," in E.B. French and K.A. Wardle (eds.), *Problems in Greek Prehistory* (Bristol, 1988; hereafter French and Wardle:1988) 11–20 [hereafter Had-

jianastasiou:1988]. See also J.F. Cherry, "The First Colonization of the Mediterranean Islands: A Review of Recent Research," *JMA* 3 (1990) 164–165 [hereafter Cherry:1990]; and J.L. Davis:1992:739–740.

41 Barber:1987:133; Cherry:1988:21; and J.L. Davis:1992:712.

42 Hadjianastasiou:1988:12 reports "no definite outlines of buildings" yet found at Grotta, but notes a "concentration of large pebbles...which might belong to the demolished foundations of houses built of mudbrick."

43 Hadjianastasiou:1988:18. For Neolithic sites in the Cyclades, see R. Hope Simpson and O.T.P.K. Dickinson, *A Gazetteer of Aegean Civilisation in the Bronze Age, Volume I: The Mainland and Islands* (Göteborg, 1979) 304–346 [hereafter Hope Simpson and Dickinson:1979].

44 Van Andel and Runnels:1988:237; also Cherry:1981:55.

45 P. Sotirakopoulou, "Early Cycladic Pottery from Akrotiri on Thera and Its Chronological Implications," *BSA* 81 (1986) 297–312 [hereafter Sotirakopoulou:1986]; P. Sotirakopoulou, "The Earliest History of Akrotiri: The Late Neolithic and Early Bronze Age Phases," *T & AW III: Chron*, 41–47 [hereafter Sotirakopoulou:1990].

46 Sotirakopoulou:1986:309.

47 Sotirakopoulou:1990:47.

48 Sotirakopoulou:1990:47.

49 C. Doumas, "Archaeological Observations at Akrotiri Relating to the Volcanic Destruction," *T & AW III: Chron*, 48 [hereafter Doumas:1990].

50 How close to the sea is difficult to say: while there is a consensus that the sea level in the Aegean was ca. 3–6 meters lower then, the matter is complicated by the fact that the LBA eruption extended the coastline in the south. Xesté 3 is located now some 250 meters from the shore (and by no means marks the southern limit of the settlement: there are traces of structures further south), and Doumas seems to believe that the Bronze Age coastline was ca. 50 meters inland from the present shore: see C. Palyvou, "Notes on the Town Plan of Late Cycladic Akrotiri, Thera," *BSA* 81 (1986) 179–181 [hereafter Palyvou:1986].

51 C. Doumas, *Thera: Pompeii of the Ancient Aegean* (London, 1983) 55–56 [hereafter Doumas:1983].

52 Doumas:1983:11.

53 It has been shown that obsidian found at Late Cycladic Akrotiri was of Melian origin; see A. Aspinall and S.W. Feather, "Neutron Activation Analysis of Aegean Obsidians," *T & AW I*, 517–521. Obsidian artefacts have also been found in Early Cycladic contexts at the site; see A.

Moundrea-Agrafioti, "Akrotiri, the Chipped Stone Industry: Reduction Techniques and Tools of the LC I Phase," *T & AW III: Arch*, 391 [hereafter Moundrea-Agrafioti:1990]. Thus there is no reason to exclude the presence of Melian obsidian from the Neolithic settlement.

54 Van Andel and Runnels:1988:236.

55 P. Faure, "Remarques sur la présence et l'emploi de la pierre ponce en Crete du Néolithique à nos jours," *Acta*, 422–427 [hereafter Faure:1971]; see also C. Renfrew, "Obsidian and Pumice: The Use of Recent Igneous Rock in Aegean Prehistory," *Acta*, 430–436 [hereafter Renfrew:1971]; and M. Artzy, "Nami: A Second Millennium International Maritime Trading Center in the Mediterranean," in S. Gitin (ed.), *Recent Excavations in Israel: A View to the West* (Dubuque, 1995; hereafter Gitin:1995) 23–25 [hereafter Artzy:1995]. It has recently been suggested that pumice may also have been used as an insecticide: see E. Panagiotakopulu, P.C. Buckland, P.M. Day, A.A. Sarpaki and C. Doumas, "Natural Insecticides and Insect Repellents in Antiquity: A Review of the Evidence," *Journal of Archaeological Science* 22 (1995) 708.

56 Faure:1971:422–423.

57 Renfrew:1971:434.

58 J.W. Sperling, *Thera and Therasia* (Athens, 1973) 32 [hereafter Sperling:1973].

59 Cherry:1988:22; Cherry:1985:16–17; and C. Renfrew, *The Emergence of Civilisation: The Cyclades and the Aegean in the Third Millennium B.C.* (London, 1972) 251 [hereafter Renfrew:1972]. It should be borne in mind, however, that population estimates for both the Neolithic and the Bronze Age are notoriously speculative, and that Renfrew's figures are sometimes considered too high.

60 C. Doumas, *Early Bronze Age Burial Habits in the Cyclades* (Göteborg, 1977) 11 [hereafter Doumas:1977a]; see also J.L. Davis:1992:740.

Chapter Two: Thera and the Emergence of the Cyclades

1 See P.P. Betancourt and B. Lawn, "The Cyclades and Radiocarbon Chronology," in J.A. MacGillivray and R.L.N. Barber (eds.), *The Prehistoric Cyclades* (Edinburgh, 1984; hereafter MacGillivray and Barber: 1984) 277. Even more controversial has been the terminology used to define the phases of the EBA: while it has long been traditional to divide the Cycladic EBA into three successive periods known as Early Cycladic

I, Early Cycladic II, and Early Cycladic III, in the 1960s Colin Renfrew adopted and advocated a "culture" terminology that replaced these three divisions with, in sequence, "Grotta-Pelos," "Keros-Syros" and "Phylakopi I." See C. Renfrew, "Crete and the Cyclades before Rhadamanthus," *Kretika Chronika* 18 (1964) 107–141 [hereafter Renfrew:1964]; C. Renfrew, "Cycladic Metallurgy and the Aegean Early Bronze Age," *AJA* 71 (1967) 1–20 [hereafter Renfrew:1967]; C. Renfrew, "The Development and Chronology of the Early Cycladic Figurines," *AJA* 73 (1969) 1–32 [hereafter Renfrew:1969]; and, especially, Renfrew:1972. Renfrew's "culture" terminology, however, has come under attack: see Coleman:1974:340; R.L.N. Barber and J.A. MacGillivray, "The Early Cycladic Period: Matters of Definition and Terminology," *AJA* 84 (1980) 141–157 [hereafter Barber and MacGillivray:1980]; Barber:1987:25; C. Doumas, "The Minoan Thalassocracy and the Cyclades," *AA* (1982) 6 [hereafter Doumas:1982]; and S.W. Manning, "The Emergence of Divergence: Development and Decline on Bronze Age Crete and the Cyclades," in C. Mathers and S. Stoddart (eds.), *Development and Decline in the Mediterranean Bronze Age* (Sheffield, 1994) 223–224 [hereafter Manning:1994].

2 See J.F. Cherry, "Four Problems in Cycladic Prehistory," in J.L. Davis and J.F. Cherry (eds.), *Papers in Cycladic Prehistory* (Los Angeles, 1979; hereafter Davis and Cherry:1979) 43. A much higher figure of ca. 34,000 was proposed by Renfrew: C. Renfrew, "Patterns of Population Growth in the Prehistoric Aegean," in P.J. Ucko, R. Tringham and G.W. Dimbleby (eds.), *Man, Settlement and Urbanism* (London, 1972; hereafter Ucko et al:1972) 394–397. For the number of settlements, see Hope Simpson and Dickinson:1979:304–346; see also Renfrew:1972: 507–525; Cherry:1988:22–23; and J.L. Davis:1992:703.

3 See Van Andel and Runnels:1988:236–240; also C.N. Runnels and J. Hansen, "The Olive in the Prehistoric Aegean: The Evidence for Domestication in the Early Bronze Age," *Oxford Journal of Archaeology* 5 (1986) 299–308 [hereafter Runnels and Hansen:1986].

4 See Renfrew:1967:4; Y. Bassiakos, V. Kilikoglou, M. Vassilaki-Grimani and A.P. Grimanis, "Provenance Studies of Theran Lead," *T & AW III: ES*, 337–345; and W.L. Friedrich and C.G. Doumas, "Was there Local Access to Certain Ores/Minerals for the Theran People before the Minoan Eruption? An Addendum," *T & AW III: Arch*, 502 [hereafter Friedrich and Doumas:1990]. Given the existence of the Lower Pumice 2 southern caldera in the EBA, it is indeed possible that the lead deposits at Athinios

were accessible.

5 Van Andel and Runnels:1988:243. Oliver Dickinson, in *The Aegean Bronze Age* (Cambridge, 1994) 296 [hereafter Dickinson:1994], writes of Neolithic "networks of contacts" inherited by the EBA islanders, adding that "the settlement of the Aegean islands surely enhanced opportunities for exchanges...and brought more materials into the distribution system." See also Manning:1994:227–229; Cunliffe:1988:11; and M.B. Cosmopoulos, "Exchange Networks in Prehistory: The Aegean and the Mediterranean in the Third Millennium B.C.," in R. Laffineur and L. Basch (eds.), *Thalassa: L'Égée préhistorique et la mer* (Liège, 1991; hereafter Laffineur and Basch:1991) 155–167.

6 Renfrew:1967:1. Dickinson:1994:209–210 also stresses the continuity between Neolithic and Early Bronze Age on the basis of burial customs.

7 Renfrew:1972:477; see C. Doumas, "The Early Cycladic Period," in G. Phylactopoulos (ed.), *Prehistory and Protohistory* (Athens, 1974; hereafter Phylactopoulos:1974) 107; and J.L. Davis:1992:703. One example of the cultural continuity evident in the transition from Neolithic to EC I can be found in the evolution of the Cycladic figurine. The marble "idols" that have become synonymous with Early Cycladic culture did not arise out of thin air: a Neolithic prototype of the schematic figurines so characteristic of EC I has been found at Saliagos: see Renfrew:1969:32 (plate 2c for the Saliagos figurine).

8 Barber:1987:70; Cherry:1988:22–23; and Manning:1994:224.

9 N.H. Gale, "Lead Isotope Analyses Applied to Provenance Studies—A Brief Review," in Maniatis:1989:492 [hereafter Gale:1989]. See also J.L. Davis:1992:728; and Z.A. Stos-Gale and C.F. Macdonald, "Sources of Metals and Trade in the Bronze Age Aegean," in N.H. Gale (ed.), *Bronze Age Trade in the Mediterranean* (Jonsered, 1991; hereafter Gale: 1991) 280 [hereafter Stos-Gale and Macdonald:1991].

10 Barber:1987:110 postulated tin being imported from the Troad, and Renfrew:1967:13 suggested the existence of tin deposits (now worked out) in that region. At the start of 1994, researchers at the University of Chicago announced the discovery of a 5,000 year old tin mine at the Turkish site of Kestel, ca. 100 km north of Tarsus; also found were traces of tin production at the nearby site of Goltepe. See also Lambrou-Phillipson: 1990:160. For tin coming from the Near East, see E.H. Cline, "Tinker, Tailor, Soldier, Sailor: Minoans and Mycenaeans Abroad," in R. Laffineur and W.-D. Niemeier (eds.), *Politeia: Society and State in the Aegean Bronze Age* (Liège, 1995; hereafter Laffineur and Niemeier:1995)

273 [hereafter Cline:1995a].

11 For Attica, see Barber:1987:136; Cherry:1988:28; and Doumas:1977a: 65–66. For Troy, see Doumas:1983:25. In southwestern Asia Minor, at Iasos in Caria, a cist grave cemetery has been dated to either EC I or EC II; see Doumas:1977a:67–68; Lambrou-Phillipson:1990:102 and 145; and Barber:1987:134. For Crete, see Doumas:1983:25. As S. Stucynski's "Cycladic 'Imports' in Crete: A Brief Survey," *TUAS* 7 (1982) 50–59 [hereafter Stucynski:1982] demonstrates, while there were a few scattered EC I imports to Crete, evidence of regular trade only appears in EC II and later.

12 C. Doumas, "Prehistoric Cycladic People in Crete," *AAA* 9 (1976) 79–80. See also Stos-Gale and Macdonald:1991:264 and 267. However, Dickinson:1994:211 and 239 notes certain non-Cycladic aspects of this cemetery, e.g., the absence of Cycladic figurines. A Cycladic enclave must thus remain speculative at best.

13 See J.E. Coleman's "Frying Pans of the Early Bronze Age Aegean," *AJA* 89 (1985) 191–219. While Coleman suspects the "frying pans" were used as plates, others see them as having had a ceremonial nature; see C. Broodbank, "The Longboat and Society in the Cyclades in the Keros-Syros Culture," *AJA* 93 (1989) 319–337.

14 The folded-arm figurines have been identified as goddesses, concubines, votaries, servants, substitute human sacrifices, etc. For general discussions on this problem, see Renfrew:1969:1–32; R.L.N. Barber, "Early Cycladic Marble Figures: Some Thoughts on Function," in J.L. Fitton (ed.), *Cycladica* (London, 1984; hereafter Fitton:1984) 10–14; J.L. Davis, "A Cycladic Figure in Chicago and the Non-funereal Use of Cycladic Marble Figures," in Fitton:1984:15–21; and C. Renfrew, "Speculations on the Use of Early Cycladic Sculpture," in Fitton:1984:24–30.

15 Barber and MacGillivray:1980:141–157 proposed the subdivision of EC III into EC IIIA and EC IIIB; see also J.A. MacGillivray's "The Relative Chronology of Early Cycladic III," in MacGillivray and Barber:1984:70–77; and Barber:1987:28–30. However, it should be noted that many scholars still prefer to speak only of EC III, believing that "EC III 'A' and 'B' each ran *through* EC III:" P. Warren and V. Hankey, *Aegean Bronze Age Chronology* (Bristol, 1989) 29 [hereafter Warren and Hankey:1989].

16 Barber:1987:70.

17 See C. Doumas, "EBA in the Cyclades: Continuity or Discontinuity?" in French and Wardle:1988:23 [hereafter Doumas:1988]; Barber:1987:28–

29 and 94; Renfrew:1972:533–534; J.B. Rutter, *Ceramic Change in the Aegean Early Bronze Age* (Los Angeles, 1979) 1; and J.B. Rutter, "Some Observations on the Cyclades in the Later Third and Early Second Millennia," *AJA* 87 (1983) 71 [hereafter Rutter:1983].

18 Doumas:1988:28; see also Lambrou-Phillipson:1990:32 and 169. For the tradition of fortified settlements in the Northeast Aegean, see Renfrew: 1972:394–399; for the disruptions in the Northeast Aegean ca. 2100 B.C., see R.L.N. Barber, "Phylakopi 1911 and the History of the Later Cycladic Bronze Age," *BSA* 69 (1974) 48 [hereafter Barber:1974]. The island of Lemnos was especially hard hit at this time, suffering almost total depopulation.

19 Gale:1989:495; see also Stos-Gale and Macdonald:1991:264; Lambrou-Phillipson:1990:100; and J.L. Davis:1992:727. The value of lead isotope analysis has, however, become a much debated topic: most of *JMA* 8 (1995) was given over to papers on the subject.

20 J.L. Davis:1992:754. The date of Kastri Ware has also been questioned: see P. Sotirakopoulou, "The Chronology of the 'Kastri Group' Reconsidered," *BSA* 88 (1993) 7–20.

21 Manning:1994:226.

22 Sotirakopoulou:1990:43.

23 Sotirakopoulou:1990:43.

24 For the 1971 find, see S. Marinatos, *Excavations at Thera V* (Athens, 1972) 23; plate 38b [hereafter Marinatos:Thera V]. See also E.B. French, "Archaeology in Greece," *Archaeological Reports* (1992–1993) 67.

25 The pillars required to support the protective roof covering the site necessitated the digging of pits below the Late Cycladic level of Akrotiri. Unhappily, the numbering of these pits has become a source of confusion: see C. Doumas, "The Stratigraphy of Akrotiri," *T & AW I*, 778 [hereafter Doumas:1978]. For the finds in the vaulted structure of pillar pit #6, see Sotirakopoulou: 1986:309; and Sotirakopoulou:1990:42.

26 For the "Fire Deposit" see A.G. Papagiannopoulou, *The Influence of Middle Minoan Pottery on the Cyclades* (Göteborg, 1991) 27, 33–34 [hereafter Papagiannopoulou:1991].

27 Sotirakopoulou:1990:47; see also the plan of the site found in Doumas: 1978:779. The discovery of three EC figurines in Xesté 3 in 1992 also indicates the lengthy inhabitation of this region of the site.

28 Sotirakopoulou:1990:47.

29 Doumas:1982:8.

30 F. Hiller von Gaertringen et al., *Thera* (Berlin, 1899–1909), volume I.

308 [hereafter Hiller]. See also Hiller's map at IG XII.3, page 69; the location of this site is presently unknown.

31 Whatever catalogue exists for the Fira Museum is now unobtainable and no labels are attached to these artefacts in the display case.

32 Renfrew:1969:12.

33 See C. Zervos, *L'Art des Cyclades* (Paris, 1957) #59.

34 I.A. Sakellarakis in J. Thimme (ed.), *Art and Culture of the Cyclades* (Karlsruhe, 1977; hereafter Thimme:1977) 146.

35 Inventory no. ABb 139; L. Ross, *Reisen auf den Griechischen Inseln* (Stuttgart and Tübingen, 1840) 181. See also Renfrew:1969:18. It should be noted that Hiller wrote of a necropolis of the "Kykladenkultur" near Megalochori (Hiller:I.307); however, Sperling:1973:26 prefers to date this cemetery (the location of which is now unknown) to the Late Bronze Age.

36 Renfrew:1969:20; and Renfrew:1972:425.

37 Inventory no. B 863 (h:15.6 cm) and B 864 (h:16.5 cm); a picture of the complete assemblage appears in Thimme:1977:figure 193. See also Doumas:1983:27; and Renfrew:1969:13-14.

38 M. Marthari, "The Local Pottery Wares with Painted Decoration from the Volcanic Destruction Level of Akrotiri, Thera," *AA* (1987) 369-370 [hereafter Marthari:1987]; also Papagiannopoulou:1991:27 and 30.

39 Marthari:1987:369; for a plan, see C. Televantou's "Ftellos," *ADeltion* 36 (1981) 374. See also Papagiannopoulou:1991:26-27.

40 M. Marthari, "Excavations at Ftellos," *AAA* 15 (1982) 95.

41 Friedrich and Doumas:1990:502.

42 Whether the island now known as Therasia also possessed settlements in the EBA remains uncertain. Given the existence in the Late Bronze Age of buildings on its present south coast, Therasia may have had a modest EC population. The only hint of this so far, though, is the somewhat vague assertion of Hiller (I.308) that *sepulcra antiquissima* existed at the southern tip of the island near Cape Trypiti.

43 S.J. Vaughan, "Petrographic Analysis of the Early Cycladic Wares from Akrotiri, Thera," *T & AW III: Arch*, 485; see also A. Papagiannopoulou, "Some Changes in the BA Pottery Production at Akrotiri and their Possible Implications," *T & AW III: Arch*, 58 [hereafter Papagiannopoulou:1990].

44 G. Papathanassopoulos, *Neolithic and Cycladic Civilization* (Athens, 1981) 104 and 106. More recently, see Manning:1994:246.

45 Barber:1987:72; see also R.L.N. Barber, "The Cyclades in the Middle

Bronze Age," *T & AW I*, 374. R. Phythyon, in "Considerations in Minoan Contacts at the Beginning of the Late Bronze Age," *TUAS* 5 (1980) 61 [hereafter Phythyon:1980], writes of "cautious growth rather than sudden decline."

46 Barber:1987:66-68.

47 Renfrew:1972:398 claims that the MC walls at Phylakopi II were "built to withstand raiders from the sea." See also Renfrew:1972:262-264; Phythyon:1980:61-62; and Barber:1974:50.

48 Dickinson:1994:241.

49 C. Doumas, "The Middle Cycladic Period," in Phylactopoulos:1974: 141.

50 Barber and MacGillivray:1980:153; Barber:1974:50; Renfrew:1972:202-203; and Renfrew:1964:139. See also J.L. Davis, "The Mainland Panelled Cup and Panelled Style," *AJA* 82 (1978) 216-222.

51 Barber:1987:146. For imported Minyan ware in the Cyclades, see also J.L. Caskey, "Greece and the Aegean Islands in the Middle Bronze Age," in *The Cambridge Ancient History* (Third Edition) Volume II, Part 1 (Cambridge, 1973) 129-130; and Dickinson:1994:242.

52 Rutter:1983:74. As to whose ships conducted the trade, Doumas favors Cycladic merchants, while Dickinson suggests merchants originating from ports on the mainland; see C. Doumas, "Trade in the Aegean in the Light of the Thera Excavations," in M. Marazzi, S. Tusa and L. Vagnetti (eds.), *Traffici Micenei nel Mediterraneo* (Taranto, 1986; hereafter Marazzi et al:1986) 237 [hereafter Doumas:1986]; and Dickinson:1994: 243. There is, of course, no reason to discount the participation of seafarers from both regions.

53 Stucynski:1982.

54 Stucynski:1982:55-57. Clay analysis confirms the Cycladic origin of these vessels, with Melos as the probable place of production; see R.E. Jones, "Composition and Provenance Studies of Cycladic Pottery with Particular Reference to Thera," *T & AW I*, 471-482 [hereafter Jones: 1978]; A. Papagiannopoulou, "Analysis of Melian and Theran Pottery: A Preliminary Report," *Hydra* 1 (1985) 59-62 [hereafter Papagiannopoulou:1985].

55 J.A. MacGillivray, "Cycladic Jars from Middle Minoan III Contexts at Knossos," in R. Hägg and N. Marinatos (eds.), *The Minoan Thalassocracy: Myth and Reality* (Stockholm, 1984; hereafter Hägg and Marinatos:1984) 153 [hereafter MacGillivray:1984].

56 MacGillivray:1984:156; see also Barber:1987:156. Of course, perishable

goods not shipped in ceramic containers would also have been exchanged, but have left little or no trace in the archaeological record: e.g., textiles.

57 Barber:1987:155; also 145–149. See also Papagiannopoulou:1991:64.

58 Doumas:1978:779.

59 For MC finds in the area of Xesté 3, see A. Papagiannopoulou in Sotira-kopoulou:1990:47; for both these finds and those in the House of the Ladies, see C. Doumas, "Ἀνασκαφὴ Θήρας," *PAE* (1987) 241–254 [hereafter Doumas:1987].

60 Papagiannopoulou:1990:58; also Papagiannopoulou:1991:28: "the plan of the MC city definitely determined the layout of the LC I successor."

61 C. Doumas, "Ἀνασκαφὴ Θήρας ('Ακρωτήρι)," *PAE* (1985) 168–176 [hereafter Doumas:1985].

62 See Doumas:1987; also M. Marthari, "The Chronology of the Last Phases of Occupation at Akrotiri in the Light of the Evidence from the West House Pottery Groups," *T & AW III: Chron*, 67 [hereafter Marthari:1990].

63 C. Doumas, *The Wall-Paintings of Thera* (Athens, 1992) 30 [hereafter Doumas:1992]. See also E.N. Davis, "The Cycladic Style of the Thera Frescoes," *T & AW III: Arch*, 226 [hereafter E.N. Davis:1990]; S.A. Immerwahr, "Swallows and Dolphins at Akrotiri: Some Thoughts on the Relationship of Vase-Painting to Wall-Painting," *T & AW III: Arch*, 237–245 [hereafter Immerwahr:1990a]; Papagiannopoulou:1990:57–66; and Marthari:1990:57–70.

64 Papagiannopoulou:1991:29 and 33–34; also Doumas:1985.

65 Immerwahr:1990a:239–240.

66 K. Bolton, "Addendum to J.V. Luce's Article: 'Thera and the Devastation of Minoan Crete: A New Interpretation of the Evidence'," *AJA* 80 (1976) 17; and G. Cadogan, "Some Middle Minoan Problems," in French and Wardle:1988:99.

67 For example, some prefer to date the Black-and-red style, including the polychrome "bird jugs," to LC I as opposed to late MC; see E. Schofield, "The Western Cyclades and Crete: A 'Special Relationship'," *Oxford Journal of Archaeology* 1 (1982) 12–13 [hereafter Schofield:1982]; and J.L. Davis, "Polychrome Bird Jugs: A Note," *AAA* 9 (1976) 83 [hereafter J.L. Davis:1976].

68 See Doumas:1990:48; Marthari:1987:370; J.L. Davis:1976:81; and V. Kilikoglou, C. Doumas, A. Papagiannopoulou, E.V. Sayre, Y. Maniatis, and A.P. Grimanis, "A Study of Middle and Late Cycladic Pottery from Akrotiri," *T & AW III: Arch*, 441–448 [hereafter Kilikoglou et al:1990].

69 R. Zahn in Hiller:III:44; and S. Marinatos, *Excavations at Thera VI* (Athens, 1974) 31 [hereafter Marinatos:Thera VI].

70 M.H. Wiener, "The Isles of Crete? The Minoan Thalassocracy Revisited," *T & AW III: Arch*, 149 [hereafter Wiener:1990].

71 MacGillivray:1984:155–156; Barber:1987:156; and Papagiannopoulou: 1985:61.

72 P.P. Betancourt, "The Middle Minoan Pottery of Southern Crete and the Question of a Middle Minoan Thalassocracy," in Hägg and Marinatos: 1984:92.

73 See J.L. Davis:1992:733.

74 MacGillivray:1984:157.

75 For contacts between Phylakopi and Akrotiri, see Kilikoglou et al:1990: 447 and Marinatos:Thera VI:68.

76 Manning:1994:245.

77 See Lambrou-Phillipson:1990; M.H. Wiener, "The Nature and Control of Minoan Foreign Trade," in Gale:1991:325–350 [hereafter Wiener: 1991]; P.M. Warren, "A Merchant Class in Bronze Age Crete?" in Gale:1991:295–301 [hereafter Warren:1991]; and Manning:1994.

Chapter Three: Thera and Crete in the Late Bronze Age

1 J.L. Davis:1992:707.

2 See Wiener:1990:128–161. See also S. Hood, "The Cretan Element on Thera in Late Minoan IA," *T & AW III: Arch*, 118–123 [hereafter Hood: 1990]; S. Hood, "A Minoan Empire in the Aegean in the 16th and 15th Centuries B.C.?" in Hägg and Marinatos:1984:33–37; and Manning: 1994:248. For Crete's need for metals, see J.L. Davis:1992:706; and N.H. Gale, "Copper Oxhide Ingots: Their Origin and their Place in the Bronze Age Metals Trade in the Mediterranean," in Gale:1991:204. For the elite demand for luxury goods, see A. Sherratt and S. Sherratt, "From Luxuries to Commodities: The Nature of Mediterranean Bronze Age Trading Systems," in Gale:1991:351–384 [hereafter Sherratt and Sherratt:1991]; and A.B. Knapp, "Thalassocracies in Bronze Age Eastern Mediterranean Trade: Making and Breaking a Myth," *World Archaeology* 24 (1992/1993) 341 [hereafter Knapp:1992/1993].

3 See Wiener:1990:128–161; the quotation is found on page 151. See also J.L. Davis:1992:706.

4 Doumas:1983:128.

5 K. Branigan, "Minoan Colonialism," *BSA* 76 (1981) 23–33 [hereafter Branigan:1981]; also K. Branigan, "Minoan Community Colonies in the Aegean?" in Hägg and Marinatos:1984:49–53 [hereafter Branigan:1984].

6 Sherratt and Sherratt:1991:368; also J.L. Davis:1992:748–749.

7 Minoan architectural features include the light well, the pier-and-door partition known as the polythyron and the sunken basin called an adyton (formerly the "lustral basin"). Cycladic features include town planning, house design, construction techniques, pottery shapes and decoration, and local features in wall-paintings that lead scholars to speak of a distinctive island iconography. See Branigan:1984:51; L. Morgan, "Island Iconography: Thera, Kea, Milos," *T & AW III: Arch*, 252–266 [hereafter Morgan:1990]; C. Televantou, "The Rendering of the Human Figure in the Theran Wall-Paintings," *AE* (1988) 135–166; and E.N. Davis:1990: 214–228. It should also be noted that some Cycladic nationalists believe that the various Minoan features noted at Phylakopi, Ayia Irini and Akrotiri in the LBA need not imply even Minoan settlers on these islands but rather exposure of the Cycladic population to Minoan culture through trade and other forms of contact. For example, in the case of Akrotiri, Palyvou has stated that "the architecture...tells us that we have a local community living in an old Cycladic town and following closely the developments in Crete, and that at some time in the Neopalatial Period they gain power and wealth and are highly influenced by all the changes that happen in Crete." [C. Palyvou, in Hood:1990:123].

8 On the "Western String" see J.L. Davis, "Minos and Dexithea: Crete and the Cyclades in the Later Bronze Age," in Davis and Cherry:1979:146; J.L. Davis:1992:706; and Schofield:1982:9–25. J.F. Cherry and J.L. Davis, in "The Cyclades and the Greek Mainland in LC I: The Evidence of the Pottery," *AJA* 86 (1982) 333, call Ayia Irini, Phylakopi and Akrotiri "the principal links in a major trade route between Crete and the mainland."

9 Barber:1987:160–161; 170–171. In her analysis of the imported pottery from the West House at Akrotiri, Marisa Marthari gives primacy to Crete but also notes mainland imports of LH I style: see Marthari:1990:57–70.

10 For example, the so-called "Swallow Ewer" from Grave Circle B, Grave Gamma, at Mycenae is Cycladic in origin. See Barber:1987:171; M. Marthari, "Akrotiri, Vases of Middle Helladic Tradition in the Destruction Level," *AE* (1980) 182–210; and Doumas:1983:131–133.

11 On these finds in general, see W.-D. Niemeier, "Minoan Artisans Travelling Overseas: the Alalakh Frescoes and the Painted Plaster Floor

at Tel Kabri (Western Galilee)," in Laffineur and Basch:1991:189–200 [hereafter Niemeier:1991]; W.-D. Niemeier, "Tel Kabri: Aegean Fresco Paintings in a Canaanite Palace," in Gitin:1995:1–15 [hereafter Niemeier:1995]; M. Bietak, "Minoan Wall-Paintings Unearthed at Ancient Avaris," *Egyptian Archaeology* 2 (1992) 26–28 [hereafter Bietak:1992]; and M. Bietak, *Avaris, The Capital of the Hyksos: Recent Excavations at Tell el-Dab'a* (London, 1996; hereafter Bietak:1996). Recently, Linear A inscriptions have come to light at Miletus; see D. Schneider, "Pot Luck," *Scientific American* 275 (1996) 20. For other evidence of Minoan contacts with the eastern Mediterranean, see Knapp: 1992a:62–67; A.B. Knapp, "Bronze Age Mediterranean Island Cultures and the Ancient Near East, Part 2," *Biblical Archaeologist* 55 (1992) 122–124 [hereafter Knapp:1992b]; and especially Lambrou-Phillipson: 1990. For the role of Minoan Crete as "gatekeeper" to the Aegean region, see E.H. Cline, *Sailing the Wine-Dark Sea: International Trade and the Late Bronze Age Aegean* (Oxford, 1994) xviii, 87 and 106 [hereafter Cline:1994].

12 For the Koan vessels, see M. Marthari, T. Marketou and R.E. Jones, "LB I Ceramic Connections between Thera and Kos," *T & AW III: Arch*, 171–184. For the Cypriot and Syro-Palestinian ware see R.L.N. Barber, "The Late Cycladic Period: A Review," *BSA* 76 (1981) 5 [hereafter Barber:1981]; P.M. Warren, "Summary of Evidence for the Absolute Chronology of the Early Part of the Aegean Late Bronze Age Derived from Historical Egyptian Sources," *T & AW III: Chron*, 24–25 [hereafter Warren:1990]; P.M. Warren, "The Stone Vessels from the Bronze Age Settlement at Akrotiri, Thera," *AE* (1979) 82–110 [hereafter Warren: 1979]; and W.-D. Niemeier, "New Archaeological Evidence for a 17th Century Date of the 'Minoan Eruption' from Israel (Tel Kabri, Western Galilee)," *T & AW III: Chron*, 120–126 [hereafter Niemeier:1990a]. Some, however, argue for direct Cycladic contact with the eastern Mediterranean: see C. Doumas, "Thera and the East Mediterranean during the First Half of the Second Millennium B.C.," in V. Karageorghis (ed.), *The Civilizations of the Aegean and their Diffusion in Cyprus and the Eastern Mediterranean, 2000-600 B.C.* (Larnaca, 1991; hereafter Karageorghis:1991) 24–26 [hereafter Doumas:1991]. Knapp:1992a:62, however, points out that "the Cycladic islands generally have revealed far less evidence of contact with areas beyond the Aegean than Crete."

13 Stucynski:1982:55–57; G. Cadogan, "Cycladic Jugs at Pyrgos," in MacGillivray and Barber:1984:162–163. See also Jones:1978:471–482.

14 For Knossos, see P.M. Warren, in Marthari:1990:70; for Rhodes and

Kos, see T. Marketou, "Santorini Tephra from Rhodes and Kos: Some Chronological Remarks Based on the Stratigraphy," *T & AW III: Chron*, 100–113 [hereafter Marketou:1990].

15 G. Cadogan, "Thera's Eruption into our Understanding of the Minoans," *T & AW III: Arch*, 95 [hereafter Cadogan:1990]; Barber:1987:171; and M. Marthari, "Investigation of the Technology of Manufacture of the Local LBA Theran Pottery: Archaeological Consideration," *T & AW III: Arch*, 450. The remaining pottery is made up of mainland LH I imports and vessels from other Cycladic islands, the Dodecanese, SW Asia Minor and the Levant.

16 Marthari:1987:359–379.

17 See M.H. Wiener, "Crete and the Cyclades in LM I: The Tale of the Conical Cups," in Hägg and Marinatos:1984:17–26. The stirrup-jar, employed in the transport of wine and oil, may also have originated on Crete and been adopted by Theran merchants. J.-C. Poursat even argues that the large number of stirrup-jars found on Thera indicate that "the oil trade was in the hands of Theran merchants, who acted as intermediaries between Crete and other parts of the Aegean world;" see J.-C. Poursat, "Craftsmen and Traders at Thera: A View from Crete," *T & AW III: Arch*, 126. See also Doumas:1986:233–239.

18 In light of the wall-paintings recently found at Tell el-Dab'a in Egypt, some scholars are now postulating the existence of itinerant Minoan artists plying their trade all over the eastern Mediterranean.

19 E.N. Davis:1990:226; and E. Sapouna-Sakellaraki, "Οἱ τοιχογραφίες τῆς Θήρας σὲ σχέση μὲ τὴν μινωϊκὴ Κρήτη," in *Acts of the Fourth International Cretological Congress* (Athens, 1981) 479–509 [hereafter Sapouna-Sakellaraki:1981].

20 C. Televantou, "Κοσμήματα 'απὸ τὴν προϊστορικὴ Θήρα," *AE* (1984) 54; Televantou notes the growing predominance of gold over silver.

21 See J.W. Shaw, "Consideration of the Site of Akrotiri as a Minoan Settlement," *T & AW I*, 429–436 [hereafter Shaw:1978]; also Cadogan: 1990:94.

22 Warren:1979:82–113.

23 Wiener:1990:151.

24 See Stos-Gale and Macdonald:1991:249–284.

25 Some lead may also have come from the island of Siphnos along the Western String and it has been suggested that the lead minerals found today on the caldera wall at Athinios on Thera may have been worked in the Bronze Age: see Friedrich and Doumas:1990:502. For the major

sources of copper, lead and silver, see Doumas:1983:120; Z.A. Stos-Gale and N.H. Gale, "The Role of Thera in the Bronze Age Trade in Metals," *T & AW III: Arch*, 72–92 [hereafter Stos-Gale and Gale:1990]; Schofield:1982:18; O.T.P.K. Dickinson, "Early Mycenaean Greece and the Mediterranean," in Marazzi et al:1986:273; and J.L. Davis:1992: 706.

26 J.L. Davis:1992:738; and Doumas:1983:45.

27 J.L. Davis and J.F. Cherry, "Spatial and Temporal Uniformitarianism in Late Cycladic I: Perspectives from Kea and Milos on the Prehistory of Akrotiri," *T & AW III: Arch*, 198 [hereafter Davis and Cherry:1990].

28 S. Marinatos, *Excavations at Thera VII* (Athens, 1976) 12 [hereafter Marinatos:Thera VII].

29 Doumas:1983:27.

30 Davis and Cherry:1990:190; Barber:1981:20. For the 1870 campaign, see F. Fouqué, *Santorin et ses éruptions* (Paris, 1879) 122 [hereafter Fouqué:1879].

31 H. Mamet and H. Gorceix, "Recherches et fouilles faite à Théra," *Bulletin de l'École Française d'Athènes* 9 (1870) 183–203; H. Mamet, *De Insula Thera* (Lille, 1874) 27–30; see also Fouqué:1879:118–123.

32 A partition wall apparently divided the northern area, but is not usually shown on plans of the site; see Sperling:1973:figure 19.

33 Doumas:1983:45; see also Barber:1981:20.

34 Doumas:1983:55–56; Sperling:1973:24 suggests the building was "the residence of some prominent or wealthy person, who chose to live outside, but conveniently near, the crowded...settlement."

35 Hiller:III.39–46. Pottery from Zahn's excavations resides in the Old Archaeological Museum in Fira (the "Fira Museum").

36 Doumas:1983:45.

37 Doumas:1983:45.

38 C. Doumas, "Ftellos," *AE* (1973) 161–166; see also Barber:1987:64–66.

39 Sperling:1973:34.

40 Doumas:1983:129.

41 On this site as a whole, see F. Fouqué, "Premier rapport sur une mission scientifique à l'île de Santorin," *Arch. Miss.* 4 (1867) 223–252; Fouqué:1879:94–103; Sperling:1973:39–40 and 56–61; see also F. Lenormant, "Découverte de constructions antéhistoriques dans l'île de Thérasia," *Revue Archéologique* 14 (1866) 423–432; and J.T. Bent, *The Cyclades* (London, 1885) 149–150. Philippson reported the site filled in when he visited the quarry in June 1896 (Hiller:I.58). An LC I juglet

from this excavation now resides in the British Museum; see V. Econo-
midou, "A Late Cycladic Juglet from Therasia in the British Museum
(BM 1926.4–10.9)," *BSA* 90 (1995) 155–156.

42 Barber:1981:20; see also K. Scholes, "The Cyclades in the Later Bronze
Age: A Synopsis," *BSA* 51 (1956) 13. For an LC I storage jar from the
area of Koloumvos, see F. Lenormant, "Reisefrüchte aus Griechenland,
2, Vase archaïque de Théra," *Archäologische Zeitung* 24 (1866) 258.

43 Sperling:1973:26; see also Hiller:I.307.

44 Rackham:1990:384–391. Dickinson:1994:25, however, thinks the prehistoric climate of the Aegean was warmer and drier than at present.

45 I. Tzachili, "All Important yet Elusive: Looking for Evidence of Cloth-
Making at Akrotiri," *T & AW III: Arch*, 386 [hereafter Tzachili:1990].

46 Kourmoulis:1990:237. On the cultivation and processing of flax, see also
Dickinson:1994:47.

47 C.S. Gamble, "Surplus and Self-Sufficiency in the Cycladic Subsistance
Economy," in Davis and Cherry:1979:123 [hereafter Gamble:1979];
Gamble notes the presence of a few dogs and equids. See also C. Gamble,
"The Bronze Age Animal Economy from Akrotiri: A Preliminary
Analysis," *T & AW I*, 745–753 [hereafter Gamble:1978].

48 L. Karali-Yannacopoulou, "Sea Shells, Land Snails and Other Marine
Remains from Akrotiri," *T & AW III: ES*, 410–415.

Chapter Four: The Late Bronze Age City at Akrotiri

1 For extensive analyses of this earthquake and its impact upon the town,
see M. Marthari, "The Destruction of the Town at Akrotiri, Thera, at the
Beginning of LCI: Definition and Chronology" [hereafter Marthari:
1984], and C. Palyvou, "The Destruction of the Town at Akrotiri, Thera
at the Beginning of LC I: Rebuilding Activities" [hereafter Palyvou:
1984], both in MacGillivray and Barber:1984:119–133 and 134–147
respectively. Palyvou estimates the debris layer to have been ca. 1.10 to
1.60 meters thick. It has become common to refer to this debris as the
"seismic destruction level" (or "SDL") in order to distinguish it from the
later "volcanic destruction level" (or "VDL"). The pottery remains in the
SDL clearly date the destruction to late MC/early LC I.

2 Doumas:1983:51. See also C. Doumas, "Notes on the Minoan Architecture of Thera," *AE* (1974) 214 [hereafter Doumas:1974]; C. Doumas,
"Town Planning and Architecture in Bronze Age Thera," *150 Jahre*

Deutsches Archäologisches Institut (Mainz, 1981) 97; and Barber:1987: 216. A. Michailidou, in "The Settlement of Akrotiri (Thera): A Theoretical Approach to the Function of the Upper Storey," in P. Darcque and R. Treuil (eds.), *L'Habitat égéen préhistorique* (Paris, 1990) 293–306, suggests that upper floors were also occasionally used for some manufacturing and storage purposes.

3 Doumas:1983:53.

4 Marinatos:Thera VII:22–28 and plate 39a; and Doumas:1992:128. S.A. Immerwahr, in *Aegean Painting in the Bronze Age* (University Park and London, 1990) 188 [hereafter Immerwahr:1990b], refers to a life-size male figure wearing a kilt and holding what looks like a cord.

5 N. Marinatos and R. Hägg, "On the Ceremonial Function of the Minoan Polythyron," *Opuscula Atheniensia* 16 (1986) 73 and 60 [hereafter N. Marinatos and Hägg:1986].

6 Doumas:1992:128; see also Immerwahr:1990b:188.

7 Doumas:1992:129–130; see also N. Marinatos, *Minoan Religion: Ritual, Image and Symbol* (Columbia, S.C., 1993) 208–209 [hereafter N. Marinatos:1993].

8 Doumas:1992:130; see also V. Karageorghis, "Rites de Passage at Thera: Some Oriental Comparanda," *T & AW III: Arch*, 67–71 [hereafter Karageorghis:1990].

9 Doumas:1992:128; see also Marinatos:Thera VII:plate 40.

10 Doumas:1992:127.

11 For the medicinal properties of the saffron crocus, see Celsus 3.18.12; 3.21.7; Pliny 21.137–138; and Hippocrates, *Steril.* 221; *Steril.* 230; *Nat. Mul.* 109; *Mul.1.* 63; *Mul. 1.* 74; *Mul. 1.* 78; *Mul.1.* 90; *Mul.2.* 179; *Mul.2.* 195; *Mul.2.* 208; *Epid.2.* 5.22; *Acut. Sp.* 66; and *Ulc.* 12. In light of the two clay tubs and the basin found in Room 2, N. Marinatos, in "Minoan Threskeiocracy on Thera," in Hägg and Marinatos:1984:175 [hereafter N. Marinatos:1984a], raised the possibility that Xesté 3 was "a workshop for the extraction of saffron from the crocus flowers." See also Morgan:1990:262.

12 N. Marinatos, *Art and Religion in Thera* (Athens, 1984) 64–65 [hereafter N. Marinatos:1984b].

13 Immerwahr:1990b:188; and N. Marinatos:1984b:68–70.

14 Doumas:1992:131. In 1993, additional fragments of this wall-painting came to light in the fill of Room 15.

15 S. Marinatos, *Excavations at Thera III* (Athens, 1970) 42–43 [hereafter Marinatos:Thera III]; and Doumas:1992:184–185.

16 Marinatos:Thera III:43–45.

17 Doumas:1983:79 speaks of rosettes "scattered at random on a plain white ground and at either side of a group of wavy bands." See also Marinatos: Thera III:63; and Doumas:1992:17.

18 Shaw:1978:433; Barber:1987:207 also inclines towards viewing Beta 1–8 as one unit. See also Palyvou:1986:188–189.

19 Barber:1987:207; and N. Marinatos:1984a:173.

20 S. Marinatos, *Excavations at Thera IV* (Athens, 1971) 29 and plate 51b [hereafter Marinatos:Thera IV]; N. Marinatos:1984b:figure 78. See also Barber:1987:207; and Doumas:1983:78–79.

21 Marinatos:Thera IV:49; N. Marinatos:1984b:109; P.P. Betancourt, "Perspective and the Third Dimension in Theran Paintings," *TUAS* 2 (1977) 21; J. Vanschoonwinkel, "Les Fresques à figuration humaine de Théra," *Revue des Archéologues et Historiens d'Art de Louvain* 16 (1983) 14.

22 Marinatos:Thera IV:29.

23 Marinatos:Thera IV:29–31; Doumas:1992:109 also postulates communication by means of a staircase between the upper and basement levels of Rooms 1 and 2.

24 Marinatos:Thera VII:20.

25 N. Marinatos:1984b:22 and 106; Marinatos believes that most, if not all, rooms with wall-paintings served as shrines.

26 N. Marinatos:1984b:112; see also Immerwahr:1990b:52.

27 Doumas:1992:131. Doumas had earlier stated (Doumas:1983:54) that "there is no direct or convincing evidence that specific rooms were used as shrines or sanctuaries." See also S.P. Morris, "A Tale of Two Cities: The Miniature Frescoes from Thera and the Origins of Greek Poetry," *AJA* 93 (1989) 511–535 [hereafter Morris:1989].

28 Marinatos:Thera III:34–36.

29 Doumas:1983:78.

30 N. Marinatos:1984b:116 and figure 83.

31 Marinatos:Thera V:37 and 45; see also Doumas:1992:111.

32 Palyvou:1986:188.

33 Marinatos:Thera III:36.

34 Doumas:1992:99; Doumas:1974:200; M. Marthari, in R.B. Koehl, "The Rhyta from Akrotiri and Some Preliminary Observations on their Functions in Selected Contexts," *T & AW III: Arch*, 361 [hereafter Koehl: 1990]; J. Vanschoonwinkel, "Les Fouilles de Théra et la protohistoire égéenne," *Les Études Classiques* 54 (1986) 229 [hereafter Vanschoonwinkel:1986]; S. Sinos, "Beobachtungen zur Siedlung von Akrotiri auf

Thera und ihrer Architektur," in H.-G. Buchholz (ed.), *Ägäische Bronze-zeit* (Darmstadt, 1987; hereafter Buchholz:1987) 298; Barber:1987:208; and C. Palyvou, "Architectural Design at Late Cycladic Akrotiri," *T & AW III: Arch*, 48 [hereafter Palyvou:1990]; Palyvou provides plans of the entrance to each unit.

35 Palyvou:1986:194. Such activities are detectable south of Room 15, east of Rooms 9, 10 and 12, and north of Room 3.

36 S. Marinatos, *Excavations at Thera* (Athens, 1968) 34–38 [hereafter Marinatos:Thera I]; and Marinatos:Thera VI:8.

37 Doumas:1974:217; Barber:1987:211; see also Palyvou:1986:184.

38 Marinatos:Thera IV:17–18.

39 Doumas:1983:53; a similar type of floor was also found in Room 18.

40 Marinatos:Thera IV:18–19.

41 Marinatos:Thera V:16.

42 Barber:1987:210; Palyvou:1986:191; and Doumas:1985:168–176.

43 Marinatos:Thera V:20 states that "the inhabitants collected every object they could find among the ruins and stored [them] in those rooms which still had their roofs preserved." But compare Doumas:1983:48 and 51.

44 Koehl:1990:356–362 favors a ritual hand-washing or anointing ceremony using perfumed oils stored in small vessels.

45 Marinatos:Thera VI:17 wrote that "it is clear here that we have an addition belonging to the period of rebuilding which the town underwent following the catastrophe" [i.e., the early earthquake]; see also Doumas: 1974:200.

46 Marinatos:Thera V:plates 49 and 64; Koehl:1990:355 has noted that Complex Delta has yielded the largest number and greatest variety of conical vases (rhyta) at Akrotiri, with eight found in Room 9 alone.

47 Koehl:1990:356.

48 Marthari:1984:119–126.

49 A minor controversy has arisen over the botanical identification of these flowers, with some identifying them as madonna lilies (*lilium candidum*), which, however, are white; others, taking the red flowers at face value, argue on behalf of the red *lilium chalcedonicum*. For madonna lilies, see S. Marinatos, "Thera, ein Neues Zentrum der Ägäischen Kultur," in Buchholz:1987:280; S. Petrakis, "Madonna Lilies in Aegean Wall Paintings," *TUAS* 5 (1980) 15; E.N. Davis:1990:219; and Immerwahr:1990b: 47. For *lilium chalcedonicum*, see M.B. Hollinshead, "The Swallows and Artists of Room Delta 2 at Akrotiri, Thera," *AJA* 93 (1989) 339–354 [hereafter Hollinshead:1989]; and also Sapouna-Sakellaraki:1981:499. It

is worth noting that the 1870 French excavations at Akrotiri also found fragments of plaster depicting red lilies; see G. Perrot and C. Chipiez, *Histoire de l'Art dans l'Antiquité* (Paris, 1894) VI:537 ff. and figures 211-212.

50 Hollinshead:1989:342.

51 Hollinshead:1989:350. This alteration may have taken place when the northern partition wall was constructed.

52 Doumas:1983:54; Doumas:1992:100. See also N. Marinatos:1984a:173-174. On the horn of consecration, see Marinatos:Thera VI:34.

53 N. Marinatos:1984b:22 and 94; and N. Marinatos:1984a:174. In support, see Immerwahr:1990b:47.

54 C. Doumas, "'Ανασκαφὴ Θήρας," *PAE* (1976) 309-329; Doumas suggested this jar may have been a "bee-hive" vessel for the collection of wax or honey.

55 Marthari:1990:67; and Palyvou:1984:135.

56 E. Schofield, "Evidence for Household Industries on Thera and Kea," *T & AW III: Arch*, 207 [hereafter Schofield:1990]. See also Marinatos: Thera VI:29-30; Doumas:1992:45; N. Marinatos, "The West House at Akrotiri as a Cult Center," *AM* 98 (1983) 17 [hereafter N. Marinatos: 1983]; Barber:1987:214. A rather different interpretation has been offered by C.S. Gillis in "Statistical Analyses and Conical Cups," *Opuscula Atheniensia* 18 (1990) 92; Gillis suggests that the West House "was owned by someone involved in the manufacture and storage and possibly even shipping of commodities such as olive oil and wine. The cellar rooms could have been used in part for the preparation, fermentation, or storing of these liquids."

57 Rooms 5, 6 and 7 yielded a great deal of pottery and Doumas reported the remains of a basket made of rushes in Room 5, suggesting that it was used in the making of cheese: C. Doumas, "'Ανασκαφὴ Θήρας," *PAE* (1977) 387-399 [hereafter Doumas:1977b].

58 Tzachili:1990:380-389.

59 See Pollux, *Onomasticon* 4.118 and 7.77.

60 Marinatos:Thera VI:19-31; but see also N. Marinatos:1984b:34-61.

61 C. Televantou, "New Light on the West House Wall-Paintings," *T & AW III: Arch*, 315 [hereafter Televantou:1990]. By far the most detailed analysis of the Miniature Frieze as a whole can be found in Lyvia Morgan's *The Miniature Wall Paintings of Thera* (Cambridge, 1988) [hereafter Morgan:1988].

62 Some of those who favor a ritual interpretation of this scene have viewed

the hill as a peak sanctuary: see L. Morgan, "Theme in the West House Paintings," *AE* (1983) 87–94 [hereafter Morgan:1983]; also S. Iakovides, "A Peak Sanctuary in Bronze Age Thera," in A. Biran (ed.), *Temples and High Places in Biblical Times* (Jerusalem, 1981) 54–60 [hereafter Iakovides:1981]. See also Morgan:1988:91 and 158; and Morgan:1990: 258. On the other hand, Morris:1989:522–523 argues for a council of war being depicted.

63 Doumas:1992:47; see also C. Doumas, "Conventions artistiques à Théra et dans la Méditerranée orientale à l'époque préhistorique," in P. Darcque and J.-C. Poursat (eds.), *L'Iconographie Minoenne* (Paris, 1985) 33; compare N. Marinatos:1984b:38–40; and Morgan:1988:90.

64 See Morgan:1983:93; N. Marinatos:1983:7–10; A. Sakellariou, "The West House Miniature Frescoes," *T & A W II*, 152 [hereafter Sakellariou: 1980]; H.-E. Giesecke, "The Akrotiri Ship Fresco," *IJNA* 12 (1983) 124 [hereafter Giesecke:1983].

65 The peculiar building to the left, at the harbor, even resembles the ship-sheds found at Kommos on Crete: see J.W. Shaw, "Bronze Age Aegean Harboursides," *T & A W III: Arch*, 430–433 [hereafter Shaw:1990].

66 For this controversy, see S. Iakovides, "Thera and Mycenaean Greece," *AJA* 83 (1979) 101–102 [hereafter Iakovides:1979]; P. M. Warren, "The Miniature Fresco from the West House at Akrotiri, Thera, and its Aegean Setting," *JHS* 99 (1979) 128–129; O. Negbi, "The 'Miniature Fresco' from Thera and the Emergence of Mycenaean Art," *T & A W I*, 645–654; S.A. Immerwahr, "Mycenaeans at Thera: Some Reflections on the Paintings from the West House," in K.H. Kinzl (ed.), *Greece and the Eastern Mediterranean in Ancient History and Prehistory* (Berlin, 1977) 182–190; R. Laffineur, "Early Mycenaean Art: Some Evidence from the West House in Thera," *BICS* 30 (1983) 111–117; W.-D. Niemeier, "Mycenaean Elements in the Miniature Fresco from Thera?" in *T & A W III: Arch*, 276 [hereafter Niemeier:1990b]; and Vanschoonwinkel:1986: 244. Morgan:1988:114 asserts that she does "not believe that it is possible to distinguish with certainty the regional identity of Aegean warriors on the basis of their gear."

67 Televantou:1990:322. On this frieze see also O. Negbi, "The 'Libyan Landscape' from Thera: A Review of Aegean Enterprises Overseas in the Late Minoan IA Period," *JMA* 7 (1994) 73–111.

68 L. Morgan Brown, "The Ship Procession in the Miniature Fresco," *T & A W I*, 629 and 639 [hereafter Morgan:1978]; also Niemeier:1990b: 275.

69 Marinatos:Thera VI:50; C.G. Reynolds, "The Thera Ships," *Mariner's*

Mirror 64 (1978) 124; Morgan:1978:629; Morgan:1988:136-137; A.F. Tilley and P. Johnstone, "A Minoan Naval Triumph?" in *IJNA* 5 (1976) 290. For other interpretations, see L. Casson, "The Thera Ships," *IJNA* 7 (1978) 233 ["a frame for making the shorelines fast to the stern"]; L. Casson, "Bronze Age Ships. The Evidence of the Thera Wall Paintings," *IJNA* 4 (1975) 9 ["a device to maintain proper trim"]; D.H. Kennedy, "A Further Note on the Thera Ships," *Mariner's Mirror* 64 (1978) 137 [intended "to counteract rolling motion at sea"]; and A. Raban, "The Thera Ships: Another Interpretation," *AJA* 88 (1984) 17 [a ram, used when these 'bi-directional' vessels were "reversed"].

70 Doumas:1983:55-56. One problem with identifying the Arrival Town as Akrotiri is the apparent presence of a defensive city wall with a large gateway. No such wall has yet been found at Akrotiri, perhaps not surprising in view of the very narrow expanse of the city so far excavated. Moreover, it is not certain that the Arrival Town is in fact protected by such a wall: Televantou:1990:322 sees too many openings in the "wall" to classify it as a defensive structure, preferring instead to see simply "edifices encircling the city." For the Akrotiri thesis, see also Doumas: 1992:49; Morgan:1983:99; Morgan:1988:92; Shaw:1990:433; and N. Marinatos:1984b:41-44. For a town on Crete, however, see J.A. Mac-Gillivray, "The Therans and Dikta," *T & AW III: Arch*, 363 [hereafter MacGillivray:1990]; Giesecke:1983:127; G.C. Gesell, "The 'Town Fresco' of Thera: A Reflection of Cretan Topography," in *Acts of the Fourth International Cretological Congress* (Athens, 1980) 197-204; and E.N. Davis, "The Iconography of the Ship Fresco from Thera," in W.G. Moon (ed.), *Ancient Greek Art and Iconography* (Madison, 1983) 8.

71 See N. Marinatos, *Minoan Sacrificial Ritual* (Stockholm, 1986) 42 [hereafter N. Marinatos:1986]; N. Marinatos:1984b:52-53; N. Marinatos, "Role and Sex Division in Ritual Scenes of Aegean Art," *Journal o. Prehistoric Religion* 1 (1987) 28. See also Sakellariou:1980:150; and M.G. Prytulak, "Weapons on the Thera Ships?" in *IJNA* 11 (1982) 3-6.

72 Morgan:1983:97-99; see also Morgan:1988:143-145; Morgan:1978: 629; and Morgan:1990:253. K.P. Foster, in "Snakes and Lions: A New Reading of the West House Frescoes from Thera," *Expedition* 30 (1989) 10-20, uses the Egyptian Sed Festival to argue for a Cycladic "jubilee" being celebrated.

73 D.L. Page, "The Miniature Frescoes from Acrotiri Thera," *PAA* 5 (1976) 148.

74 See Morgan:1990:254; L. Morgan, "The Wall-Paintings of Ayia Irini

Kea," *BICS* 40 (1995) 243-244; A. Kempinski and W.-D. Niemeier, "Kabri, 1991," *Israel Exploration Journal* 42 (1992) 260-265 [hereafter Kempinski and Niemeier:1992]; Niemeier:1991:189-200; Niemeier: 1995:1-15; W.-D. Niemeier, "Minoans and Hyksos: Aegean Frescoes in the Levant," *BICS* 40 (1995) 258-260. Reconstructions of the Tell el-Dab'a fragments can now be found in Bietak:1996.

75 An excellent examination of narrative in Aegean art has been carried out by C. Dawn Cain in *The Question of Narrative in Aegean Bronze Age Art*, unpublished Ph.D. thesis, University of Toronto (1997); I am most grateful to Dr. Cain for giving me access to her study. For other work in this area see C.G. Thomas, "Aegean Bronze Age Iconography: Poetic Art?" in R. Laffineur and J.L. Crowley (eds.), Εἰκών. *Aegean Bronze Age Iconography: Shaping a Methodology* (Liège, 1992; hereafter Laffineur and Crowley:1992) 213-219; and Morris:1989:511-535.

76 Marinatos:Thera VI:38-57; and Doumas:1992:47 and 49.

77 Televantou:1990:323-324. Nanno Marinatos has also accepted a "semi-narrative character" for the frieze, stating that it "depicts the adventures of the Minoan fleet as it was sailing around the Aegean;" see N. Marinatos, "Divine Kingship in Minoan Crete," in P. Rehak (ed.), *The Role of the Ruler in the Prehistoric Aegean* (Liège, 1995; hereafter Rehak:1995) 39 [hereafter N. Marinatos:1995].

78 There has been some controversy about the exact location of this painting; see Televantou:1990:313; Doumas:1992:47; Doumas:1983:83-84; N. Marinatos:1984b:46; and Morgan:1988:143-144.

79 Marinatos:Thera VI:19-31.

80 Morgan:1978:640.

81 Marinatos:Thera VI:19-28; also Doumas:1992:28, 46 and 49; Palyvou: 1986:184; Morris:1989:511-535; and Televantou:1990:312. In contrast, Nanno Marinatos has argued that the architecture of the rooms and the presence of wall-paintings (as well as various ritual vessels) indicate a shrine complex: see N. Marinatos:1984b:15-16 and 46-49; N. Marinatos and Hägg:1986:72; and N. Marinatos:1983:4-5 and 13-14.

82 A. Michailidou, "The Lead Weights from Akrotiri: The Archaeological Record," *T & AW III: Arch*, 416 [hereafter Michailidou:1990].

83 Recent excavations, however, have revealed a double wall in the south of Rooms 8 and 5, suggesting either the existence of two independent units or the addition of a new unit to a pre-existing core. See T. Sali-Axioti, "The Lightwell of the House of the Ladies and its Structural Behaviour," *T & AW III: Arch*, 437 [hereafter Sali-Axioti:1990].

84 Doumas:1983:81–82.

85 Marinatos:Thera V:15. Some scholars have argued that the plants, depicted in clumps of three each, were actually papyrus; see P. Warren, "Did Papyrus Grow in the Aegean?" in *AAA* 9 (1976) 89–95; N. Marinatos:1984b:94–96; and Immerwahr:1990b:49. Those who favor the pancratium lily (*Pancratium Maritimum*, or "sea daffodils") include Doumas:1992:34; and C. Diapoulis, "Prehistoric Plants of the Islands of the Aegean Sea," *T & A W II*, 129–140.

86 S. Peterson, "A Costuming Scene from the Room of the Ladies on Thera," *AJA* 85 (1981) 211; see also Doumas:1992:35.

87 Doumas:1992:130.

88 Immerwahr:1990b:209; see Doumas:1983:74 for the celestial arc.

89 N. Marinatos:1984b:97.

90 Marinatos:Thera VI:8. The light well is only 1.7 x 1.5 meters.

91 Sali-Axioti:1990:437–440; Doumas:1987:241–254. An unexpected discovery was that the "lower section of the light-well had fallen into disuse during the final phase of the settlement and had been infilled with debris from an earlier destruction" (Doumas:1992:185). This debris included a small piece of plaster decorated with parallel red lines.

92 Doumas:1992:185; the presence of this building was noted in Thera V:15–16, where Marinatos provisionally called it the "Kitchen."

93 S. Marinatos, *Excavations at Thera II* (Athens, 1969) 22 [hereafter Marinatos:Thera II].

94 Part of the western facade of this wing was in fact located by tunnelling in the early years of the excavation. A door and window were found, in front of which ran the pavement of a road or courtyard; even a terracotta water spout was found *in situ*. The space beyond the door was full of pumice and was not excavated. As tunnelling continued, the walls of at least three different buildings were located. Clearly this part of the settlement was as densely inhabited as the rest. See Marinatos:Thera II:32–33; and Marinatos:Thera III:15–17 and 33.

95 See Barber:1987:216; Doumas:1983:55; and Palyvou:1986:184. The juxtaposition of a mill room with a lavatory seems unusual, and Marinatos regarded the Mill House as having had a religious function, perhaps being used for the milling of "holy flour" intended for ritual ceremonies: see Marinatos:Thera III:15.

96 Marinatos:Thera II:19 and 31; and N. Marinatos:1984b:20.

97 See N. Marinatos, "The 'African' of Thera Reconsidered," *Opuscula Atheniensia* 17 (1988) 137 [hereafter N. Marinatos:1988]; and N. Marin-

atos, "The Monkey in the Shrine: A Fresco Fragment from Thera," Εἰλαπινή. Τόμος Τιμητικὸς γιὰ τὸν Καθηγητὴ Νικολαο Πλατωνα (Heraklion, 1987; hereafter Platon:1987) 417–421.

98 Marinatos:Thera II:27–29; and Marinatos:Thera V:8.

99 Michailidou:1990:416–417.

100 Marinatos:Thera V:9; Marinatos:Thera VI:14; Palyvou:1986:191–193; and Marthari:1984:119–133.

101 Marinatos:Thera III:19.

102 Marthari:1984:119 and 126.

103 Marinatos:Thera VI:14 and plate 83b.

104 Marinatos:Thera VI:31; the seeds were not identified.

105 Palyvou:1990:55; also Palyvou:1984:147.

106 Marinatos:Thera VII:21 and plate 31; C. Doumas, "'Ανασκαφὴ Θήρας," *PAE* (1975) 212–229; and Doumas:1977b:387–399.

107 Doumas:1992:176. Additional fragments of this composition were found in the stairwell in 1993 and 1996. Also, incised on fragments of this wall-painting were child-like sketches of ships: see C. Televantou, "Incised Representations of Ships on Theran Wall-Painting," *AAA* 20 (1987) 115–122.

108 See Wiener:1990:141; N. Marinatos and Hägg:1986:58; and Doumas: 1992:176.

109 C. Palyvou has written that "the most important E.-W. street lies to the south of Xesté 4...It is 2-3 m wide and is bordered by imposing ashlar facades, giving the impression of a major street that may prove to be even more important than Telchines Road." See Palyvou:1986:191, and figure 3. More clearing was carried out in this area in 1995.

Chapter Five: The Late Bronze Age Society of Thera

1 For einkorn wheat, see A. Sarpaki, "A Palaeoethnobotanical Study of the West House, Akrotiri, Thera," *BSA* 87 (1992) 224 [hereafter Sarpaki: 1992]. For a discussion of when the olive was domesticated, see Runnels and Hansen:1986:299–308; in response, see Manning:1994:231–232.

2 Gamble:1978:745–753; and Gamble:1979:122–133. Gamble has found the bones of dogs, red deer and donkeys in very small numbers.

3 Sarpaki:1992:227; see also A. Sarpaki, "'Small Fields or Big Fields?' That is the Question," *T & AW III: ES*, 422–432.

4 Sarpaki:1992:227.

5 Doumas:1991:25. L. Katsa-Tomara speaks of Akrotiri as "an exchange-geared society" in "The Pottery-Producing System at Akrotiri: An Index of Exchange and Social Activity," *T & AW III: Arch*, 32 [hereafter Katsa-Tomara:1990]. See also Wiener:1991:341; and Warren:1979:108. For an extensive examination of the economic role of trade in the Bronze Age see Sherratt and Sherratt:1991:351–384.

6 Warren:1979:108; see also T.D. Devetzi, "The Stone Industry at Akrotiri: A Theoretical Approach," *T & AW III: Arch*, 23.

7 Katsa-Tomara:1990:31–40; see also Papagiannopoulou:1991:64.

8 Schofield:1990:204. See also Moundrea-Agrafioti:1990:390–406; Stos-Gale and Gale:1990:72–91; N. Marinatos:1984a:175; and C. Doumas, "The Elements at Akrotiri," *T & AW III: Arch*, 29.

9 See E.H. Cline, "'My Brother, My Son': Rulership and Trade between the LBA Aegean, Egypt and the Near East," in Rehak:1995:150 [hereafter Cline:1995b]; see also Niemeier:1991:189–200; Niemeier:1995:1–15; and Wiener:1991:325. Bietak:1992:26–28 postulated not only the presence of skilled artists from Crete but even a community of Minoans living at Avaris; see also Bietak:1996:75: "There is no doubt that Minoan artists were employed."

10 Schofield:1990:201; see also Michailidou:1990:418.

11 See Knapp:1992/1993:332–347; Warren:1991:295–301; E. H. Cline and M.J. Cline, "Of Shoes and Ships and Sealing Wax," *Expedition* 33 (1991) 46–54; Cline:1994; Cline:1995b:143–150; and Sherratt and Sherratt:1991:376.

12 Warren:1991:295 calls this the Ugaritic or tamkar model; Wiener:1991:327 points to the "merchant ambassadors of Zimri-Lim of Mari in the 18th century B.C., some of whom used the occasion of royal journeys to make private purchases for future sales." See also A.B. Knapp, "Spice, Drugs, Grain and Grog: Organic Goods in Bronze Age East Mediterranean Trade," in Gale:1991:50–52 [hereafter Knapp:1991]; Knapp:1992b:128; and Katsa-Tomara:1990:32.

13 Knapp:1992/1993:332–347.

14 See Niemeier:1995:1–15; M. Bietak, "Connections between Egypt and the Minoan World: New Results from Tell el-Dab'a/Avaris," in W.V. Davies and L. Schofield (eds.), *Egypt, the Aegean and the Levant* (London, 1995; hereafter Davies and Schofield:1995) 19–28 [hereafter Bietak:1995].

15 Doumas:1991:25; E. Panayiotakopoulou, *A Palaeoentomological Study from the West House at Akrotiri, Santorini, Greece* (Sheffield, 1989); the

recent identification of a wild silk cocoon also seems relevant. For the Nami finds, see Artzy:1995:20; compare A. Sarpaki and G. Jones, "Ancient and Modern Cultivation of *Lathyrus Clymenum L.* in the Greek Islands," *BSA* 85 (1990) 363-368; and Sarpaki:1992:219-230.

16 For Bronze Age sea routes, see E.K. Mantzourani and A.J. Theodorou, "An Attempt to Delineate the Sea-Routes between Crete and Cyprus during the Bronze Age," in Karageorghis:1991:46-51; Cline:1994:91; and C. Lambrou-Phillipson, "Seafaring in the Bronze Age Mediterranean: The Parameters Involved in Maritime Travel," in Laffineur and Basch:1991:11-19. The cargo of the Ulu Burun wreck (14th century B.C.) included items that were Mycenaean, Egyptian, Cypriot, Levantine and Nubian; see G.F. Bass, "Evidence of Trade from Bronze Age Shipwrecks," in Gale:1991:69-82; G.F. Bass, "A Bronze Age Shipwreck at Ulu Burun (Kas): 1984 Campaign," *AJA* 90 (1986) 269-296; C. Pulak, "The Bronze Age Shipwreck at Ulu Burun, Turkey: 1985 Campaign," *AJA* 92 (1988) 1-37; G.F. Bass, C. Pulak, D. Collon and J. Weinstein, "The Bronze Age Shipwreck at Ulu Burun: 1986 Campaign," *AJA* 93 (1989) 1-29. For tramping in the Bronze Age, see Sherratt and Sherratt:1991:357.

17 Knapp:1992/1993:341; see also Lambrou-Phillipson:1990.

18 The existence of "rulers" on Crete is also attested by paintings in the Egyptian tomb of Menkheperesenb; see Cline:1995b:146.

19 The seminal work is N. Marinatos:1984b. See also N. Marinatos:1995: 37-47; and N. Marinatos, "Formalism and Gender Roles: A Comparison of Minoan and Egyptian Art," in Laffineur and Niemeier:1995:577-584.

20 E.N. Davis, "Art and Politics in the Aegean: The Missing Ruler," in Rehak:1995:19; see also R.B. Koehl, "The Nature of Minoan Kingship," in Rehak:1995:23-35 [hereafter Koehl:1995].

21 N. Marinatos:1995:41-45. Koehl:1995:31-35 prefers to speak of "priest-chiefs" who were "primi inter pares" as opposed to absolute monarchs; he suggests (31) that "the figures whom we see depicted in Minoan art that may be identified as priests are also kings or chiefs."

22 See Wiener:1990:144.

23 Although she does admit the likely existence of private enterprise as well: see N. Marinatos:1984a:168 and 175.

24 N. Marinatos, "Minoan-Cycladic Syncretism," *T & AW III: Arch*, 370-377 [hereafter N. Marinatos:1990]. Recent important works on Minoan religion include P. Warren, *Minoan Religion as Ritual Action* (Gothenburg, 1988; hereafter Warren:1988a); P. Warren, "Crete: The Minoans

and their Gods," in Cunliffe:1988:30–41 [hereafter Warren:Crete]; N. Marinatos:1986; and N. Marinatos:1993.

25 See N. Marinatos:1984a:174. Such role-playing has been seen in Minoan Crete by H. Reusch in "Zum Wandschmuck des Thronsaales in Knossos," *Minoica: Festschrift J. Sundwall* (Berlin, 1958) 334–358; Reusch argued that a priestess playing the role of the goddess sat on the famous throne at Knossos. See also W.-D. Niemeier, "Zum Deuting des Thronraumes im Palast von Knossos," *AM* 101 (1986) 63–95.

26 The throne at Knossos was flanked by painted griffins so that whoever sat there would be in a position similar to that of the goddess depicted in Xesté 3. The iconography of the griffin and of other creatures associated with powerful figures in Minoan art has been thoroughly documented by John G. Younger, "The Iconography of Rulership: A Conspectus," in Rehak:1995:151–211; see especially plates LXXIIId and LXXV; see also M.C. Shaw, "The Aegean Garden," *AJA* 97 (1993) 661–685, figure 16; and A. Peatfield, "Water, Fertility, and Purification in Minoan Religion," in C. Morris (ed.), *Klados. Essays in Honour of J.N. Coldstream* (London, 1995) 218 [hereafter Peatfield:1995]. It should be noted that griffins similar in appearance to that at Xesté 3 were painted at Tell el-Dab'a: see Bietak:1995:24.

27 Another wall-painting from Xesté 3 depicts monkeys engaged in human activities and a fresco fragment from Complex Alpha depicts monkeys in a sacred area marked by horns of consecration; see N. Marinatos, "An Offering of Saffron to the Minoan Goddess of Nature," in T. Linders and G. Nordquist (eds.), *Gifts to the Gods* (Uppsala, 1987) 126; and N. Marinatos:1988:137–141.

28 Apparent evidence of human sacrifice has come from two sites on Crete: the building at Anemospilia (see Warren:1988a:4–6) and a house roughly 350 meters west of the palace at Knossos, where the bones of allegedly sacrificed children were discovered (see Warren:1988a:7–9). Both sites have created considerable controversy over the practice of human sacrifice on Crete. See also Peatfield:1995:217–227.

29 E.N. Davis, "Youth and Age in the Thera Frescoes,"*AJA* 90 (1986) 399–406 [hereafter E.N. Davis:1986]; breast development seems to be another measure of the age of a female figure. See also D. Withee, "Physical Growth and Aging Characteristics Depicted in the Theran Frescoes," *AJA* 96 (1992) 336. It is important to bear in mind, when speaking of "youth and age," that life expectancy in the LBA Aegean was about 31 for men and 28 for women: see P.J.P. McGeorge, "Health and Diet in Minoan

Times," in R.E. Jones and H.W. Catling (eds.), *New Aspects of Archaeological Science in Greece* (London, 1988) 48; and also P.J.P. McGeorge, "Biosocial Evolution in Bronze Age Crete," in Platon:1987: 408.

30 E.N. Davis:1986:401; see also N. Marinatos, "The 'Export' Significance of Minoan Bull Hunting and Bull Leaping Scenes," *Ägypten und Levante* 4 (1994) 92; MacGillivray:1990:363; and Karageorghis:1990:67–70. R.B. Koehl, in "The Chieftain Cup and a Minoan Rite of Passage," *JHS* 106 (1986) 101–104, has suggested that not all Therans participated in this practice; rather, this sequence of hairstyles could have denoted social status and thus might have been restricted to members of the elite class. Koehl points out that Egyptian youths who wore "Horus Locks" seem to have held privileged positions in their society.

31 Warren:Crete:40.

32 N. Marinatos:1986:36. On similar pits at Akrotiri, see Papagiannopoulou:1991:33.

33 Warren:Crete:35–36.

34 Koehl:1990:350–362 postulates the existence of beer-making and beer-drinking ceremonies.

35 A pit discovered under the West House contained nippled ewers that might have been intended as a foundation deposit to ensure the prosperity and fertility of the occupants; see Papagiannopoulou:1991:33–34; and N. Marinatos:1990:370–372.

36 N. Marinatos:1984a:174.

37 The men in the procession along the staircase of Xesté 4 also seem to hold objects; see P. Rehak, "Aegean Breechcloths, Kilts, and the Keftiu Paintings," *AJA* 100 (1996) 47.

38 Warren:Crete:38.

39 Morgan:1983:88; see also Iakovides:1981:54–60. For peak sanctuaries in general see L. Vance Watrous, "Some Observations on Minoan Peak Sanctuaries," in Laffineur and Niemeier:1995:393–402.

40 N. Marinatos:1990:370–377.

41 N. Marinatos:1990:375.

42 See S. Hiller, "Minoan Qe-Ra-Si-Ja. The Religious Impact of the Thera Volcano on Minoan Crete," *T & AW I*, 675–679 [hereafter S. Hiller: 1978]; and M. Artzy, "Conical Cups and Pumice, Aegean Cult at Tel Nami, Israel," in Laffineur and Basch:1991:203–205 [hereafter Artzy: 1991]. This, of course, would establish that the name of the island prior to the LBA eruption was indeed Thera.

Chapter Six: Apocalypse

1 C. Doumas, "The Minoan Eruption of the Santorini Volcano," *Antiquity* 48 (1974) 111.

2 Heiken and McCoy:1984:8461. See also G. Heiken and F. McCoy, "Precursory Activity to the Minoan Eruption, Thera, Greece," *T & AW III: ES*, 82 [hereafter Heiken and McCoy:1990]; and R.S.J. Sparks and C.J. N. Wilson, "The Minoan Deposits: A Review of their Characteristics and Interpretation," *T & AW III: ES*, 90 [hereafter Sparks and Wilson: 1990].

3 Heiken and McCoy:1990:79–88.

4 For the phenomenon of base surge, see A. Bond and R.S.J. Sparks, "The Minoan Eruption of Santorini, Greece," *Journal of the Geological Society, London* 132 (1976) 4; Sparks and Wilson:1990:89; and E. McClelland and R. Thomas, "A Palaeomagnetic Study of Minoan Age Tephra from Thera," *T & AW III: ES*, 129 [hereafter McClelland and Thomas: 1990].

5 Sparks and Wilson:1990:97.

6 Eriksen et al:1990:140.

7 Heiken and McCoy:1984:8441 and 8454.

8 Huijsmans and Barton:1990:440.

9 Sparks and Wilson:1990:97–98. Such a scenario would support the belief of Heiken and McCoy that caldera collapse continued after the fourth phase; see Heiken and McCoy:1984:8441.

10 H. Sigurdsson, S. Carey and J.D. Devine, "Assessment of Mass, Dynamics and Environmental Effects of the Minoan Eruption of Santorini Volcano," *T & AW III: ES*, 109; Sparks and Wilson:1990:97; J. Keller, "Summary of the Progress in Volcanology," *T & AW III: ES*, 486; and McClelland and Thomas:1990:129.

11 Dense Rock Equivalent, commonly abbreviated as DRE, may be defined as the volume of the tephra expelled expressed in cubic kilometers of magma.

12 For a discussion of volume estimates see Pyle:1990:113–121.

13 S.W. Manning, "The Thera Eruption: The Third Congress and the Problem of the Date," *Archaeometry* 32 (1990) 95 [hereafter Manning:1990a]. See also W.L. Friedrich, P. Wagner and H. Tauber, "Radiocarbon Dated Plant Remains from the Akrotiri Excavation on Santorini, Greece," *T & AW III: Chron*, 193 [hereafter Friedrich et al: 1990]; H.-W. Hubberten, M. Bruns, M. Calamiotou, C. Apostolakis, S. Filippakis and A. Grimanis, "Radiocarbon Dates from the Akrotiri Excavations," *T & AW*

III: Chron, 186 [hereafter Hubberten et al:1990]; and B. Weninger, "Theoretical Radiocarbon Discrepancies," *T & AW III: Chron,* 216–219 [hereafter Weninger:1990].

14 The most prominent critic of the radiocarbon results has been Peter Warren: see especially P.M. Warren, "The Minoan Civilisation of Crete and the Volcano of Thera," *The Journal of the Ancient Chronology Forum* 4 (1990/1991) 33–34 [hereafter Warren:1990/1991]; Warren concludes (34) that "there is at the moment far too much imprecision in the Aegean LB 1 C-14 picture for a convincing absolute chronology to be derived from it." See also P.M. Warren, "Further Arguments against an Early Date," *Archaeometry* 30 (1988) 176–179 [hereafter Warren:1988b]; P.M. Warren, "Absolute Dating of the Aegean Late Bronze Age," *Archaeometry* 29 (1987) 208–209 [hereafter Warren:1987]; and P.M. Warren, "Absolute Dating of the Bronze Age Eruption of Thera (Santorini)," *Nature* 308 (1984) 492–493 [hereafter Warren:1984]. See also Weninger: 1990:216–231; and J.D. Muhly, "Egypt, the Aegean and Late Bronze Age Chronology in the Eastern Mediterranean: A Review Article," *JMA* 4 (1991) 235–247. *Contra* Muhly's article, see S.W. Manning, "Response to J.D. Muhly on Problems of Chronology in the Aegean Late Bronze Age," *JMA* 4 (1991) 249–262. That any preservatives had been applied to the samples was denied by the excavators; see D.E. Nelson, J.S. Vogel and J.R. Southon, "Another Suite of Confusing Radiocarbon Dates for the Destruction of Akrotiri," *T & AW III: Chron,* 206.

15 S.W. Manning, "The Bronze Age Eruption of Thera: Absolute Dating, Aegean Chronology and Mediterranean Cultural Interrelations," *JMA* 1 (1988) 61 [hereafter Manning:1988].

16 H.N. Michael and P.P. Betancourt, "Further Arguments for an Early Date," *Archaeometry* 30 (1988) 174.

17 R.A. Housley, R.E.M. Hedges, I.A. Law and C.R. Bronk, "Radiocarbon Dating by AMS of the Destruction of Akrotiri," *T & AW III: Chron,* 213. In the same volume, Friedrich et al:1990:188 reported on new results from Copenhagen which also support the high chronology; they offer a calibrated date of 1675 B.C., with a 1σ deviation range between 1690 and 1625 B.C. Likewise, Hubberten et al:1990:179 reported that "eleven new radiocarbon dates obtained on material from the Akrotiri excavations cluster about a mean value of 1670 B.C."

18 Warren:1988b:178. It should also be noted that the generally conservative Sinclair Hood, in his article on "The Third International Congress on Santorini (Thera)," *Kadmos* 29 (1990) 85, summed up the results of the

Congress well by stating that "the calibrated dates obtained by different laboratories are not in total agreement, but they converge to suggest a date for the eruption well back in the 17th century, somewhere between *c.* 1675 and 1625 BC, over a hundred years earlier than the conventional date..." On the other hand, Sturt Manning, a staunch adherent of the high chronology, admits that "it must also be acknowledged that the data at present are such that a lower, mid-sixteenth-century B.C. date for the eruption, and for the close of the LMIA period, remain an unlikely possibility": Manning:1990a:98.

19 M.G.L. Baillie, *A Slice through Time* (London, 1995) 109 [hereafter Baillie:1995]; see also S.W. Manning, *The Absolute Chronology of the Aegean Early Bronze Age* (Sheffield, 1995) Appendix 7: "Dating the Eruption of Thera and the LMIA Period," 200–216 [hereafter Manning: 1995].

20 P.P. Betancourt, "Dating the Aegean Late Bronze Age with Radiocarbon," *Archaeometry* 29 (1987) 47 [hereafter Betancourt:1987]. See also P.P. Betancourt, "High Chronology or Low Chronology: The Archaeological Evidence," *T & AW III: Chron*, 19–23. Betancourt's suggested revision has not yet won over most traditionalists but it has received support from Manning: see S.W. Manning, "The Santorini Eruption: An Up-date," *JMA* 2 (1989) 303–313 [hereafter Manning: 1989a]; S.W. Manning, "A New Age for Minoan Crete," *New Scientist* (11 February 1989) 60–63 [hereafter Manning:1989b]; S.W. Manning, "The Eruption of Thera: Date and Implications," *T & AW III: Chron*, 29–40 [hereafter Manning:1990b]; and also Manning:1988:17–82.

21 A. Kempinski and W.-D. Niemeier, *Excavations at Kabri. Preliminary Report of 1990 Season* (Tel Aviv, 1991) 24; see also A. Kempinski and W.-D. Niemeier, "Tel Kabri, 1989–1990," *Israel Exploration Journal* 41 (1991) 192; Kempinski and Niemeier:1992:260–265; A. Kempinski and W.-D. Niemeier, *Excavations at Kabri. Preliminary Report of 1991 Season* (Tel Aviv, 1992) 8–9; Niemeier:1991:196–200; and Niemeier: 1995:1–15.

22 Niemeier:1990a:124.

23 V.C. LaMarche, Jr. and K.K. Hirschboeck, "Frost Rings in Trees as Records of Major Volcanic Eruptions," *Nature* 307 (1984) 121–126.

24 Weninger:1990:219.

25 See J.R. Pilcher, M.G.L. Baillie, B. Schmidt and B. Becker, "A 7272-year Tree-ring Chronology for Western Europe," *Nature* 312 (1984) 150–152; M.G.L. Baillie and J.R. Pilcher, "The Belfast 'Long Chrono-

logy' Project," in R.G.W. Ward (ed.), *Applications of Tree-ring Studies* (Oxford, 1987) 203–214; M. Baillie, "Irish Oaks Record Volcanic Dust Veils Drama," *Archaeology Ireland* 2 (1988) 71–74 [hereafter Baillie: 1988a]; M. Baillie, "Marker Dates—Turning Prehistory into History," *Archaeology Ireland* 2 (1988) 154–155 [hereafter Baillie:1988b]; M.G.L. Baillie and D.M. Brown, "An Overview of Oak Chronologies," in E.A. Slater and J.O. Tate (eds.), *Science and Archaeology: Glasgow 1987* (Oxford, 1988) 543–548; M.G.L. Baillie and M.A.R. Munro, "Irish Tree Rings, Santorini and Volcanic Dust Veils," *Nature* 332 (1988) 344–346 [hereafter Baillie and Munro:1988]; M.G.L. Baillie, "Irish Tree Rings and an Event in 1628 BC," *T & AW III: Chron*, 160–166 [hereafter Baillie:1990]; and M.G.L. Baillie, "Marking in Marker Dates: towards an Archaeology with Historical Precision," *World Archaeology* 23 (1991) 233–243. For the German chronology, see H.H. von Leuschner and A. Delorme, "Verlängerung der Göttinger Eichenjahrringchronologien für Nord- und Süddeutschland bis zum Jahr 4008 v. Chr.," in *Forstarchiv* 55 (1984) 3–5.

26 Baillie:1990:160.
27 See Baillie and Munro:1988:344; and Baillie:1988a:73.
28 P.I. Kuniholm, B. Kromer, S.W. Manning, M. Newton, C.E. Latini and M.J. Bruce, "Anatolian Tree Rings and the Absolute Chronology of the Eastern Mediterranean, 2220–718 BC," *Nature* 381 (1996) 780–783 [hereafter Kuniholm et al:1996]. See also C. Renfrew, "Kings, Tree Rings and the Old World," *Nature* 381 (1996) 733–734 [hereafter Renfrew:1996].
29 Kuniholm et al:1996:782.
30 J.S. Vogel, W. Cornell, D.E. Nelson and J.R. Southon, "Vesuvius/ Avellino, One Possible Source of Seventeenth Century BC Climatic Disturbances," *Nature* 344 (1990) 535 [hereafter Vogel et al: 1990].
31 See S.W. Manning, "Thera, Sulphur, and Climatic Anomalies," *Oxford Journal of Archaeology* 11 (1992) 245–253 [hereafter Manning:1992].
32 See C.U. Hammer, H.B. Clausen and W. Dansgaard, "Greenland Ice Sheet Evidence of Post-Glacial Volcanism and its Climatic Impact," *Nature* 288 (1980) 230–235.
33 C.U. Hammer, H.B. Clausen, W.L. Friedrich and H. Tauber, "The Minoan Eruption of Santorini in Greece Dated to 1645 BC ?" in *Nature* 328 (1987) 517–519; see also C.U. Hammer and H.B. Clausen, "The Precision of Ice-Core Dating," *T & AW III: Chron*, 174–178.
34 D.M. Pyle, "The Application of Tree-Ring and Ice-Core Studies to the

Notes for pages 111 to 113

Dating of the Minoan Eruption," *T & AW III: Chron*, 169–171; also
D.M. Pyle, "Ice-Core Acidity Peaks, Retarded Tree Growth and Putative
Eruptions," *Archaeometry* 31 (1989) 88–91. Vogel et al:1990:536 state
that "recent petrological calculations of the sulphur emissions from Thera
account for only 3–6% of the amount expected from the concentration of
acid in the ice layer." Other researchers, however, discount the accuracy
of these petrological studies: see Kuniholm et al:1996:782; Manning:
1992:245–253; and Manning:1995:215–216.

35 Manning:1992:246; see, more recently, Manning:1995:200–216.

36 On the possibility of multiple eruptions, see Baillie:1995:114–115.

37 G.A. Zielinski, P.A. Mayewski, L.D. Meeker, S. Whitlow, M.S. Twickler, M. Morrison, D.A. Meese, A.J. Gow and R.B. Alley, "Record of
Volcanism Since 7000 B.C. from the GISP2 Greenland Ice Core and
Implications for the Volcano-Climate System," *Science* 264 (1994) 948–
952 [hereafter Zielinski et al:1994]. It should be noted, however, that
Zielinski et al. also found "events" at 1577, 1594, 1600 and 1602 B.C.
that are not attributed to any specific volcano (see Table 2, page 950).

38 Renfrew:1996:734 writes that "one grain of Theran tephra at the appropriate point in a single Greenland ice core would be enough to establish a
sound link going beyond mere supposition." See also Manning:1995:
203; and Baillie:1995:121.

39 Baillie:1990:160; Baillie:1995:112 puts it another way: "It looks as
though something volcanic and environmental is going on in the later
seventeenth century BC. The tree-rings specify some environmental
effects at 1628 BC and it is not impossible that the 1645 ± 20 BC acidity
layer represents the same event. Given the radiocarbon evidence Santorini
has to be a possible candidate."

40 A recent example of such reluctance is given by H. Matthäus, "Representations of Keftiu in Egyptian Tombs and the Absolute Chronology of
the Aegean Late Bronze Age," *BICS* 40 (1995) 177–186.

41 Warren:1990:26; and Warren:1987:205.

42 Warren:1990/1991:36; Warren:1984:492; see also V. Hankey, "The
Chronology of the Aegean Late Bronze Age," in P. Åström (ed.), *High,
Middle or Low: Acts of an International Colloquium Held at the
University of Gothenburg, 20th-22nd August 1987* (Gothenburg, 1987;
hereafter High, Middle or Low:1987) 40. J.L. Davis:1992:736 states that
"there are very few artifactual synchronisms between Greece and Egypt
during the early LBA. The dates and contexts of relevant imports and
exports are in almost all cases disputable."

43 Manning:1988:68; see also Manning:1990b:33; and Manning:1995:203–206. After the debate on chronology at the Third International Congress, Manning wrote that "the Congress papers of Betancourt, Warren, and Manning left it clear that the existing evidence is both sparse and not particularly precise...It must also be noted that the Egyptian chronology...has been highlighted as less precise than often assumed by Aegean scholars." (Manning:1990a:92) For a good examination of the problems within Egyptian chronology, see K.A. Kitchen, "The Basics of Egyptian Chronology in Relation to the Bronze Age," in High, Middle or Low: 1987:37–55 [hereafter Kitchen:1987].

44 R.S. Merrillees, "Aegean Bronze Age Relations with Egypt," *AJA* 76 (1972) 282.

45 D.G. Sullivan, "The Discovery of Santorini Minoan Tephra in Western Turkey," *Nature* 333 (1988) 552–554; and D.G. Sullivan, "Minoan Tephra in Lake Sediments in Western Turkey: Dating the Eruption and Assessing the Atmospheric Dispersal of the Ash," *T & AW III: Chron*, 114–119. At the Third International Congress, it was reported that W. Voightlander had discovered Theran ash at Teichioussa on the coast of Turkey: see P. Kuniholm, "Overview and Assessment of the Evidence for the Date of the Eruption of Thera," *T & AW III: Chron*, 16.

46 Marketou:1990:100–113; C. Doumas and L. Papazoglou, "Santorini Tephra from Rhodes," *Nature* 287 (1980) 322–324 [hereafter Doumas and Papazoglou:1980].

47 C. Doumas, "The Prehistoric Eruption of Thera and Its Effects. The Evidence from Rhodes," in S. Dietz and I. Papachristodoulou (eds.), *Archaeology in the Dodecanese* (Copenhagen, 1988) 36.

48 D.J. Stanley and H. Sheng, "Volcanic Shards from Santorini (Upper Minoan Ash) in the Nile Delta, Egypt," *Nature* 320 (1986) 733–735.

49 For an examination of the "Thera as Atlantis" theory, see P.Y. Forsyth, *Atlantis: The Making of Myth* (Montreal, 1980).

50 Kitchen:1987:52.

51 E.N. Davis, "A Storm in Egypt during the Reign of Ahmose," *T & AW III: Chron*, 232–235; K.P. Foster and R.K. Ritner, "Texts, Storms, and the Thera Eruption," *Journal of Near Eastern Studies* 55 (1996) 1–14.

52 On this see Manning:1995:206; and Baillie:1995:116 and 154–155.

53 Bietak:1996:76–78; see also Renfrew:1996:734.

54 S. Marinatos, "The Volcanic Destruction of Minoan Crete," *Antiquity* 13 (1939) 425–439; J.V. Luce, *The End of Atlantis* (London, 1969).

55 A notable exception is found in the work of W.S. Downey and D.H.

Tarling: see W.S. Downey and D.H. Tarling, "Archaeomagnetic Dating of Santorini Volcanic Eruptions and Fired Destruction Levels of Late Minoan Civilization," *Nature* 309 (1984) 519-523; W. Downey and D. Tarling, "The End of the Minoan Civilisation," *New Scientist* 103 (1984) 49-52; and D.H. Tarling and W.S. Downey, "Archaeomagnetic Results from Late Minoan Destruction Levels on Crete and the 'Minoan' Tephra on Thera," *T & AW III: Chron*, 146-158. Their advocacy of a two-stage Theran eruption, however, has not won many converts: see, for example, R.S.J. Sparks, "Archaeomagnetism, Santorini Volcanic Eruptions and Fired Destruction Levels on Crete," *Nature* 313 (1985) 74-75; and Y. Liritzis, "Archaeomagnetism, Santorini Volcanic Eruptions and Fired Destruction Levels on Crete," *Nature* 313 (1985) 75-76.

56 See Doumas and Papazoglou:1980:323; and Watkins et al:1978:122-126.

57 See Warren:1990/1991.

58 C. Lambrou-Phillipson, "Thera in the Mythology of the Classical Tradition: An Archaeological Approach," *T & AW III: Arch*, 162-170; S. Hiller:1978:675-679; and I. Tzedakis, "Ponce de la Canée," *AAA* (1968) 313-314. Pumice in conjunction with conical cups and other religious artefacts has been discovered in a sanctuary at Nami: see Artzy:1991.

59 See G. Rapp, Jr. and S.B. Cooke, "Thera Pumice Recovered from LH IIA Stratum at Nichoria," *AAA* 6 (1973) 136-137; and G. Rapp, Jr., S. R.B. Cooke and E. Henrickson, "Pumice from Thera (Santorini) Identified from a Greek Mainland Archeological Excavation," *Science* 179 (1973) 471-473.

60 See Iakovides:1979:101-102; and J.L. Crowley, "More on Mycenaeans at Thera," *AJA* 87 (1983) 83-85.

61 See C. Doumas and P. Warren, "Thera: A Late Cycladic III Settlement at Monolithos," *AAA* 12 (1979) 232-236; and Sperling:1973:27-28.

BIBLIOGRAPHY

Artzy, M. "Conical Cups and Pumice, Aegean Cult at Tel Nami, Israel." *Thalassa. L'Égée préhistorique et la mer.* Eds. R. Laffineur and L. Basch. Liège: Aegaeum 7, 1991. 203–206.

_____. "Nami: A Second Millennium International Maritime Trading Center in the Mediterranean." *Recent Excavations in Israel: A View to the West.* Ed. S. Gitin. Dubuque: Archaeological Institute of America, 1995. 17–40.

Aspinall, A. and S.W. Feather. "Neutron Activation Analysis of Aegean Obsidians." *Thera and the Aegean World I.* Ed. C. Doumas. London: Thera and the Aegean World, 1978. 517–521.

Aston, M.A. and P.G. Hardy. "The Pre-Minoan Landscape of Thera: a Preliminary Statement." *Thera and the Aegean World III: Earth Sciences.* Ed. D.A. Hardy. London: The Thera Foundation, 1990. 348–361.

Baillie, M.G.L. "Irish Oaks Record Volcanic Dust Veils Drama." *Archaeology Ireland* 2 (1988): 71–74.

_____. "Irish Tree Rings and an Event in 1628 BC." *Thera and the Aegean World III: Chronology.* Ed. D.A. Hardy. London: The Thera Foundation, 1990. 160–166.

_____. "Marking in Marker Dates: Towards an Archaeology with Historical Precision." *World Archaeology* 23 (1991): 233–243.

_____. *A Slice through Time.* London: B.T. Batsford Ltd, 1995.

Baillie, M.G.L. and M.A.R. Munro. "Irish Tree Rings, Santorini and Volcanic Dust Veils." *Nature* 332 (1988): 344–346.

Barber, R.L.N. "Phylakopi 1911 and the History of the Later Cycladic Bronze Age." *BSA* 69 (1974): 1–53.

_____. "The Cyclades in the Middle Bronze Age." *Thera and the Aegean World I.* Ed. C. Doumas. London: Thera and the Aegean World, 1978. 367–379.

_____. "The Late Cycladic Period: A Review." *BSA* 76 (1981): 1–21.

158   *Bibliography*

_____. "Early Cycladic Marble Figures: Some Thoughts on Function." *Cycladica*. Ed. J.L. Fitton. London: The British Museum, 1984. 10-14.

_____. *The Cyclades in the Bronze Age*. London: Duckworth, 1987.

Barber, R.L.N. and J.A. MacGillivray. "The Early Cycladic Period: Matters of Definition and Terminology." *AJA* 84 (1980): 141-157.

Bass, G.F. "Evidence of Trade from Bronze Age Shipwrecks." *Bronze Age Trade in the Mediterranean*. Ed. N.H. Gale. Jonsered: Paul Åströms Förlag, 1991. 69-82.

Bassiakos, Y., V. Kilikoglou, M. Vassilaki-Grimani and A.P. Grimanis. "Provenance Studies of Theran Lead." *Thera and the Aegean World III: Earth Sciences*. Ed. D.A. Hardy. London: The Thera Foundation, 1990. 337-345.

Betancourt, P.P. "Perspective and the Third Dimension in Theran Paintings." *Temple University Aegean Symposium 2*. Ed. P.P. Betancourt. Philadelphia: Temple University, 1977. 19-22.

_____. "The Middle Minoan Pottery of Southern Crete and the Question of a Middle Minoan Thalassocracy." *The Minoan Thalassocracy: Myth and Reality*. Eds. R. Hägg and N. Marinatos. Stockholm: Paul Åströms Förlag, 1984. 89-92.

_____. "Dating the Aegean Late Bronze Age with Radiocarbon." *Archaeometry* 29 (1987): 45-49.

_____. "High Chronology or Low Chronology: The Archaeological Evidence." *Thera and the Aegean World III: Chronology*. Ed. D.A. Hardy. London: The Thera Foundation, 1990. 19-23.

Betancourt, P.P. and B. Lawn. "The Cyclades and Radiocarbon Chronology." *The Prehistoric Cyclades*. Eds. J.A. MacGillivray and R.L.N. Barber. Edinburgh: University of Edinburgh, 1984. 277-295.

Bietak, M. "Connections between Egypt and the Minoan World: New Results from Tell el-Dab'a/Avaris." *Egypt, the Aegean and the Levant*. Eds. W.V.

Davies and L. Schofield. London: The British Museum, 1995. 19-28.

_____. *Avaris, The Capital of the Hyksos: Recent Excavations at Tell el-Dab'a*. London: The British Museum, 1996.

Bolton, K. "Addendum to J.V. Luce's Article: 'Thera and the Devastation of Minoan Crete: A New Interpretation of the Evidence'." *AJA* 80 (1976): 17-18.

Bond, A. and R.S.J. Sparks. "The Minoan Eruption of Santorini, Greece." *Journal of the Geological Society, London* 132 (1976): 1-16.

Branigan, K. "Minoan Colonialism." *BSA* 76 (1981): 23-33.

_____. "Minoan Community Colonies in the Aegean?" *The Minoan Thalassocracy: Myth and Reality*. Eds. R. Hägg and N. Marinatos. Stockholm: Paul Åströms Förlag, 1984. 49-53.

Broodbank, C. "The Longboat and Society in the Cyclades in the Keros-Syros Culture." *AJA* 93 (1989): 319-337.

Cadogan, G. "Thera's Eruption into our Understanding of the Minoans." *Thera and the Aegean World III: Archaeology*. Ed. D.A. Hardy. London: The Thera Foundation, 1990. 93-97.

Casson, L. "Bronze Age Ships. The Evidence of the Thera Wall Paintings." *IJNA* 4 (1975): 3-10.

_____. "The Thera Ships." *IJNA* 7 (1978): 232-233.

Cherry, J.F. "Four Problems in Cycladic Prehistory." *Papers in Cycladic Prehistory*. Eds. J.L. Davis and J.F. Cherry. Los Angeles: University of California, 1979. 22-47.

_____. "Pattern and Process in the Earliest Colonization of the Mediterranean Islands." *Proceedings of the Prehistoric Society* 47 (1981): 41-68.

_____. "Islands out of the Stream: Isolation and Interaction in Early East Mediterranean Insular Prehistory." *Prehistoric Production and Exchange:*

The Aegean and Eastern Mediterranean. Eds. A.B. Knapp and T. Stech. Los Angeles: University of California, 1985. 12–29.

_____. "Island Origins: The Early Prehistoric Cyclades." *Origins: The Roots of European Civilisation.* Ed. B. Cunliffe. Chicago: The Dorsey Press, 1988. 16–29.

_____. "The First Colonization of the Mediterranean Islands: A Review of Recent Research." *JMA* 3 (1990): 145–221.

Cherry, J.F. and J.L. Davis. "The Cyclades and the Greek Mainland in LC I: The Evidence of the Pottery." *AJA* 86 (1982): 333–341.

Cline, E.H. *Sailing the Wine-Dark Sea: International Trade and the Late Bronze Age Aegean.* Oxford: British Archaeological Reports, 1994.

_____. "'My Brother, My Son': Rulership and Trade between the LBA Aegean, Egypt and the Near East." *The Role of the Ruler in the Prehistoric Aegean.* Ed. P. Rehak. Liège: Aegaeum 11, 1995. 143–150.

_____. "Tinker, Tailor, Soldier, Sailor: Minoans and Mycenaeans Abroad." *Politeia: Society and State in the Aegean Bronze Age.* Eds. R. Laffineur and W.-D. Niemeier. Liège: Aegaeum 12, 1995. 265–287.

Cline, E.H. and M.J. Cline. "Of Shoes and Ships and Sealing Wax." *Expedition* 33 (1991): 46–54.

Coleman, J.E. "The Chronology and Interconnections of the Cycladic Islands in the Neolithic and the Early Bronze Age." *AJA* 78 (1974): 333–343.

_____. "Frying Pans of the Early Bronze Age Aegean." *AJA* 89 (1985): 191–219.

Cosmopoulos, M.B. "Exchange Networks in Prehistory: The Aegean and the Mediterranean in the Third Millennium B.C." *Thalassa. L'Égée préhistorique et la mer.* Eds. R. Laffineur and L. Basch. Liège: Aegaeum 7, 1991. 155–167.

Crowley, J.L. "More on Mycenaeans at Thera." *AJA* 87 (1983): 83–85.

Davis, E.N. "The Iconography of the Ship Fresco from Thera." *Ancient Greek Art and Iconography*. Ed. W.G. Moon. Madison: University of Wisconsin, 1983. 1–14.

_____. "Youth and Age in the Thera Frescoes." *AJA* 90 (1986): 399–406.

_____. "A Storm in Egypt during the Reign of Ahmose." *Thera and the Aegean World III: Chronology*. Ed. D.A. Hardy. London: The Thera Foundation, 1990. 232–235.

_____. "The Cycladic Style of the Thera Frescoes." *Thera and the Aegean World III: Archaeology*. Ed. D.A. Hardy. London: The Thera Foundation, 1990. 214–228.

_____. "Art and Politics in the Aegean: The Missing Ruler." *The Role of the Ruler in the Prehistoric Aegean*. Ed. P. Rehak. Liège: Aegaeum 11, 1995. 11–19.

Davis, J.L. "Polychrome Bird Jugs: A Note." *AAA* 9 (1976): 81–83.

_____. "The Mainland Panelled Cup and Panelled Style." *AJA* 82 (1978): 216–222.

_____. "Minos and Dexithea: Crete and the Cyclades in the Later Bronze Age." *Papers in Cycladic Prehistory*. Ed. J.L. Davis and J.F. Cherry. Los Angeles: University of California, 1979. 143–157.

_____. "A Cycladic Figure in Chicago and the Non-funereal Use of Cycladic Marble Figures." *Cycladica*. Ed. J.L. Fitton. London: The British Museum, 1984. 15–21.

_____. "Review of Aegean Prehistory I: The Islands of the Aegean." *AJA* 96 (1992): 699–756.

Davis, J.L. and J.F. Cherry. "Spatial and Temporal Uniformitarianism in Late Cycladic I: Perspectives from Kea and Milos on the Prehistory of Akrotiri." *Thera and the Aegean World III: Archaeology*. Ed. D.A. Hardy. London: The Thera Foundation, 1990. 185–200.

Devetzi, T.D. "The Stone Industry at Akrotiri: A Theoretical Approach." *Thera and the Aegean World III: Archaeology.* Ed. D.A. Hardy. London: The Thera Foundation, 1990. 19-23.

Diapoulis, C. "Prehistoric Plants of the Islands of the Aegean Sea." *Thera and the Aegean World II.* Ed. C. Doumas. London: Thera and the Aegean World, 1980. 129-140.

Dickinson, O.T.P.K. "Early Mycenaean Greece and the Mediterranean." *Traffici Micenei nel Mediterraneo.* Eds. M. Marazzi, S. Tusa and L. Vagnetti. Taranto: Istituto per la Storia e l'Archeologia della Magna Grecia, 1986. 271-276.

_____. *The Aegean Bronze Age.* Cambridge: Cambridge University Press, 1994.

Doumas, C. "Ftellos." *AE* (1973): 161-166.

_____. "The Minoan Eruption of the Santorini Volcano." *Antiquity* 48 (1974): 110-115.

_____. "Notes on the Minoan Architecture of Thera." *AE* (1974): 199-219.

_____. "᾿Ανασκαφὴ Θήρας." *PAE* (1975): 212-229.

_____. "᾿Ανασκαφὴ Θήρας." *PAE* (1976): 309-329.

_____. "Prehistoric Cycladic People in Crete." *AAA* 9 (1976): 69-80.

_____. "᾿Ανασκαφὴ Θήρας." *PAE* (1977): 387-399.

_____. *Early Bronze Age Burial Habits in the Cyclades.* Göteborg: Paul Åströms Förlag, 1977.

_____. "The Stratigraphy of Akrotiri." *Thera and the Aegean World I.* Ed. C. Doumas. London: Thera and the Aegean World, 1978. 777-784.

_____. "Town Planning and Architecture in Bronze Age Thera." *150 Jahre Deutsches Archäologisches Institut.* Mainz, 1981. 95-98.

_____. "The Minoan Thalassocracy and the Cyclades." *AA* (1982): 5–14.

_____. *Thera: Pompeii of the Ancient Aegean*. London: Thames and Hudson, 1983.

_____. "'Ανασκαφὴ Θήρας ('Ακρωτήρι)." *PAE* (1985): 168–176.

_____. "Conventions artistiques à Théra et dans la Méditerranée orientale à l'époque préhistorique." *L'Iconographie Minoenne*. Eds. P. Darcque and J.-C. Poursat. Paris: BCH Supplement 11, 1985. 29–34.

_____. "Trade in the Aegean in the Light of the Thera Excavations." *Traffici Micenei nel Mediterraneo*. Eds. M. Marazzi, S. Tusa and L. Vagnetti. Taranto: Istituto per la Storia e l'Archeologia della Magna Grecia, 1986. 233–240.

_____. "'Ανασκαφὴ Θήρας." *PAE* (1987): 241–254.

_____. "EBA in the Cyclades: Continuity or Discontinuity?" *Problems in Greek Prehistory*. Eds. E.B. French and K.A. Wardle. Bristol: Bristol Classical Press, 1988. 21–29.

_____. "The Prehistoric Eruption of Thera and Its Effects. The Evidence from Rhodes." *Archaeology in the Dodecanese*. Eds. S. Dietz and I. Papachristodoulou. Copenhagen: The National Museum of Denmark, 1988. 34–38.

_____. "The Transition from Late Neolithic to Early Bronze Age: The Evidence from the Islands." *Archaeometry: Proceedings of the 25th International Symposium*. Ed. Y. Maniatis. Amsterdam: Elsevier, 1989. 705–708.

_____. "Archaeological Observations at Akrotiri Relating to the Volcanic Destruction." *Thera and the Aegean World III: Chronology*. Ed. D.A. Hardy. London: The Thera Foundation, 1990. 48–50.

_____. "The Elements at Akrotiri." *Thera and the Aegean World III: Archaeology*. Ed. D.A. Hardy. London: The Thera Foundation, 1990. 24–30.

_____. "Thera and the East Mediterranean during the First Half of the

Second Millennium B.C." *The Civilizations of the Aegean and their Diffu-sion in Cyprus and the Eastern Mediterranean, 2000–600 B.C.* Ed. V. Karageorghis. Larnaca: Pierides Foundation, 1991. 24–27.

————. *The Wall-Paintings of Thera.* Athens: The Thera Foundation, 1992.

Doumas, C. and L. Papazoglou. "Santorini Tephra from Rhodes." *Nature* 287 (1980): 322–324.

Doumas, C. and P. Warren. "Thera: A Late Cycladic III Settlement at Mono-lithos." *AAA* 12 (1979): 232–236.

Druitt, T.H. "Vent Evolution and Lag Breccia Formation during the Cape Riva Eruption of Santorini, Greece." *Journal of Geology* 93 (1985): 439–454.

Druitt, T.H. and V. Francaviglia. "An Ancient Caldera Cliff Line at Phira, and its Significance for the Topography and Geology of Pre-Minoan San-torini." *Thera and the Aegean World III: Earth Sciences.* Ed. D.A. Hardy. London: The Thera Foundation, 1990. 362–369.

Druitt, T.H., R.A. Mellors, D.M. Pyle and R.S.J. Sparks. "Explosive Vol-canism on Santorini, Greece." *Geological Magazine* 126 (1989): 95–126.

Eriksen, U., W.L. Friedrich, B. Buchardt, H. Tauber and M.S. Thomsen. "The Stronghyle Caldera: Geological, Palaeontological and Stable Isotope Evidence from Radiocarbon Dated Stromatolites from Santorini." *Thera and the Aegean World III: Earth Sciences.* Ed. D.A. Hardy. London: The Thera Foundation, 1990. 139–150.

Faure, P. "Remarques sur la présence et l'emploi de la pierre ponce en Crete du Néolithique à nos jours." *Acta of the 1st International Scientific Con-gress on the Volcano of Thera.* Ed. A. Kaloyeropoulou. Athens: Archae-ological Services of Greece, 1971. 422–429.

Foster, K.P. and R.K. Ritner. "Texts, Storms, and the Thera Eruption." *Journal of Near Eastern Studies* 55 (1996): 1–14.

Fouqué, F. *Santorin et ses éruptions.* Paris: Masson, 1879.

Friedrich, W.L. and C. Doumas. "Was there Local Access to Certain Ores/Minerals for the Theran People before the Minoan Eruption? An Addendum." *Thera and the Aegean World III: Archaeology.* Ed. D.A. Hardy. London: The Thera Foundation, 1990. 502–503.

Friedrich, W.L., U. Eriksen, H. Tauber, J. Heinemeier, N. Rud, M.S. Thomsen and B. Buchardt. "Existence of a Water-Filled Caldera Prior to the Minoan Eruption of Santorini, Greece." *Naturwissenschaften* 75 (1988): 567–569.

Friedrich, W.L., P. Wagner and H. Tauber. "Radiocarbon Dated Plant Remains from the Akrotiri Excavation on Santorini, Greece." *Thera and the Aegean World III: Chronology.* Ed. D.A. Hardy. London: The Thera Foundation, 1990. 188–196.

Gale, N.H. "Lead Isotope Analyses Applied to Provenance Studies—A Brief Review." *Archaeometry: Proceedings of the 25th International Symposium.* Ed. Y. Maniatis. Amsterdam: Elsevier, 1989. 469–502.

_____. "Copper Oxhide Ingots: Their Origin and their Place in the Bronze Age Metals Trade in the Mediterranean." *Bronze Age Trade in the Mediterranean.* Ed. N.H. Gale. Jonsered: Paul Åströms Förlag, 1991. 197–233.

Gamble, C. "The Bronze Age Animal Economy from Akrotiri: A Preliminary Analysis." *Thera and the Aegean World I.* Ed. C. Doumas. London: Thera and the Aegean World, 1978. 745–753.

_____. "Surplus and Self-Sufficiency in the Cycladic Subsistance Economy." *Papers in Cycladic Prehistory.* Eds. J.L. Davis and J.F. Cherry. Los Angeles: University of California, 1979. 122–134.

Georgiou, H.S. "Bronze Age Ships and Rigging." *Thalassa. L'Égée préhistorique et la mer.* Eds. R. Laffineur and L. Basch. Liège: Aegaeum 7, 1991. 61–70.

Gesell, G.C. "The 'Town Fresco' of Thera: A Reflection of Cretan Topography." *Acts of the Fourth International Cretological Congress.* Athens, 1980. 197–204.

Giesecke, H.-E. "The Akrotiri Ship Fresco." *IJNA* 12 (1983): 123-143.

Hadjianastasiou, O. "A Late Neolithic Settlement at Grotta, Naxos." *Problems in Greek Prehistory*. Eds. E.B. French and K.A. Wardle. Bristol: Bristol Classical Press, 1988. 11-20.

Hammer, C.U. and H.B. Clausen. "The Precision of Ice-Core Dating." *Thera and the Aegean World III: Chronology*. Ed. D.A. Hardy. London: The Thera Foundation, 1990. 174-178.

Hammer, C.U., H.B. Clausen and W. Dansgaard. "Greenland Ice Sheet Evidence of Post-Glacial Volcanism and its Climatic Impact." *Nature* 288 (1980): 230-235.

Hammer, C.U., H.B. Clausen, W.L. Friedrich and H. Tauber. "The Minoan Eruption of Santorini in Greece Dated to 1645 BC ?" *Nature* 328 (1987): 517-519.

Heiken, G. and F. McCoy. "Caldera Development during the Minoan Eruption, Thira, Cyclades, Greece." *Journal of Geophysical Research* 89 (1984): 8441-8462.

_____. "Precursory Activity to the Minoan Eruption, Thera, Greece." *Thera and the Aegean World III: Earth Sciences*. Ed. D.A. Hardy. London: The Thera Foundation, 1990. 79-88.

Heiken, G., F. McCoy and M. Sheridan. "Palaeotopographic and Palaeogeologic Reconstruction of Minoan Thera." *Thera and the Aegean World III: Earth Sciences*. Ed. D.A. Hardy. London: The Thera Foundation, 1990. 370-376.

Hiller, S. "Minoan Qe-Ra-Si-Ja. The Religious Impact of the Thera Volcano on Minoan Crete." *Acta of the 1st International Scientific Congress on the Volcano of Thera*. Ed. A. Kaloyeropoulou. Athens: Archaeological Services of Greece, 1971. 675-679.

Hiller von Gaertringen, F. *Thera*. Volumes I-IV. Berlin: Reimer, 1899-1909.

Hollinshead, M.B. "The Swallows and Artists of Room Delta 2 at Akrotiri,

Thera." *AJA* 93 (1989): 339–354.

Hood, S. "A Minoan Empire in the Aegean in the 16th and 15th Centuries B.C.?" *The Minoan Thalassocracy: Myth and Reality.* Eds. R. Hägg and N. Marinatos. Stockholm: Paul Åströms Förlag, 1984. 33–37.

———. "The Third International Congress on Santorini (Thera)." *Kadmos* 29 (1990): 84–86.

———. "The Cretan Element on Thera in Late Minoan IA." *Thera and the Aegean World III: Archaeology.* Ed. D.A. Hardy. London: The Thera Foundation, 1990. 118–123.

Housley, R.A., R.E.M. Hedges, I.A. Law and C.R. Bronk. "Radiocarbon Dating by AMS of the Destruction of Akrotiri." *Thera and the Aegean World III: Chronology.* Ed. D.A. Hardy. London: The Thera Foundation, 1990. 207–215.

Hubberten, H.-W., M. Bruns, M. Calamiotou, C. Apostolakis, S. Filippakis and A. Grimanis. "Radiocarbon Dates from the Akrotiri Excavations." *Thera and the Aegean World III: Chronology.* Ed. D.A. Hardy. London: The Thera Foundation, 1990. 179–187.

Huijsmans, J.P.P. and M. Barton. "New Stratigraphic and Geochemical Data for the Megalo Vouno Complex: a Dominating Volcanic Landform in Minoan Times." *Thera and the Aegean World III: Earth Sciences.* Ed. D.A. Hardy. London: The Thera Foundation, 1990. 433–441.

Iakovides, S. "Thera and Mycenaean Greece." *AJA* 83 (1979): 101–102.

———. "A Peak Sanctuary in Bronze Age Thera." *Temples and High Places in Biblical Times.* Ed. A. Biran. Jerusalem: Hebrew Union College, 1981. 54–60.

Immerwahr, S.A. "Mycenaeans at Thera: Some Reflections on the Paintings from the West House." *Greece and the Eastern Mediterranean in Ancient History and Prehistory.* Ed. K.H. Kinzl. Berlin: Walter de Gruyter, 1977. 173–191.

_____. *Aegean Painting in the Bronze Age*. University Park and London: The Pennsylvania State University Press, 1990.

_____. "Swallows and Dolphins at Akrotiri: Some Thoughts on the Relationship of Vase-Painting to Wall-Painting." *Thera and the Aegean World III: Archaeology*. Ed. D.A. Hardy. London: The Thera Foundation, 1990. 237–245.

Jones, R.E. "Composition and Provenance Studies of Cycladic Pottery with Particular Reference to Thera." *Thera and the Aegean World I*. Ed. C. Doumas. London: Thera and the Aegean World, 1978. 471–482.

Kalogeropoulos, S. and S. Paritsis. "Geological and Geochemical Evolution of the Santorini Volcano: a Review." *Thera and the Aegean World III: Earth Sciences*. Ed. D.A. Hardy. London: The Thera Foundation, 1990. 164–171.

Karageorghis, V. "Rites de Passage at Thera: Some Oriental Comparanda." *Thera and the Aegean World III: Archaeology*. Ed. D.A. Hardy. London: The Thera Foundation, 1990. 67–71.

Karali-Yannacopoulou, L. "Sea Shells, Land Snails and Other Marine Remains from Akrotiri." *Thera and the Aegean World III: Earth Sciences*. Ed. D.A. Hardy. London: The Thera Foundation, 1990. 410–415.

Katsa-Tomara, L. "The Pottery-Producing System at Akrotiri: An Index of Exchange and Social Activity." *Thera and the Aegean World III: Archaeology*. Ed. D.A. Hardy. London: The Thera Foundation, 1990. 31–40.

Keller, J. "Summary of the Progress in Volcanology." *Thera and the Aegean World III: Earth Sciences*. Ed. D.A. Hardy. London: The Thera Foundation, 1990. 486–487.

Keller, J., Th. Rehren and E. Stadlbauer. "Explosive Volcanism in the Hellenic Arc: a Summary and Review." *Thera and the Aegean World III: Earth Sciences*. Ed. D.A. Hardy. London: The Thera Foundation, 1990. 13–26.

Kempinski, A. and W.-D. Niemeier. *Excavations at Kabri. Preliminary*

Report of 1990 Season. Tel Aviv: Tel Kabri Expedition, 1991.

_____. *Excavations at Kabri. Preliminary Report of 1991 Season.* Tel Aviv: Tel Kabri Expedition, 1992.

Kennedy, D.H. "A Further Note on the Thera Ships." *Mariner's Mirror* 64 (1978): 135–137.

Kilikoglou, V., C. Doumas, A. Papagiannopoulou, E.V. Sayre, Y. Maniatis and A.P. Grimanis. "A Study of Middle and Late Cycladic Pottery from Akrotiri." *Thera and the Aegean World III: Archaeology.* Ed. D.A. Hardy. London: The Thera Foundation, 1990. 441–448.

Knapp, A.B. "Spice, Drugs, Grain and Grog: Organic Goods in Bronze Age East Mediterranean Trade." *Bronze Age Trade in the Mediterranean.* Ed. N.H. Gale. Jonsered: Paul Åströms Förlag, 1991. 21–68.

_____. "Bronze Age Mediterranean Island Cultures and the Ancient Near East, Part 1." *Biblical Archaeologist* 55 (1992): 52–72.

_____. "Bronze Age Mediterranean Island Cultures and the Ancient Near East, Part 2." *Biblical Archaeologist* 55 (1992): 112–128.

_____. "Thalassocracies in Bronze Age Eastern Mediterranean Trade: Making and Breaking a Myth." *World Archaeology* 24 (1992/1993): 332–347.

Koehl, R.B. "The Rhyta from Akrotiri and Some Preliminary Observations on their Functions in Selected Contexts." *Thera and the Aegean World III: Archaeology.* Ed. D.A. Hardy. London: The Thera Foundation, 1990. 350–362.

_____. "The Nature of Minoan Kingship." *The Role of the Ruler in the Prehistoric Aegean.* Ed. P. Rehak. Liège: Aegaeum 11, 1995. 23–36.

Kourmoulis, N. "The Consequences of Volcanic Activity of the Minoan Period on the Hydrogeological Conditions of the Island of Thera." *Thera and the Aegean World III: Earth Sciences.* Ed. D.A. Hardy. London: The Thera Foundation, 1990. 237–240.

Kuniholm, P.I. "Overview and Assessment of the Evidence for the Date of the Eruption of Thera." *Thera and the Aegean World III: Chronology*. Ed. D.A. Hardy. London: The Thera Foundation, 1990. 13-18.

Kuniholm, P.I., B. Kromer, S.W. Manning, M. Newton, C.E. Latini and M.J. Bruce. "Anatolian Tree Rings and the Absolute Chronology of the Eastern Mediterranean, 2220-718 BC." *Nature* 381 (1996): 780-783.

Laffineur, R. "Early Mycenaean Art: Some Evidence from the West House in Thera." *BICS* 30 (1983): 111-122.

LaMarche, V.C. and K.K. Hirschboeck. "Frost Rings in Trees as Records of Major Volcanic Eruptions." *Nature* 307 (1984): 121-126.

Lambrou-Phillipson, C. *Hellenorientalia: The Near Eastern Presence in the Bronze Age Aegean, ca. 3000-1100 B.C.*. Göteborg: Paul Åströms Förlag, 1990.

_____. "Thera in the Mythology of the Classical Tradition: An Archaeological Approach." *Thera and the Aegean World III: Archaeology*. Ed. D.A. Hardy. London: The Thera Foundation, 1990. 162-170.

_____. "Seafaring in the Bronze Age Mediterranean: The Parameters Involved in Maritime Travel." *Thalassa. L'Égée préhistorique et la mer*. Eds. R. Laffineur and L. Basch. Liège: Aegaeum 7, 1991. 11-19.

Leuschner, H.H. von and A. Delorme. "Verlängerung der Göttinger Eichenjahrringchronologien für Nord- und Süddeutschland bis zum Jahr 4008 v. Chr." *Forstarchiv* 55 (1984): 3-5.

Limbrey, S. "Soil Studies at Akrotiri." *Thera and the Aegean World III: Earth Sciences*. Ed. D.A. Hardy. London: The Thera Foundation, 1990. 377-383.

Liritzis, Y. "Archaeomagnetism, Santorini Volcanic Eruptions and Fired Destruction Levels on Crete." *Nature* 313 (1985): 75-76.

MacGillivray, J.A. "Cycladic Jars from Middle Minoan III Contexts a Knossos." *The Minoan Thalassocracy: Myth and Reality*. Eds. R. Häg and N. Marinatos. Stockholm: Paul Åströms Förlag, 1984. 153–158.

_____. "The Relative Chronology of Early Cycladic III." *The Prehistoric Cyclades.* Eds. J.A. MacGillivray and R.L.N. Barber. Edinburgh: University of Edinburgh, 1984. 70–77.

_____. "The Therans and Dikta." *Thera and the Aegean World III: Archaeology.* Ed. D.A. Hardy. London: The Thera Foundation, 1990. 363–369.

Manning, S.W. "The Bronze Age Eruption of Thera: Absolute Dating, Aegean Chronology and Mediterranean Cultural Interrelations." *JMA* 1 (1988): 17–82.

_____. "A New Age for Minoan Crete." *New Scientist* (11 February 1989): 60–63.

_____. "The Santorini Eruption: An Up-date." *JMA* 2 (1989): 303–313.

_____. "The Eruption of Thera: Date and Implications." *Thera and the Aegean World III: Chronology.* Ed. D.A. Hardy. London: The Thera Foundation, 1990. 29–40.

_____. "The Thera Eruption: The Third Congress and the Problem of the Date." *Archaeometry* 32 (1990): 91–100.

_____. "Response to J.D. Muhly on Problems of Chronology in the Aegean Late Bronze Age." *JMA* 4 (1991): 249–262.

_____. "Thera, Sulphur, and Climatic Anomalies." *Oxford Journal of Archaeology* 11 (1992): 245–253.

_____. "The Emergence of Divergence: Development and Decline on Bronze Age Crete and the Cyclades." *Development and Decline in the Mediterranean Bronze Age.* Eds. C. Mathers and S. Stoddart. Sheffield: J.R. Collis, 1994. 221–270.

_____. *The Absolute Chronology of the Aegean Early Bronze Age.* Sheffield: Sheffield Academic Press, 1995.

Marinatos, N. "The West House at Akrotiri as a Cult Center." *AM* 98 (1983): 1-19.

_____. *Art and Religion in Thera*. Athens: Mathioulakis, 1984.

_____. "Minoan Threskeiocracy on Thera." *The Minoan Thalassocracy: Myth and Reality*. Eds. R. Hägg and N. Marinatos. Stockholm: Paul Åströms Förlag, 1984. 167-178.

_____. *Minoan Sacrificial Ritual*. Stockholm: Paul Åströms Förlag, 1986.

_____. "Role and Sex Division in Ritual Scenes of Aegean Art." *Journal of Prehistoric Religion* 1 (1987): 23-34.

_____. "The Monkey in the Shrine: A Fresco Fragment from Thera." Εἰλαπινή. Τόμος Τιμητικὸς γιὰ τὸν Καθηγητὴ Νικολαο Πλατωνα. Heraklion, 1987. 417-421.

_____. "An Offering of Saffron to the Minoan Goddess of Nature." *Gifts to the Gods*. Eds. T. Linders and G. Nordquist. Uppsala: Uppsala University, 1987. 123-132.

_____. "The 'African' of Thera Reconsidered." *Opuscula Atheniensia* 17 (1988): 137-141.

_____. "Minoan-Cycladic Syncretism." *Thera and the Aegean World III: Archaeology*. Ed. D.A. Hardy. London: The Thera Foundation, 1990. 370-377.

_____. *Minoan Religion: Ritual, Image and Symbol*. Columbia, S.C.: University of South Carolina Press, 1993.

_____. "The 'Export' Significance of Minoan Bull Hunting and Bull Leaping Scenes." *Ägypten und Levante* 4 (1994): 89-93.

_____. "Divine Kingship in Minoan Crete." *The Role of the Ruler in the Prehistoric Aegean*. Ed. P. Rehak. Liège: Aegaeum 11, 1995. 37-47.

_____. "Formalism and Gender Roles: A Comparison of Minoan and Egyptian Art." *Politeia: Society and State in the Aegean Bronze Age*. Eds. R. Laffineur and W.-D. Niemeier. Liège: Aegaeum 12, 1995. 577-584.

Marinatos, N. and R. Hägg. "On the Ceremonial Function of the Minoan Polythyron." *Opuscula Atheniensia* 16 (1986): 57-73.

Marinatos, S. "The Volcanic Destruction of Minoan Crete." *Antiquity* 13 (1939): 425-439.

_____. *Excavations at Thera*. Athens: Archaeological Society, 1968.

_____. *Excavations at Thera II*. Athens: Archaeological Society, 1969.

_____. *Excavations at Thera III*. Athens: Archaeological Society, 1970.

_____. *Excavations at Thera IV*. Athens: Archaeological Society, 1971.

_____. *Excavations at Thera V*. Athens: Archaeological Society, 1972.

_____. *Excavations at Thera VI*. Athens: Archaeological Society, 1974.

_____. *Excavations at Thera VII*. Athens: Archaeological Society, 1976.

_____. "Thera, ein Neues Zentrum der Ägäischen Kultur." *Ägäische Bronzezeit*. Ed. H.-G. Buchholz. Darmstadt: Wissenschaftliche Buchgesellschaft, 1987. 275-287.

Marketou, T. "Santorini Tephra from Rhodes and Kos: Some Chronological Remarks Based on the Stratigraphy." *Thera and the Aegean World III: Chronology*. Ed. D.A. Hardy. London: The Thera Foundation, 1990. 100-113.

Marthari, M. "Akrotiri, Vases of Middle Helladic Tradition in the Destruction Level." *AE* (1980): 182-211.

_____. "Excavations at Ftellos." *AAA* 15 (1982): 86-101.

_____. "The Destruction of the Town at Akrotiri, Thera, at the Beginning of LCI: Definition and Chronology." *The Prehistoric Cyclades*. Eds. J.A.

MacGillivray and R.L.N. Barber. Edinburgh: University of Edinburgh, 1984. 119–133.

_____. "The Local Pottery Wares with Painted Decoration from the Volcanic Destruction Level of Akrotiri, Thera." *AA* (1987): 359–370.

_____. "Investigation of the Technology of Manufacture of the Local LBA Theran Pottery: Archaeological Consideration." *Thera and the Aegean World III: Archaeology*. Ed. D.A. Hardy. London: The Thera Foundation, 1990. 449–458.

_____. "The Chronology of the Last Phases of Occupation at Akrotiri in the Light of the Evidence from the West House Pottery Groups." *Thera and the Aegean World III: Chronology*. Ed. D.A. Hardy. London: The Thera Foundation, 1990. 57–70.

Marthari, M., T. Marketou and R.E. Jones. "LB I Ceramic Connections between Thera and Kos." *Thera and the Aegean World III: Archaeology*. Ed. D.A. Hardy. London: The Thera Foundation, 1990. 171–184.

McClelland, E. and R. Thomas. "A Palaeomagnetic Study of Minoan Age Tephra from Thera." *Thera and the Aegean World III: Earth Sciences*. Ed. D.A. Hardy. London: The Thera Foundation, 1990. 129–138.

Michael, H.N. and P.P. Betancourt. "Further Arguments for an Early Date." *Archaeometry* 30 (1988): 169–175.

Michailidou, A. "The Settlement of Akrotiri (Thera): A Theoretical Approach to the Function of the Upper Storey." *L'Habitat égéen préhistorique*. Eds. P. Darcque and R. Treuil. Paris: Boccard, 1990. 293–306.

_____. "The Lead Weights from Akrotiri: The Archaeological Record." *Thera and the Aegean World III: Archaeology*. Ed. D.A. Hardy. London: The Thera Foundation, 1990. 407–419.

Morgan Brown, L. "The Ship Procession in the Miniature Fresco." *Thera and the Aegean World I*. Ed. C. Doumas. London: Thera and the Aegean World, 1978. 629–644.

Morgan, L. "Theme in the West House Paintings." *AE* (1983): 85–105.

_____. *The Miniature Wall Paintings of Thera*. Cambridge: Cambridge University Press, 1988.

_____. "Island Iconography: Thera, Kea, Milos." *Thera and the Aegean World III: Archaeology*. Ed. D.A. Hardy. London: The Thera Foundation, 1990. 252–266.

_____. "The Wall-Paintings of Ayia Irini, Kea." *BICS* 40 (1995): 243–244.

_____. "Of Animals and Men: The Symbolic Parallel." *Klados. Essays in Honour of J.N. Coldstream*. Ed. C. Morris. London: University of London, 1995. 171–184.

Morris, S.P. "A Tale of Two Cities: The Miniature Frescoes from Thera and the Origins of Greek Poetry." *AJA* 93 (1989): 511–535.

Moundrea-Agrafioti, A. "Akrotiri, the Chipped Stone Industry: Reduction Techniques and Tools of the LC I Phase." *Thera and the Aegean World III: Archaeology*. Ed. D.A. Hardy. London: The Thera Foundation, 1990. 390–406.

Muhly, J.D. "Egypt, the Aegean and Late Bronze Age Chronology in the Eastern Mediterranean: A Review Article." *JMA* 4 (1991): 235–247.

Negbi, O. "The 'Miniature Fresco' from Thera and the Emergence of Mycenaean Art." *Thera and the Aegean I*. Ed. C. Doumas. London: Thera and the Aegean World, 1978. 645–656.

_____. "The 'Libyan Landscape' from Thera: A Review of Aegean Enterprises Overseas in the Late Minoan IA Period." *JMA* 7 (1994): 73–111.

Nelson, D.E., J.S. Vogel and J.R. Southon. "Another Suite of Confusing Radiocarbon Dates for the Destruction of Akrotiri." *Thera and the Aegean World III: Chronology*. Ed. D.A. Hardy. London: The Thera Foundation, 1990. 197–206.

Niemeier, W.-D. "Mycenaean Elements in the Miniature Fresco from Thera?"

Thera and the Aegean World III: Archaeology. Ed. D.A. Hardy. London: The Thera Foundation, 1990. 267–284.

_____. "New Archaeological Evidence for a 17th Century Date of the 'Minoan Eruption' from Israel (Tel Kabri, Western Galilee)." *Thera and the Aegean World III: Chronology.* Ed. D.A. Hardy. London: The Thera Foundation, 1990. 120–126.

_____. "Minoan Artisans Travelling Overseas: the Alalakh Frescoes and the Painted Plaster Floor at Tel Kabri (Western Galilee)." *Thalassa. L'Égée préhistorique et la mer.* Eds. R. Laffineur and L. Basch. Liège: Aegaeum 7, 1991. 189–200.

_____. "Minoans and Hyksos: Aegean Frescoes in the Levant." *BICS* 40 (1995): 258–260.

_____. "Tel Kabri: Aegean Fresco Paintings in a Canaanite Palace." *Recent Excavations in Israel: A View to the West* Ed. S. Gitin. Dubuque: Archaeological Institute of America, 1995. 1–15.

Page, D.L. "The Miniature Frescoes from Acrotiri Thera." *PAA* 51 (1976): 135–152.

Palyvou, C. "The Destruction of the Town at Akrotiri, Thera at the Beginning of LC I: Rebuilding Activities." *The Prehistoric Cyclades.* Eds. J.A. MacGillivray and R.L.N. Barber. Edinburgh: University of Edinburgh, 1984. 134–147.

_____. "Notes on the Town Plan of Late Cycladic Akrotiri, Thera." *BSA* 81 (1986): 179–194.

_____. "Architectural Design at Late Cycladic Akrotiri." *Thera and the Aegean World III: Archaeology.* Ed. D.A. Hardy. London: The Thera Foundation, 1990. 44–56.

Papagiannopoulou, A. "Some Changes in the BA Pottery Production at Akrotiri and their Possible Implications." *Thera and the Aegean World III: Archaeology.* Ed. D.A. Hardy. London: The Thera Foundation, 1990. 57–66.

_____. *The Influence of Middle Minoan Pottery on the Cyclades.* Göteborg: Paul Åströms Förlag, 1991.

_____. "Xesté 3, Akrotiri, Thera: The Pottery." *Klados. Essays in Honour of J.N. Coldstream.* Ed. C. Morris. London: University of London, 1995. 209–215.

Peatfield, A. "Water, Fertility, and Purification in Minoan Religion." *Klados. Essays in Honour of J.N. Coldstream.* Ed. C. Morris. London: University of London, 1995. 217–227.

Peterson, S. "A Costuming Scene from the Room of the Ladies on Thera." *AJA* 85 (1981): 211.

Petrakis, S. "Madonna Lilies in Aegean Wall Paintings." *Temple University Aegean Symposium 5.* Ed. P.P. Betancourt. Philadelphia: Temple University, 1980. 15–21.

Phythyon, R. "Considerations in Minoan Contacts at the Beginning of the Late Bronze Age." *Temple University Aegean Symposium 5.* Ed. P.P. Betancourt. Philadelphia: Temple University, 1980. 61–65.

Pichler, H. and S. Kussmaul. "Comments on the Geological Map of the Santorini Islands." *Thera and the Aegean World II.* Ed. C. Doumas. London: Thera and the Aegean World, 1980. 413–427.

Pilcher, J.R., M.G.L. Baillie, B. Schmidt and B. Becker. "A 7272-year Tree-ring Chronology for Western Europe." *Nature* 312 (1984) 150–152.

Poursat, J.-C. "Craftsmen and Traders at Thera: A View from Crete." *Thera and the Aegean World III: Archaeology.* Ed. D.A. Hardy. London: The Thera Foundation, 1990. 124–127.

Prytulak, M.G. "Weapons on the Thera Ships?" *IJNA* 11 (1982): 3–6.

Pyle, D.M. "Ice-Core Acidity Peaks, Retarded Tree Growth and Putative Eruptions." *Archaeometry* 31 (1989): 88–91.

_____. "New Estimates for the Volume of the Minoan Eruption." *Thera and the Aegean World III: Earth Sciences.* Ed. D.A. Hardy. London: The Thera Foundation, 1990. 113–121.

_____. "The Application of Tree-Ring and Ice-Core Studies to the Dating of the Minoan Eruption." *Thera and the Aegean World III: Chronology.* Ed. D.A. Hardy. London: The Thera Foundation, 1990. 167–173.

Raban, A. "The Thera Ships: Another Interpretation." *AJA* 88 (1984): 11–19.

Rackham, O. "Observations on the Historical Ecology of Santorini." *Thera and the Aegean World III: Earth Sciences.* Ed. D.A. Hardy. London: The Thera Foundation, 1990. 384–391.

Rapp, G. and S.B. Cooke. "Thera Pumice Recovered from LH IIA Stratum at Nichoria." *AAA* 6 (1973): 136–137.

Rapp, G., S.R.B. Cooke and E. Henrickson. "Pumice from Thera (Santorini) Identified from a Greek Mainland Archeological Excavation." *Science* 179 (1973): 471–473.

Renfrew, C. "Crete and the Cyclades before Rhadamanthus." *Kretika Chronika* 18 (1964): 107–141.

_____. "Cycladic Metallurgy and the Aegean Early Bronze Age." *AJA* 71 (1967): 1–20.

_____. "The Development and Chronology of the Early Cycladic Figurines." *AJA* 73 (1969): 1–32.

_____. "Saliagos—A Neolithic Settlement in the Cyclades." *Actes du VII Congrès International des Sciences Préhistoriques et Protohistoriques 1.* Ed. J. Filip. Prague: Institut d'Archéologie de l'Académie Tchécoslovaque des Sciences à Prague, 1970. 393–394.

_____. "Obsidian and Pumice: The Use of Recent Igneous Rock in Aegean Prehistory." *Acta of the 1st International Scientific Congress on the Volcano of Thera.* Ed. A. Kaloyeropoulou. Athens: Archaeological Services of Greece, 1971. 430–436.

_____. "Patterns of Population Growth in the Prehistoric Aegean." *Man, Settlement and Urbanism.* Eds. P.J. Ucko, R. Tringham and G.W. Dimbleby. London: Duckworth, 1972. 383-399.

_____. *The Emergence of Civilisation: The Cyclades and the Aegean in the Third Millennium B.C.* London: Methuen, 1972.

_____. "Speculations on the Use of Early Cycladic Sculpture." *Cycladica.* Ed. J.L. Fitton. London: The British Museum, 1984. 24-30.

_____. "Kings, Tree Rings and the Old World." *Nature* 381 (1996): 733-734.

Runnels, C.N. and J. Hansen. "The Olive in the Prehistoric Aegean: The Evidence for Domestication in the Early Bronze Age." *Oxford Journal of Archaeology* 5 (1986): 299-308.

Rutkowski, B. "Religious Elements in the Theran Frescoes." *Thera and the Aegean World I.* Ed. C. Doumas. London: Thera and the Aegean World, 1978. 661-664.

Rutter, J.B. *Ceramic Change in the Aegean Early Bronze Age.* Los Angeles: Institute of Archaeology, UCLA, 1979.

_____. "Some Observations on the Cyclades in the Later Third and Early Second Millennia." *AJA* 87 (1983): 69-76.

Sakellariou, A. "The West House Miniature Frescoes." *Thera and the Aegean World II.* Ed. C. Doumas. London: Thera and the Aegean World, 1980. 147-153.

Sali-Axioti, T. "The Lightwell of the House of the Ladies and its Structural Behaviour." *Thera and the Aegean World III: Archaeology.* Ed. D.A. Hardy. London: The Thera Foundation, 1990. 437-440.

Sapouna-Sakellaraki, E. "Οἱ τοιχογραφίες τῆς Θήρας σὲ σχέση μὲ τὴν μινωϊκὴ Κρήτη." *Acts of the Fourth International Cretological Congress.* Athens, 1981. 479-509.

Sarpaki, A. "'Small Fields or Big Fields ?' That is the Question." *Thera and the Aegean World III: Earth Sciences.* Ed. D.A. Hardy. London: The Thera Foundation, 1990. 422–432.

_____. "A Palaeoethnobotanical Study of the West House, Akrotiri, Thera." *BSA* 87 (1992): 219–230.

Sarpaki, A. and G. Jones. "Ancient and Modern Cultivation of *Lathyrus Clymenum L.* in the Greek Islands." *BSA* 85 (1990): 363–368.

Schofield, E. "The Western Cyclades and Crete: A 'Special Relationship'." *Oxford Journal of Archaeology* 1 (1982): 9–25.

_____. "Evidence for Household Industries on Thera and Kea." *Thera and the Aegean World III: Archaeology.* Ed. D.A. Hardy. London: The Thera Foundation, 1990. 201–211.

Shaw, J.W. "Consideration of the Site of Akrotiri as a Minoan Settlement." *Thera and the Aegean World I.* Ed. C. Doumas. London: Thera and the Aegean World, 1978. 429–436.

_____. "Bronze Age Aegean Harboursides." *Thera and the Aegean World III: Archaeology.* Ed. D.A. Hardy. London: The Thera Foundation, 1990. 420–436.

Sherratt, A. and S. Sherratt. "From Luxuries to Commodities: The Nature of Mediterranean Bronze Age Trading Systems." *Bronze Age Trade in the Mediterranean.* Ed. N.H. Gale. Jonsered: Paul Åströms Förlag, 1991. 351–384.

Sigurdsson, H., S. Carey and J.D. Devine. "Assessment of Mass, Dynamics and Environmental Effects of the Minoan Eruption of Santorini Volcano." *Thera and the Aegean World III: Earth Sciences.* Ed. D.A. Hardy. London: The Thera Foundation, 1990. 100–112.

Sotirakopoulou, P. "Early Cycladic Pottery from Akrotiri on Thera and Its Chronological Implications." *BSA* 81 (1986): 297–312.

_____. "The Earliest History of Akrotiri: The Late Neolithic and Early

Bronze Age Phases." *Thera and the Aegean World III: Chronology.* Ed. D.A. Hardy. London: The Thera Foundation, 1990. 41–47.

_____. "The Chronology of the 'Kastri Group' Reconsidered." *BSA* 88 (1993): 7–20.

Sparks, R.S.J. "Archaeomagnetism, Santorini Volcanic Eruptions and Fired Destruction Levels on Crete." *Nature* 313 (1985): 74–75.

Sparks, R.S.J. and C.J.N. Wilson. "The Minoan Deposits: A Review of their Characteristics and Interpretation." *Thera and the Aegean World III: Earth Sciences.* Ed. D.A. Hardy. London: The Thera Foundation, 1990. 89–99.

Sperling, J.W. *Thera and Therasia.* Athens: Athens Centre of Ekistics, 1973.

Stanley, D.J. and H. Sheng. "Volcanic Shards from Santorini (Upper Minoan Ash) in the Nile Delta, Egypt." *Nature* 320 (1986): 733–735.

Stos-Gale, Z.A. and N.H. Gale. "The Role of Thera in the Bronze Age Trade in Metals." *Thera and the Aegean World III: Archaeology.* Ed. D.A. Hardy. London: The Thera Foundation, 1990. 72–92.

Stos-Gale, Z.A. and C.F. Macdonald. "Sources of Metals and Trade in the Bronze Age Aegean." *Bronze Age Trade in the Mediterranean.* Ed. N.H. Gale. Jonsered: Paul Åströms Förlag, 1991. 249–287.

Stucynski, S. "Cycladic 'Imports' in Crete: A Brief Survey." *Temple University Aegean Symposium 7.* Ed. P.P. Betancourt. Philadelphia: Temple University, 1982. 50–59.

Sullivan, D.G. "The Discovery of Santorini Minoan Tephra in Western Turkey." *Nature* 333 (1988): 552–554.

_____. "Minoan Tephra in Lake Sediments in Western Turkey: Dating the Eruption and Assessing the Atmospheric Dispersal of the Ash." *Thera and the Aegean World III: Chronology.* Ed. D.A. Hardy. London: The Thera Foundation, 1990. 114–119.

Tarling, D.H. and W.S. Downey. "Archaeomagnetic Results from Late

Minoan Destruction Levels on Crete and the 'Minoan' Tephra on Thera." *Thera and the Aegean World III: Chronology.* Ed. D.A. Hardy. London: The Thera Foundation, 1990. 146–159.

Televantou, C. A. "Ftellos." *ADeltion* 36 (1981): 373–377.

―――. "Κοσμήματα 'από την προϊστορική Θήρα." *AE* (1984): 14–54.

―――. "The Rendering of the Human Figure in the Theran Wall-Paintings," *AE* (1988): 135–166.

―――. "New Light on the West House Wall-Paintings." *Thera and the Aegean World III: Archaeology.* Ed. D.A. Hardy. London: The Thera Foundation, 1990. 309–326.

―――. "Theran Wall-Painting: Artistic Tendencies and Painters." Εἰκών. *Aegean Bronze Age Iconography: Shaping a Methodology.* Eds. R. Laffineur and J.L. Crowley. Liège: Aegaeum 8, 1992. 145–158.

Thimme, J., ed. *Art and Culture of the Cyclades.* Karlsruhe: Müller, 1977.

Thomas, C.G. "Aegean Bronze Age Iconography: Poetic Art?" Εἰκών. *Aegean Bronze Age Iconography: Shaping a Methodology.* Eds. R. Laffineur and J.L. Crowley. Liège: Aegaeum 8, 1992. 213–219.

Tilley, A.F. and P. Johnstone. "A Minoan Naval Triumph?" *IJNA* 5 (1976): 285–292.

Tzachili, I. "All Important yet Elusive: Looking for Evidence of Cloth-Making at Akrotiri." *Thera and the Aegean World III: Archaeology.* Ed. D.A. Hardy. London: The Thera Foundation, 1990. 380–389.

Van Andel, T.H. and C.N. Runnels. "An Essay on the 'Emergence of Civilization' in the Aegean World." *Antiquity* 62 (1988): 234–247.

Vanschoonwinkel, J. "Les Fresques à figuration humaine de Théra." *Revue des Archéologues et Historiens d'Art de Louvain* 16 (1983): 9–50.

―――. "Les Fouilles de Théra et la protohistoire égéene." *Les Études Class-*

iques 54 (1986): 223-252.

Vaughan, S.J. "Petrographic Analysis of the Early Cycladic Wares from Akrotiri, Thera." *Thera and the Aegean World III: Archaeology.* Ed. D.A. Hardy. London: The Thera Foundation, 1990. 470-487.

Vogel, J.S., W. Cornell, D.E. Nelson and J.R. Southon. "Vesuvius/Avellino, One Possible Source of Seventeenth Century BC Climatic Disturbances." *Nature* 344 (1990): 534-537.

Warren, P.M. "Did Papyrus Grow in the Aegean?" *AAA* 9 (1976): 89-95.

_____. "The Miniature Fresco from the West House at Akrotiri, Thera, and its Aegean Setting." *JHS* 99 (1979): 115-129.

_____. "The Stone Vessels from the Bronze Age Settlement at Akrotiri, Thera." *AE* (1979): 82-113.

_____. "Absolute Dating of the Bronze Age Eruption of Thera (Santorini)." *Nature* 308 (1984): 492-493.

_____. "Absolute Dating of the Aegean Late Bronze Age." *Archaeometry* 29 (1987): 205-211.

_____. "Crete: The Minoans and their Gods." *Origins: The Roots of European Civilisation.* Ed. B. Cunliffe. Chicago: Dorsey Press, 1988. 30-41.

_____. "Further Arguments against an Early Date." *Archaeometry* 30 (1988): 176-179.

_____. *Minoan Religion as Ritual Action.* Gothenburg: Paul Åströms Förlag, 1988.

_____. "Summary of Evidence for the Absolute Chronology of the Early Part of the Aegean Late Bronze Age Derived from Historical Egyptian Sources." *Thera and the Aegean World III: Chronology.* Ed. D.A. Hardy. London: The Thera Foundation, 1990. 24-26.

_____. "The Minoan Civilisation of Crete and the Volcano of Thera." *The*

Journal of the Ancient Chronology Forum 4 (1990/1991): 29-39.

_____. "A Merchant Class in Bronze Age Crete?" *Bronze Age Trade in the Mediterranean*. Ed. N.H. Gale. Jonsered: Paul Åströms Förlag, 1991. 295-301.

Warren, P.M. and V. Hankey. *Aegean Bronze Age Chronology*. Bristol: Bristol Classical Press, 1989.

Watkins, N.D., R.S.J. Sparks, H. Sigurdsson, T.C. Huang, A. Federman, S. Carey and D. Ninkovich. "Volume and Extent of the Minoan Tephra from Santorini Volcano: New Evidence from the Deep-sea Sediment Cores." *Nature* 271 (1978): 122-126.

Weninger, B. "Theoretical Radiocarbon Discrepancies." *Thera and the Aegean World III: Chronology*. Ed. D.A. Hardy. London: The Thera Foundation, 1990. 216-231.

Wiener, M.H. "Crete and the Cyclades in LM I: The Tale of the Conical Cups." *The Minoan Thalassocracy: Myth and Reality*. Eds. R. Hägg and N. Marinatos. Stockholm: Paul Åströms Förlag, 1984. 17-26.

_____. "The Isles of Crete? The Minoan Thalassocracy Revisited." *Thera and the Aegean World III: Archaeology*. Ed. D.A. Hardy. London: The Thera Foundation, 1990. 128-161.

_____. "The Nature and Control of Minoan Foreign Trade." *Bronze Age Trade in the Mediterranean*. Ed. N.H. Gale. Jonsered: Paul Åströms Förlag, 1991. 325-350.

Younger, J.G. "The Iconography of Rulership: A Conspectus." *The Role of the Ruler in the Prehistoric Aegean*. Ed. P. Rehak. Liège: Aegaeum 11, 1995. 151-211.

Zielinski, G.A., P.A. Mayewski, L.D. Meeker, S. Whitlow, M.S. Twickler, M. Morrison, D.A. Meese, A.J. Gow and R.B. Alley. "Record of Volcanism Since 7000 B.C. from the GISP2 Greenland Ice Core and Implications for the Volcano-Climate System." *Science* 264 (1994): 948-952.

INDEX

adyton, 44, 55–59, 64, 96, 98, 100, 101
"African," wall-painting, 85–86
agriculture, 12, 16, 19, 91–92
Agrilia, 15
Ahmose, 114
Akrotiri, excavation site, 2, 15–18, 25–27, 30, 33–37, 38, 39–47, 49–50, 51–90, 91, 92, 93, 95, 96, 99, 100, 102, 106, 108, 112, 115
Akrotiri, peninsula, 2, 10, 11, 29, 77, 91
Akrotiri, volcanoes, 2, 3
Alalakh, 41, 115
Alaphouzos Quarry, 47–48, 51, 91
Anaphe, 20, 94
Aniakchak, 110, 112
"Antelopes," wall-painting, 62–63
Antiparos, 14, 15, 20
Archangelos, 27, 45, 51, 101
Argolid, 12, 41
Asia Minor, 1, 14, 20, 22, 24, 38, 40, 94, 110
Aspronisi, 1, 2, 11, 49, 77
Athinios, 1, 2, 29
Attica, 15, 20, 22, 24, 41, 44
Avaris, see Tell el-Dab'a
Avellino/Vesuvius, 110, 111
Ayia Irini, 15, 24, 25, 31, 33, 38, 39–42, 45, 78
Ayia Photia, 22

Baillie, M.G.L., 108, 110, 112
Balos, 2, 46, 51, 91
Barber, R.L.N., 23, 33
base surge, 104–105
Betancourt, P.P., 37, 108, 113
Bolton, K., 35

"Boxing Boys," wall-painting, 62–63
Branigan, K., 40

Cadogan, G., 35
caldera, 2, 28, 29, 46, 47, 105, 106
Cape Akrotiri, 27, 45, 76
Cape Riva, 2, 6, 8–11
Cape Riva, caldera, 6, 9, 10, 105
Cape Therma, 29
Cape Trypiti, 2, 4
Carians, 39
Cherry, J.F., 12, 14, 15, 17
climate, 11, 49, 109, 111, 112, 113
Complex Alpha, 70, 73, 84–86, 93, 100
Complex Beta, 26, 61–65, 70
Complex Delta, 26, 27, 34, 35, 61, 65–71, 81, 86, 89, 100
Complex Gamma, 60–61
copper, 15, 20, 22, 40, 41, 44, 46
Crete, 1, 16, 17, 22, 24, 26, 28, 30–33, 36–38, 39–45, 51, 56, 59, 64, 74, 91, 93–101, 106, 113, 115
Cyclades, 12–18, 19–38, 39–42, 49
Cycladic White Ware, 32
Cyprus, 38, 44, 94

Dark Burnished Ware, 32, 37
Dark-faced Ware, 24
Davis, E.N., 43, 96, 98, 114
Davis, J.L., 24, 25
dendrochronology, 109–111, 112
Dickinson, O., 32
Doumas, C., 14, 16, 24, 26, 27, 29, 32, 34, 40, 45, 46, 47, 51, 56, 57, 60, 64, 68, 71, 74, 76, 78, 84, 89, 92, 103

Plate I: Harpists (Courtesy: Badisches Landesmuseum)

Plates

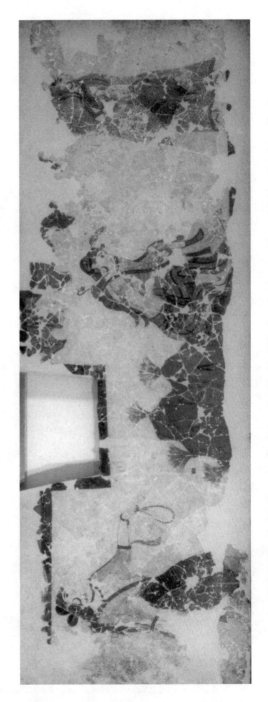

Plate II: North Wall, Adyton, Xesté 3 (Courtesy: Athens, Idryma Theras, Petros M. Nomikos)

Plate III: Goddess, Xesté 3 (Courtesy: Athens, Idryma Theras, Petros M. Nomikos)

Plate IV: Boxing Boys and Antelopes (Courtesy: TAP Service)

Plate V: Monkeys (Courtesy: TAP Service)

Plates

Plate VI: Spring Fresco (Courtesy: TAP Service)

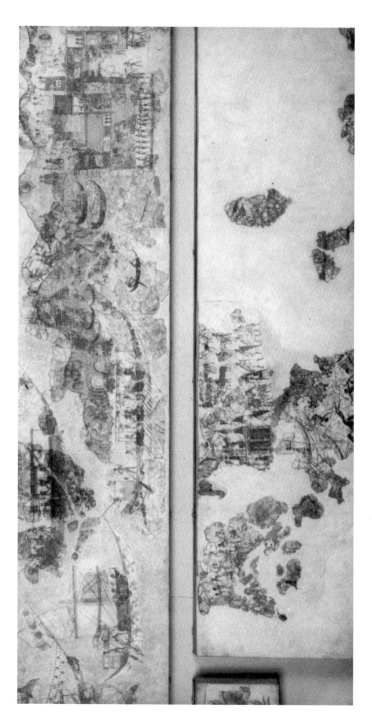

Plate VIIa (above): South Wall, Room 5, West House (Courtesy: TAP Service)
Plate VIIb (below): North Wall, Room 5, West House (Courtesy: TAP Service)

Plate VIIIa (above): South Wall, Room 5, West House (Courtesy: TAP Service)
Plate VIIIb (below): East Wall, Room 5, West House (Courtesy: TAP Service)

Plate IX: Priestess, West House (Courtesy: TAP Service)

Plate X: South Wall, Room 1, House of the Ladies (Courtesy: TAP Service)

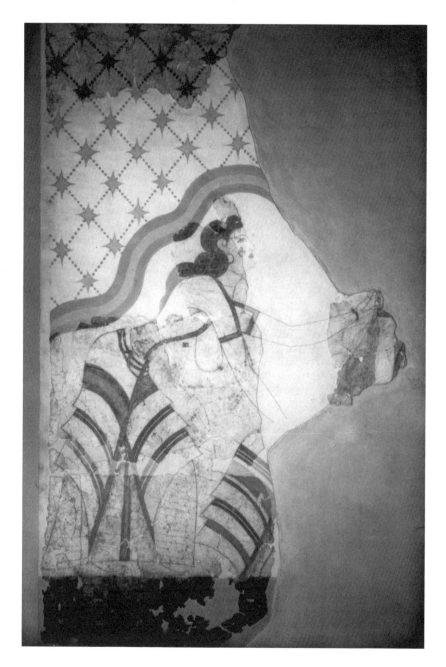

Plate XI: North Wall, Room 1, House of the Ladies (Courtesy: TAP Service)

`VARD COMMUNITY COLL`
`BOURNE CAMPUS LIF`
`FL. MICH`
`ELBOURN, FL 3295`

BREVARD COMMUNITY COLLEGE
MELBOURNE CAMPUS LIBRARY
3865 N. WICKHAM ROAD
MELBOURNE, FL 32935